HOW CANCER CROSSED THE COLOR LINE

How Cancer Crossed the Color Line

KEITH WAILOO

UNIVERSITY PRESS

2011

OXFORD
UNIVERSITY PRESS

Oxford University Press, Inc., publishes works that further
Oxford University's objective of excellence
in research, scholarship, and education.

Oxford   New York
Auckland   Cape Town   Dar es Salaam   Hong Kong   Karachi
Kuala Lumpur   Madrid   Melbourne   Mexico City   Nairobi
New Delhi   Shanghai   Taipei   Toronto

With offices in
Argentina   Austria   Brazil   Chile   Czech Republic   France   Greece
Guatemala   Hungary   Italy   Japan   Poland   Portugal   Singapore
South Korea   Switzerland   Thailand   Turkey   Ukraine   Vietnam

Published by Oxford University Press, Inc.
198 Madison Avenue, New York, NY 10016

www.oup.com

Oxford is a registered trademark of Oxford University Press

Library of Congress Cataloging-in-Publication Data
Wailoo, Keith.
How cancer crossed the color line / Keith Wailoo.
    p.   cm.
Includes bibliographical references and index.
ISBN 978-0-19-517017-7
1. Cancer—United States. 2. Cancer in women—United States.
3. Minorities—Health and hygiene—United States. I. Title.
[DNLM: 1. Neoplasms—history—United States. 2. African Americans—United States.
3. Health Education—history—United States. 4. History, 20th Century—United States.
5. Neoplasms—ethnology—United States. 6. Neoplasms—prevention & control—United States.
7. Women's Health—United States. QZ 11 AA1 W215h 2011]
RC276.W35   2011
362.196′994—dc22   2010018126

9 8 7 6 5 4 3 2 1

Printed in the United States of America
on acid-free paper

To Elliot and Myla Wailoo

CONTENTS

HOW CANCER CROSSED THE COLOR LINE

INTRODUCTION: HEALTH AWARENESS
AND THE COLOR LINE

In the spring of 1977, Minnie Riperton's health battles offered stark proof that cancer awareness was changing, and that the disease was (in the words of one observer) "not a white disease anymore."[1] The national press portrayed the twenty-nine-year-old African-American soul singer with a five-and-a-half-octave range as a remarkable cancer survivor. "Very much in tune with [her] body," Riperton had "found [the breast lump] herself" and benefited from early detection.[2] Her subsequent efforts to help other women "by publicizing her own personal experience with breast cancer" exemplified courageous outreach.[3] She appeared on the *Tonight Show*, lectured nationally, and became an honorary chairman of the American Cancer Society's education crusade.[4] The disease was not a death sentence, she would tell her audiences: "I got cancer, I lost a breast, but I saved the rest of my life because I examined myself early, now I'm healthy, I picked up my life where it left off."[5] In a White House ceremony in 1977, President Jimmy Carter honored her as a tenacious new model, not only for black Americans but for all those who faced the "constant combined hope and fear" surrounding cancer.[6]

When Riperton's cancer returned in 1979, it transformed her from a model of determination and survival to "a symbol of the disease's growing and tragic destruction of Black people . . . a metaphor for the tens of thousands of cancer deaths in Black America each year," according to *Ebony*.[7] The recurrence had come suddenly, when she felt what she thought to be a pinched nerve in her shoulder. Treatments resumed. Confined to bed, the indomitable performer still hoped to get well and go out on the road after the release of her new album. When Riperton died in July 1979 at Cedar-Sinai Medical Center in Los Angeles, her manager recalled her heroism: "She was still doing phone interviews from home. But she was getting worse. She was in real pain. I think she knew she was going to die."[8] The surgeon LaSalle D. Leffall Jr., the first African American appointed as president of the American Cancer Society, eulogized her as "a symbol of hope and courage to many."[9] On the one-year anniversary of her death, Los Angeles mayor Tom Bradley declared July "Minnie Riperton Month" to spread breast cancer awareness in the black community, a group once seen as less vulnerable but now understood to be in harm's way.[10]

Minnie Riperton's story is important for more than her stalwart public example: she was the first black woman to achieve national prominence as a cancer victim or survivor. Although blacks had suffered and died from cancer throughout the twentieth century, the images associated with cancer—particularly cancer awareness and prevention—had been for more than fifty years overwhelmingly of white Americans. From the early years of a stigmatized and hush-hush disease to the lifting of taboos in the decades after the 1950s, the faces and spokespeople for this transformation were always white and female. Just two years before Riperton's case became news, a *Chicago Tribune* editorial insisted that First Lady Betty Ford's breast cancer battle was a signal moment—"surely no women now can forget about the menace of breast cancer. Awareness of the danger is more than halfway toward safety from it."[11] Now with Riperton's death, a host of issues that had once been linked only to whites (breast self-examination, surgery, cancer awareness, early diagnosis, chemotherapy, recovery, life after cancer, and death) were now publicly tied to the African-American experience. Cancer, to adapt W. E. B. Du Bois's famous formulation, had crossed "the color line."[12]

A half-century earlier, cancer was said by experts to be rare in people of color—because, on average, African Americans and so-called primitive people did not live long enough to reach the so-called cancer age in great numbers. "It should be remembered," ran the common refrain in the 1920s, "that cancer is mostly a product of civilization."[13] "Civilization" was shorthand for the high educational attainment, the middle- and upper-class lifestyles, the urban living, and the longer life span that so often characterized well-to-do

Anglo-Americans. At that time these factors were associated with rising cancer rates, and so the message to be aware of the threat, crafted by physicians, biologists, and public health scholars, carried its strongest resonances for whites, and even more so for white women. As cancer specialists saw these women not only as the bearers of the next generation but also as the carriers of civilization, the public health messages urging cancer awareness counseled them in intimate fashion to safeguard their breasts and uteruses as delicate organs of maternity and reproduction. Importantly, these women were understood to possess an inner life upon which responsible health awareness could be built. In contrast, the less vulnerable nonwhites across the color line were largely viewed as lacking these interior qualities. Cancer awareness was far more than a health campaign; it was an expertly targeted social ideology with potent racial undercurrents.

In the 1970s, a particular way of speaking publicly about cancer—as a personal experience concerning blacks as well as whites—emerged in American health discourse. The novelty of Riperton's story was that she was seen as an individual, one with psychological dimensions and intimate experiences that hitherto (for over half a century) had been associated in the popular imagination only with white women. This moment had deep social and political roots. As sociologist Nikolas Rose rightly observed, the process of personalizing health is a long and complex one, for "over the first sixty years or so of the twentieth century, human beings came to understand themselves as inhabited by a deep interior psychological space, and to evaluate themselves and act upon themselves in terms of this belief."[14] That process, in the case of cancer, was also laced with racial meanings.

For many decades, medical authorities contended that the interior psychic space upon which awareness, self-monitoring, and health were built was the possession of whites. How that assumption came into being, how it evolved in the epidemiological imagination nurtured by statistics, and how it fragmented is the historical puzzle taken up in this book. As epidemiologists and cancer specialists saw it, the path to health awareness and from awareness to self-knowledge, self-control, and good systems of health management was not available to every man and woman. How cancer crossed the color line is therefore also the story of the evolution of professional and popular beliefs—about color, vulnerability, and the different capacities of individuals and groups to safeguard themselves.

But had cancer truly been a "white disease" in earlier decades, suddenly changing its racial profile in the 1970s? Had the epidemiology of disease abruptly shifted, with blacks dying in greater numbers than ever because of shifts in exposure to cancer-causing agents, aging of the population, or other factors? Or was this shift only now becoming noticeable in the wake of the Civil Rights era—perhaps because of increased political and cultural attention to the African-American condition? To be sure, the public focus on Minnie Riperton's experience reflected the politics of the times, with its intense concern about racial inequality. But many other factors—scientific, demographic, cultural, and political—shaped the transformation in the diseases we call cancer. It is impossible to rewind the clock and uncover the statistical truth of who actually experienced what kind of cancer in earlier decades when the standards of diagnosis were so different. Looking back, uncertainties abound about when, where, how, and why cancer "crossed the color line." Was this crossing a real epidemiological shift? Was it a slow and systematic decade-by-decade shift? Was it an abrupt transition? Or was the mortality shift really a matter of evolving epidemiological and social perception in which statisticians became more attuned to people who had once been off their radar? In seeking to answer these questions, the story told herein becomes a portrait not of the numbers per se but of the many life stories behind the statistics and of the way statistical trends create ideologies of race, gender, and difference.[15]

Cancer awareness took generations to build. For individuals, to be *aware* of cancer meant believing that one was "at risk," altering one's behavior, changing one's diet and lifestyle, or even mobilizing others to act. But this awareness did not emerge without powerful outside forces pushing the individual—education, public campaigns, expert counseling, and various institutions with their targeted messages. As the cancer awareness campaign emerged in the 1910s and 1920s and matured in the 1930s, 1940s, and 1950s, most of these outside forces contended that educated women stood vulnerable before the gathering health menace. Accordingly, these were the women whose images, psyches, and inner anxieties featured centrally in the posters, films, articles, and news coverage of the campaign. The message resonated with broader ideas of white vulnerability and risk in an era marked by hardening Jim Crow, the exclusion of Chinese immigrants, angry white supremacy movements, and contests for fitter families through good breeding and eugenics. It was in this context that media campaigns and professional writings routinely portrayed (usually privileged) white women as at risk for cancer. Even though these depictions showed class and regional variations, a particular kind of woman—well-to-do or middle-class, modern, and capable of safeguarding self and family—was almost always the central target of cancer awareness. As we shall see, cancer awareness in these early days was as much about projecting, shaping, and nurturing white norms as it was about defining nonwhite others; and these ideas of race and risk spoke intimately to women's beliefs about class and security. Indeed, communications about cancer did not so much speak *to* existing fears as it constructed them—building awareness by fostering the anxieties, the intimate ideals, the fears, and the concerns that became associated with upper- and middle-class Anglo-American femininity.

The birth of cancer awareness early in the twentieth century opened a long-lasting racial divide in how experts understood the impact of modernity on health. While early twentieth-century authorities imagined white women as biologically prone to cancer, focusing on them as individuals with intimate fears, they saw African Americans as a stereotyped, homogeneous social group lacking such an interior life. Theories about these social groupings pervaded cancer discourse, fueling speculation about biological and ecological differences that made blacks almost "immune" from the disease. Specialists such as the surgeon Willy Meyer imbued this civilization-primitivism dichotomy with sweeping importance in the early 1930s, imagining "primitive" nonwhite people as not only immune from cancer "on a par with the fish of the ocean" but also as incapable of internalizing cancer awareness. Each generation adopted theories of color and disease that were fitted to the era's cultural sensibilities, political currents, and social tensions. After World War II, by contrast, the African-American radiologist John Moseley insisted that "cancer is a great democrat. It does not discriminate because of race, creed, sex or age." This egalitarian outlook on cancer—the idea that no group was truly immune or uniquely vulnerable—gained a firm foothold in the 1940s and 1950s, echoing the values of the time. It would take another two decades before Minnie Riperton's personal story, the first such intimate portrait of a nonwhite woman's cancer story, could gain wide coverage. Riperton's story is a landmark in that it adapted mainstream images of cancer awareness—feminine courage, loss, and forbearance in the face of death—to the post–Civil Rights era.

Most of the historical studies of cancer in America treat race as a minor variable—a footnote or a distraction in the disease's scientific, social, and medical history. Such studies, regardless of the specific type of cancer, make only faint efforts to examine how theories of racial biology or genetic difference have featured in the debate over cancer differences. Fewer still examine the links between racial discrimination and disparities in prevention, treatment, and survival. By default, such accounts lean heavily toward narratives of white mainstream Americans' struggles with cancer, leaving questions of difference at the margins.[16] While it is beyond the scope of this book to completely fill this historical gap, the chapters ahead open a much-needed line of investigation in asking how, when, and why did cancer cross the color line. Race, ethnicity, and gender were never marginal to the story of cancer; from the start, they were central organizing motifs in how cancer awareness came about, how it evolved, and how the "war on cancer" has been waged in twentieth century America.[17]

Early twentieth-century epidemiologists and health statisticians were certain that race played an important role in cancer disparities; what they meant by "race," however, kept changing. As the century began, health statisticians paid earnest attention to the "colored" and "white" cancer profiles. By the 1950s, other racial sensibilities emerged, and the binary categories of "white" and "nonwhite" came into vogue. "Nonwhites" (a category championed by the U.S. Census in the 1950s) numbered around 16 million—about 10.5 percent of the American population in the 1950s. Most were African American, but only because Mexican Americans were classified as part of the "white" population at the time.[18] Ten years later, the nonwhite population category had grown more complicated, with groups such as Asians growing rapidly. By 1970, when Mexican Americans were reclassified (along with Cubans, Central Americans, and Puerto Rican Americans) as Hispanic, the "nonwhite" category was now seen as internally diverse and lost its value as a Census and health indicator. By 2000, nonwhites accounted for nearly 30 percent of the U.S. population, and the category was broken down further into sub categories (12.6 percent Hispanic, 12.1 percent Black, 3.6 percent Asian, and so on).[19] The white category, meanwhile, had remained in constant use—enduring even if the types of people labeled white were different in 2000 than in 1920.

Any history of race and cancer awareness must acknowledge that these constantly shifting racial constructs wreak havoc with the search for epidemiological truth, especially when combined with major changes in the diagnosis and disease classification. An earnest search for a single epidemiological truth would be futile; but to ignore the numbers entirely would also be a mistake. Instead, the pages ahead examine how the numbers generated debate, shaped anxiety, fed controversy, fear, and hope, and laid the groundwork for theories of difference. Those who monitored cancer trends knew full well the limitations, but they also were not shy about making sweeping pronouncements, for nothing less than the future health of the nation and the character of its people was at stake.

Epidemiological "facts" are notoriously unreliable, and statistics on cancer epidemiology have proven particularly tricky.[20] Early in the century, many health experts scoffed at all the public hand-wringing over cancer, insisting that what some were calling an epidemic was only an illusion. While some statisticians insisted that "cancer is relatively on the increase in the civilized world," physicians and surgeons remained "somewhat skeptical and inclined to attribute the increase largely to better methods of diagnosis of internal cancer and to the lengthening of the average life which increases the number of individuals reaching the cancerous age."[21] The skeptics proposed that it was the "diminution in the numbers of deaths certified as due to senility, and to 'ill-defined' causes" that gave the mistaken impression of a new, deadly and emerging scourge.[22] Classification, in other words, determined what was seen and what remained unseen. The proper diagnosis and classification of cancer, one scholar noted in the 1930s, was itself "a battleground for the conflicting interests and desires of various medical groups."[23] From the age of the biopsy into the era of the prostate-specific antigen test in the 1990s, improved diagnosis continued playing games with perception.[24] In the late 1950s, for example, Louisiana cancer surgeon Alton Ochsner was convinced that the unprecedented increase in lung cancer was "due almost entirely to cigarette smoking," but other medical experts believed "the development of black-top highways and streets" were to blame and that the disease's lower incidence in women was due to their lower exposure to such outdoor pollutants.[25] Such debates over the evidence and its meaning, in one cancer after another, cast long shadows over the search for truth.

One of the stories told in this book is about how cancer and race evolved in the epidemiological imagination. A field dating as far back as the time of Hippocrates, the statistical study of disease trends in the population became increasingly sophisticated in the nineteenth century and became critically important in the development of the public health professions in the twentieth. The collection of data on health experiences involved, of course, categorizing both diseases and dividing and categorizing population. Thus, as epidemiology and health statistics developed in the twentieth century—in schools of public health, in health departments, in insurance companies, and in many other realms of society—the field offered increasingly compelling pictures of disease trends, while also generating particular ideas of the population itself and its health challenges. Categorizing race and defining cancer—two complex and ever-shifting realities—proved to be especially challenging for the field.

Even today, although the statistics have vastly improved, one physician (a correspondent for the journal *Gynecologic Oncology*) could observe that "cancer statistics are usually not based on an accurate count of cases but on estimations derived from various sources. There is no national cancer registry that counts every cancer diagnosed each year." With estimates often compiled from many local registries and extrapolated to the entire population, the numbers are elaborate, expert guesses. And, "like all statistics," concluded this observer, "cancer numbers can be misused and misunderstood."[26] Cancer posed a profound paradox, for the statistics were as mobile as the people, and each form (breast, prostate, colon, leukemia) seemed to tell its own story about demographics, vulnerable populations, and the color line. Today, for example, breast cancer rates are higher in white women than in black women. This had been true for the last hundred years. But in recent decades it has become clear that despite their lower incidence, black women suffered from a higher mortality from cancer than white women. Explaining these epidemiological mysteries required speculation beyond the numbers and statistics themselves; it required theories of difference and of social change, and an active racial imagination.

Spanning more than a century and using a wide range of sources, this story tells how cancer began the century as an intensely individualized and personal experience linked to whites, while similarly intimate, personal dimensions of the cancer experience remained obscure when experts looked across the color line. Popular and scientific evidence (congressional testimony, films, novels, newspapers, magazines, medical and public health studies, as well as less well-known biographical and autobiographical writings) tell an account of why it took so long for Minnie Riperton to emerge as a dramatic figure in the American cancer story. To track cancer awareness over time, then, we move outward from scientific discoveries and individual patients to what sociologists Barney Glaser and Anselm Strauss call "awareness contexts": "the total combination of what specific people, groups, organizations, communities or nations know . . . about a specific issue."[27] Focusing on individuals, ideologies, and social forces, the pages ahead reveal strong continuities in American racial ideologies and disease beliefs, striking discontinuities, and abrupt changes in how race, cancer, and the relation of one to the other was conceptualized.[28]

Chapters 1 and 2 examine the birth of a dichotomy in American cancer awareness—the emergence of a disparity between how experts, organizations, and communities worried about cancer awareness in whites as an individualized, inner psychological issue, and how they worried over blacks as a demographic type, paying little attention to inner sensibilities.[29] Chapter 1 explores the central place of well-to-do white women in the birth of cancer awareness and its links to a conservative conception of femininity. Experts insisted that whenever women turned away from traditional breast-feeding, shunned proper hygiene, or produced fewer children or had too many, cancer followed. From its beginnings, then, cancer awareness highlighted the special vulnerability of women. This would have many long-term implications for doctors, patients, and the American war on cancer from the 1910s when the American Society for the Control of Cancer (now the American Cancer Society) was founded, into the 1930s with the National Cancer Act, and through the "War on Cancer" that has been waged in recent decades.

Most scientists (few of whom were people of color) drew a very different portrait when they looked across the color line. Chapter 2 explores how ideologies of black-white difference factored into the ways in which epidemiologists and others interpreted rising mortality rates and supposed declining immunity among blacks.[30] Statisticians, physicians, biologists, and surgeons imagined African Americans not as individuals but as a homogeneous group that was carefree and protected from cancer, living as they did in "primitive," stress-free environments that made them less vulnerable to the modern scourge. At the same time, however, authors such as J. Ellis Barker insisted that the black death rates from cancer were rising because "when they live like white men, they die freely from cancer"; in short, new dangers faced blacks as they migrated from primitivism to civilization, and from the South into urban, northern America.[31] But in time, as this chapter shows, authorities were forced by social and scientific events to abandon these old theories of civilization, primitivism, race, and disease, and to formulate new theories about disease in keeping with the changing times.

Old ideas did not die, however. Chapter 3 examines how the dominant image of white women and cancer was adapted to a new era in medicine and in popular culture during World War II and the Cold War. On one hand, a new, egalitarian view of cancer began to emerge. As Clarence C. Little (president of the American Society for the Control of Cancer and also president of the American Eugenics Society) insisted in the late 1930s, the disease was a great equalizer of people. "At a time when our country is inclined to develop class, race or creed animosities or hatreds," he argued, the disease was a common enemy to all.[32] Yet new imagery in the *Saturday Evening Post*, *Reader's Digest*, and on the silver screen also updated the classic image of the female cancer fighter for postwar culture. These and other cultural trends had a sweeping impact for women and for cancer awareness, giving rise for example to the breast self-examination movement, to new prevention and self-surveillance practices, and to new disparities of perception. The link between gender and cancer was also changing by the mid-1940s, when diagnostic improvements pushed physicians to find more male cancers (the so-called internal cancers) than female ones and to rethink the trends.[33] One eminent doctor insisted in *Reader's Digest* in 1955 that the higher rate of cancer in women was only an illusion: "More cancer is reported among women than among men, but because the disease most frequently strikes women in external or accessible organs, it can be detected earlier than in men and more effectively treated."[34]

As we learn in chapter 4, the 1950s was also a transitional era in medical thought about race and cancer—a time of professional confusion over the meanings of race, the identity of cancer itself, and the impact of behaviors like sex and smoking, rather than race, on cancer. Even as white women continued to be at the epicenter of American cancer anxieties, disagreement increased about the true gender and racial distribution of the disease.[35] New cancer anomalies in nonwhites were becoming visible as well—in Mexican Americans and Asians in cities like Los Angeles, in Jewish women with their surprisingly low cervical cancer rates, and in black Americans' mortality trends—and confusion emerged as well over which racial categories best characterized the changing American population and whether old stereotypes would hold. As statistician Sigismund Peller commented in 1952, "the study of cancer in nonwhite races is not advanced enough to make it possible to point out differentiating characteristics."[36] The civilization thesis and its associated racial presumptions were dying quietly, for, as Charles Cameron, medical director of the American Cancer Society, insisted, if cancer was a disease of civilization, it was only because "civilization . . . permits more comprehensive reporting of cancer, encourages more accurate diagnosis of cancer, and enables people to live long enough to have cancer."[37] Cancer, once the ninth leading cause of death in America, was now second only to heart disease as a killer. As therapeutic hope grew, Americans began to see access to drugs and surgery as a new social and economic dividing line, separating those who survived and those who died early from the disease. The challenge for many authorities was how to study and track this process as it was unfolding on different sides of the color line.

Chapter 5 reveals how the social movements of the 1960s and a new politicization of cancer opened another stage in American disease awareness—slowly leading patients, activists, and scholars to attend closely to the black experience of cancer. As early as 1956, for example, the American Cancer Society, acknowledging the need to take cancer awareness across this color line, announced it was hiring one African-American man to "broaden the base of the cancer control movement . . . by working directly with Negro groups and leaders."[38] Meanwhile, a new antiestablishment activism was disrupting the complacency of the burgeoning community of cancer specialists and researchers, with patients and politicians demanding greater honest, fair, and responsive cancer care. These two developments—working at first separately and then in tandem—gradually altered the politics of cancer awareness and created a culture of public criticism of the cancer establishment. The culmination of these trends was the stunning discovery in early 1970 by a team of Howard University researchers that a two-decade-long increase in black cancer mortality had gone unseen by the nation's foremost cancer authorities.[39] Cancer had apparently crossed the black-white color line in the 1950s without professional awareness or public concern.

In the 1980s, the 1990s, and the first decade of the twenty-first century, a new identity politics emerged around race, gender, and cancer. Chapter 6 turns to this recent era, symbolized by pink ribbons, walkathons, disease awareness months, and public fund-raising by famous survivors, when cancer awareness emerged as a dominant theme in the nation's health. The lines between the private experience of cancer and its political meanings had become thoroughly blurred, and the politics of the disease were being played out in an atmosphere of intense competition for public attention and resources. The chapter examines three "epidemics" that gained wide attention through these decades—the spike in breast cancer incidence in wealthy white Marin County, California, the rise of prostate cancer mortality among African-American men, and the unusually high rate of cervical cancer among Vietnamese-American women (alongside the low rate among Japanese-American women)—to examine the complexities of racial awareness and cancer disparities in our own time. For example, in the case of prostate cancer the growing use of the new prostate-specific antigen (PSA) diagnostic test became a problematic tool not only for rallying patients and building awareness but also for inventing new truths about black biological difference—turning old theories of racial immunity on their head. Such examples reveal how far race thinking and awareness had come since the early days, when white women sat nearly alone at the center of the psychologically traumatic cancer crusade. What was also remarkable about these three still-unfolding epidemics, this chapter shows, was how each was shaped by its own gender, ethnic, and racial politics, and how each gave rise to different resentments, to unorthodox ideologies and familiar confusions about race classification, biology, migration, and civilization.

Following chapter 6, this book's conclusion turns to the future, asking what forms of race and cancer awareness we might expect to emerge in years to come, given the nation's new and ever-evolving politics and demographics of race and disease.[40]

To say that cancer "crossed the color line" raises a critical question—what line, exactly, and between what colors?—because the very definition of the color line changed constantly with the times. Over the course of the twentieth century, a dominant black-white dichotomy legitimized by segregation increasingly became characterized by more complex socially defined ethnic boundaries. The very notion of the "color line" articulated by Du Bois became more varied as new *colored* populations grew, and as Jim Crow laws met their legal demise in the 1950s and 1960s. Moreover, the color line has been historically malleable by allowing, for example, groups once labeled as nonwhite, such as the Jews and the Irish, to "become white," and permitting other groups such as Latinos to navigate back and forth across the white line. In theorizing about race differences, experts could not ignore the realities of assimilation, racial mixing and intermarriage across groups, and the ever-shifting race classification practices in the Census and society. All these factors became important variables that made one era's theories of race and cancer discontinuous with the next era's beliefs. Thus did the "one-drop rule" that applied to blacks (according to which any hint of African-American ancestry made one black by law) gradually give rise to more subtle forms of racial labeling. As we shall see in the pages ahead, this changing landscape of race theory would have far-reaching implications in epidemiology, the health sciences, and American society at large.

1

WHITE PLAGUE

In 1923, Louis Dublin worried over cancer. Not his own, but the rising toll of disease in the general American public. As chief statistician at the Metropolitan Life Insurance Company, Dublin pondered the grim cancer mortality trends showing that women—particularly those who were white, well-to-do, and advancing in years—would have much to fear in the future. "We are now confronted with a new situation," he later wrote, for with "the reduction in the mortality from other conditions . . . [and] with every improvement in the condition of life in the early ages, more and more people will approach the later period [of life] when the population is exposed to the cancer menace."[1] As Dublin lifted his head from the morbid statistics, he would have noticed accounts from real life echoing these tragic numbers. The American social reformer Jane Addams, for instance, also worried about cancer in 1923. At age 62, single and childless, she had experienced a recent scare.[2] On tour in Peking, China, Addams had been thrown violently from a rickshaw. Badly bruised and in much pain, she soon discovered that "a sensation of discomfort in her right breast was due, not to the general bruising from the fall but to a small tumor." Without hesitating, a doctor was summoned.[3] During a hasty trip to Tokyo, which had the best hospitals and surgeons in the region, doctors advised Addams that "complete amputation of the breast" would be necessary. As her travel companion explained in a letter to Addams's nephew back in Chicago, "It may not be malignant, but they insist on breast amputation and the removal of all the glands which may become involved."[4] The surgery was performed without delay, and only after the surgery was the tumor sent to pathology for testing. Addams survived the procedure and lived to be a co-winner of the Nobel Peace Prize in 1931; she died in 1935.

The strongest warnings that women should be aware of the risks of cancer went out from statistical experts such as Louis Dublin to people like Addams: well-to-do white women who were said to be prone to cancer and who lived amid a fearful ambiguity about why they seemed so vulnerable.[5] Such women were urged to understand that they were more vulnerable than men simply because they were women. "Unfortunately," cautioned the Philadelphia specialist Francis C. Wood in 1927, "cancer afflicts women in a very much larger proportion than it does men, for the simple reason that there are two organs in women [in] which cancer frequently occurs that raise the percentage—the breast and the womb."[6] And as a spokesman for the American Society for the Control of Cancer (ASCC) insisted in 1924, "nor can it be questioned that cancer is more common among the well-to-do and the prosperous than among the poor."[7] To such learned men it was no mystery that cancer sought out a particular class of woman. Its rise, many contended, was obviously intertwined with growing female political and economic independence, the decline of traditional motherhood and with it breast-feeding and large families, and the alleged misuse of organs of maternity and reproduction.

This modern script for cancer awareness was written during the 1910s, '20s, and '30s, with white women of a certain class as its central actors and with popular and scientific understandings of the disease intimately linked to concerns about changing gender roles. "Cancer of the breast is the penalty women pay for failing to bear and particularly to nurse children," opined California doctor Emil Bogen at the 1934 American Public Health Association annual convention. Herbert Lombard of the Massachusetts Department of Public Health rallied women to see that fertility and maternity were keys to their protection. Psychological, social, and biological specialists wove many such theories from the statistics: cancer patients were frustrated as mothers; love had eluded them; cancer appeared when physical lacerations or deep psychic wounds lay untreated. While some believed that having too many children exposed women to some cancers, others held that, on the contrary, large families insulated them against the dreaded disease. One publication, *Science News Letter*, suggested that the "greater tendency on the part of women with small families to develop cancer is probably linked with biological inferiority" and "their relative inability to have larger families."[8] Whatever theory one preferred, women and their reproductive lives were the central focus of early-twentieth-century explanations of cancer.[9] Statistician Louis Dublin himself bemoaned that the death rate for breast cancer had risen in the five years before 1937 and suggested that reproductive trends put women into a double bind. "It is quite conceivable," he wrote, "that the marked falling off of the birth rate is partly responsible for this increase in cancer of the breast, just as it may well explain the downward trend in mortality for cancers of the female genital organs."[10] Cancer, in short, was a paradox for modern women who were navigating a new world of family possibilities.

Early-twentieth-century public discourse placed not only womanhood but also privileged, civilized whiteness at the core of emerging cancer awareness. Cancer was thought to be a disease caused by white women's modernity. Although the typical cancer victim was not generically white, cancer discourse revolved around a particular class image of femininity and whiteness. Where the uneducated might have seen cancer as repulsive and awful, where the superstitious might not have spoken its name for fear of contracting the disease, and where black women were entirely absent from much of the discussion, the white middle classes were coached to cultivate new ideas about their bodies, themselves, and the cancer threat.

Addressing this imagined white, female victim, cancer awareness campaigns of the era preached that danger came with every choice a woman made. Maintaining a well-balanced maternal and sexual life and safeguarding the organs of maternity became crucial in the fight against cancer. Cancer risks were thought to be inherent to womanhood, although these risks could also be elevated by neglect, violations of hygiene, and ignorance about the responsibilities of maternity, reproduction, and sexual activity.[11] Even though cancer was not among the five leading causes of death in the general population, scientists, doctors, and lay observers agreed that "probably the disease that women dread most of all, and rightly so, is cancer."[12] As a result, the lives of well-to-do women—their progress in society, their repressions and fears, their modesty or vanity, and their upward trajectory—were scrutinized closely. Anxious that the future of the race was at stake, some experts even imagined that lower rates of births and breast-feeding were responsible. To them, the rising cancer death rates represented one face of white race suicide—a particular preoccupation of American nativists in the 1910s, '20s, and '30s.

Whether in the newspapers, medical reports, or novels of the era, cancer was known as a specialized assassin, exploiting white women's most intimate vulnerabilities, their organs of sexuality and maternity. Elsie, one author's caricature in the American Medical Association's popular health magazine, *Hygeia*, was a typical carefree victim who failed to heed this targeted message about cancer awareness. "Run down and pale, she thought she could take care of her own condition," explained the author. "For months she tried drug store remedies, but the ailment persisted and became steadily worse. After suffering much mental and physical anguish, Elsie determined to see a doctor and tell him everything." But sitting across from the physician, she lost her nerve. Restrained by false modesty and coyness, Elsie allowed her prudish discomfort to stop her from speaking about her symptoms. These young unmarried women were "the most serious offenders of the 'I won't talk' class," the author insisted.[13] Failure to talk about their breasts, their vaginas, bleeding from the rectum, or other intimate matters would be their undoing. As one commentator put it, "How much better the attitude of those who come to the physician and say 'I thought I ought to show you this lump. Of course, I don't want to be operated on, but I would rather go through that ordeal than have cancer."[14] Married women were different, claimed another *Hygeia* article in 1941. Aware of their responsibilities to family, these women (particularly those in the better-off classes) were "the health officer(s) of the family . . . [with] the patience and persistence needed to bring information about cancer to everyone."[15]

It was a compelling script, one with lasting significance for how Americans imagined the interior lives and public portraits of cancer victims.[16] The mystery of race and cancer opens in this uncharted space between simmering eugenic fears, statistics, and theories about how civilized whiteness, women's biology and behavior, and modern life created this rising health threat. In the view of Clarence C. Little, the influential president of the ASCC and of the American Eugenics Society, there was hope yet for these women to become cancer aware; indeed, awareness had a eugenic feature in that it weeded out those who were less educated and incapable of becoming alert to the looming danger. "The threat of cancer has, under certain circumstances, a positive selective value . . . ," he wrote, "at a time when all other social influences are operating to the discouragement of individual responsibility and initiative." The intelligent would survive because in cancer "intelligence and courage will pay direct and vital dividends . . . [while] ignorance and procrastination will take a stern toll."[17] Through the 1920s, '30s, and '40s, the ASCC and other anti-cancer crusaders coached, cajoled, and lectured women about appropriate lifestyles and dangerous behaviors, about monitoring themselves and their families for warning signs, and about the suicidal "danger . . . [of] waiting for time to render the decision."[18] Educated women of initiative were encouraged to be psychologically attuned to the "challenge of a problem of this kind."[19] They were counseled to be discreet but not too modest or vain, and to be alert and fearful but not to the point of hysteria.[20] The cancer awareness playbook not only spoke to these women, their psychological concerns, their modesty, and their domestic anxieties; it also mobilized their fears, portraying these publicly so that women might recognize themselves in the script.

WHY WOMEN? SPECIAL ORGANS

Cancer began the century as the ninth leading cause of mortality, far behind the leading killer, tuberculosis. By the 1920s, however, it had moved up to sixth place.[21] On both sides of the Atlantic, scientists wondered why cancer was "everywhere increasing through the civilised world," and why women seemed to be affected more than men. All statistical evidence from Dublin's records and other sources suggested that women were bearing a disproportionate amount of the mortality, with breast, ovarian, and cervical cancer outpacing other forms. When the word "cancer" was uttered, speakers were not thinking of cancers of the lung, colon, prostate, liver, or stomach, which were deemed to be less common and, as internal disorders, more difficult to diagnose. By cancer, they mostly meant the diseases of women. According to the London surgeon Herbert Snow in 1920, "women are the principal sufferers, and possess special organs whose cell-structures normally undergo a process of involution, of withering-up and shrinking when their natural work is done." Medical men, biologists, and statisticians saw these organs of maternity and reproduction as primary targets of the dread pathology. "Men are not exempt from its ravages," Snow continued, "but suffer in a far minor degree."[22] The coincidence between the arrival of menopause (the end of a woman's reproductive years) and the rise of cancer rates was too great for him to ignore. The woman's troubled navigation through life's many stages seemed to increase her exposure to risk. Doctors had grown comfortable playing the role of moral manager to women with such worries, guiding and attempting to control their choices: the threat of cancer became another opportunity to exert such influence.[23]

But was the gender gap in cancer real? How much of it stemmed from medical hypersensitivity about white women and their changing social roles, or from the relative difficulty in diagnosing men's cancers? Theories on these questions were constantly shifting as cancer came into clearer view. Many types of so-called internal cancer were difficult to diagnose. But this too was changing with advances in diagnosis, making specialists' theories highly unstable. Many internal pathologies, such as gastrointestinal cancers, killed without ever being diagnosed. Breast and uterine cancers, by contrast, were much easier to diagnose because "the symptoms and signs could be more definitely taught," and "attract the patients' attention earlier; [and] admit of easier diagnosis."[24] Thus the characterization of cancer as a woman's disease derived from the fact that women's cancers were more clinically obvious, and more socially visible, than many men's cancers. This was statistician Walter Willcox's argument in 1917. He insisted that male deaths were simply not accurately recorded; "[A]ll the new evidence supports the conclusion . . . that the death rates from cancer in the two sexes are approaching equality," Willcox contended, "as the inaccessible cancers typical in men were subject to better diagnosis."[25] In truth, the question of whether cancer was really more prevalent in women was (and is) unanswerable because of this vast diagnostic uncertainty. But in an era deeply attentive to, perhaps even obsessed with, the fate of white women, this lack of evidence could not impede speculation. The insightful Willcox was in a tiny minority. The consensus opinion saw cancer as the post-Victorian woman's special vulnerability—a rising challenge for a new era.[26]

However unreliable the evidence might be, cancer trends nevertheless generated grandiose theories about women and civilization. The renowned economist Irving Fisher saw the disease as a product of a new political economy. "One of the boasts of civilization is the abundance and variety of our food," he wrote in 1916, "and yet it is to this very abundance and variety that we must attribute a large number of the degenerative diseases . . . This is Nature's revenge . . . Mr. Hoffman, [Prudential Life's chief statistician] in his exhaustive treatise on the statistics of cancer, has established a strong presumption that this frightful malady is due in large part to what we have falsely regarded as a sign of economic strength."[27] Other scholars voiced skepticism about these easily spun theories on women's new roles and economic prosperity linked to cancer, insisting that the cancer statistics could not be trusted. "Even under optimum conditions—in the great hospitals of Chicago, London, and Berlin . . . there is still an error of some thirty per cent," wrote one authority in the late 1920s, "because it is so difficult to recognize cancer when it involves the less accessible organs."[28] American cancer statistics were arguably worse because of huge gaps in its system of health monitoring. As one spokesman for the ASCC argued, "the rates for particular [U.S.] cities are, to a certain extent, affected by hospital admissions, providing special facilities for cancer treatment, but there is no doubt that cancer is more frequent in large cities than in rural districts."[29]

Although social factors could have explained why urban, well-off women's cancers were diagnosed and cancers in other populations remained hidden, biological theories about the vulnerability of modern women had strong appeal. According to the above-quoted Emil Bogen, cancer rates were higher among unmarried women and among married women who had borne no children. (Jane Addams fit the profile precisely.) In the 1920s and '30s, new lifestyles and freedoms for women such as cosmetics, dance halls, the pursuit of higher education, fewer children, and a more public life as citizens were said to have created fertile soil for disease. Biological theories supported social anxieties; medical theories intertwined with gender debates; and cancer discourse was infused with a social potency. The method for avoiding cancer was clear: "childbearing and nursing," Bogen argued, "is a natural preventive measure." Never mind that Bogen's expertise came from studies of the nursing practices and milk ducts of mice; he extrapolated from his research to theorize on the broader concerns of the day surrounding modern women. As *Science* reported, Bogen's findings suggested that the main cancer culprit was a little-known substance called "cholesterol" found in the milk ducts of the breast. Usually harmless when the milk was flowing, it was capable of producing cancer when breast-feeding ceased.[30]

Despite the considerable leap from mouse to man, such studies were treated as authoritative. They confirmed what many already believed: that bearing children, safeguarding the breasts during maternity, and attending to her body after menopause was a woman's duty. "On entering her forties," J. H. J. Upham wrote, "when child bearing usually ceases, a woman owes it to herself and to her family to have a thorough physical examination so that she may get an estimate of the functional and organic damage that may have occurred." The subject of cancer was suffused with blame, guilt, shame, and personal responsibility—for not pursuing the right path in breast-feeding and unwisely managing reproduction and maternity. Moreover, knowledgeable, educated women—precisely those seen as at risk—were deemed to be most responsible for their own failures of prevention. As one typical cancer awareness message warned, "You cannot be blamed for what you don't know, but you can be blamed for what you do know but fail to act upon."[31]

Cancer awareness for women meant being alert to the tiniest signs (from lumps or unusual discharges), preparing for the worst, and moving aggressively—even preemptively—against suspected tumors. After Jane Addams's radical mastectomy in 1923, no one doubted the wisdom of the operation, even though careful postoperative analysis confirmed that the tumor was benign.[32] Of course, not everyone agreed that preemptive removal was the best policy. One aggrieved woman, having had a similar operation around the same time, complained to her doctor that "my operation was a dreadful mistake, and entirely unnecessary, because I did not have cancer anyway." Jane Addams, however, and many like her, did not appear to complain. Whether or not the operation was a "success" remained vexingly unclear, but given the threat, they believed aggressive prevention was sound policy.[33] One Dr. J. C. Barnett noted in 1930, "a discharge—either blood or watery—from the nipple is sometimes the first sign of breast cancer." He admitted, however, that such a discharge "may occur in the absence of cancer."[34] To resolve any confusion, physicians like Barnett urged prompt medical consultation. If any tumor was detected, aggressive preemptive surgery often followed. By 1930, because pathological analysis was becoming speedier, a tissue sample from the patient could be rushed straight from the operating table to the laboratory for analysis. "If cancer is found at the exploratory operation," noted Barnett, "the entire breast may then be excised under the same anesthesia." A woman with a tiny suspicious lump before surgery might awaken from her sleep to find an entire breast removed.[35]

In private, women learned to be fearful, and well-to-do women were especially counseled that they had one key option within their grasp: fast, aggressive surgery. "You may remember," wrote Mrs. Mabel Willard to Richard Cabot in 1912, "that on the second of last October, I came to you for examination of the left breast—that you discovered a growth, which you were confident was not malignant, but which you said should be removed at once." Operating surgically on the slightest hint of danger became the focus of cancer awareness campaigns. "Dr. Richardson performed the operation the fifth of October," Willard wrote, "removing the entire left breast, and at the time of the operation he thought it was 'purely malignant.'" To be sure, these operations (or radium or X-ray treatments) were costly, with frequent trips to the hospital provoking financial worry for people who lacked the means.[36] As I. S. Falk commented in the early 1930s: "at one extreme [of expense] medical care for a 'cold' or an attack of some other minor respiratory disease . . . [cost] on average, $6." But "at the other extreme, a cancer $342 [could be] a financial catastrophe for the family of small or modest means."[37] In the painful throes of recovery, Mrs. Willard likely did not worry over the cost. She believed she had dodged a bullet by her hasty action. But even here, ambiguity reigned. She soon learned that "Dr. Whitney's report of the microscopic examination proved it to be non-malignant, for which I am profoundly grateful."[38] Rather than bemoan losing the entire breast unnecessarily and the high cost, Willard focused on the positive: the threat had not been real.

Where internal organs were concerned, uncertainty magnified the fear and speculation. In one case of a fifty-eight-year-old woman complaining of lethargy, Dr. Richard Cabot's suspicion ran the gamut from ulcer to kidney disease, and from nervous fatigue to stomach cancer. "I was anxious not to alarm her at all," he wrote in 1912, "and so I have not expressed to her any of my fears, and told her quite truthfully that all the examinations I made were negative."[39] Until the 1930s, for a woman or man to suspect cancer was to live in this gray zone of uncertainty, in a kind of purgatory between life and death. There was also a gray zone after diagnosis and therapy, as physician-historian Robert Aronowitz makes clear in his 2007 study of breast cancer.[40] Thus, in 1935, when Jane Addams lay ailing in her Chicago home again suffering with cancer, the extent of the disease was unclear.[41] The surgeons sought to resolve ambiguities on the operating table. But in this case, the findings were dire: "the extent to which the growth had spread . . . had not been suspected," and it was during the surgical investigation to determine the disease's extent that Addams died.[42] Nor was this uncertainty limited to the female cancers. In 1913, when the seventy-year-old A. M. Burt wrote to Richard Cabot to give him an update on his own condition, he chided the learned physician: "When you talked with me you said you could not tell the nature of the trouble[;] it was all guess work . . . [but] you made a bad guess. I have proved beyond all doubt that I had no cancer . . . the trouble was the liver."[43] These ambiguities were typical of the situation surrounding cancer in the 1920s and 1930s. Detecting true cancers (especially where internal tumors were concerned) put specialists and laypersons in uncharted terrain. Uncertainty, fear, skepticism, and anxiety became the backdrop upon which cancer awareness would develop, particularly for women.

RACE, MODERNITY, AND "RIGHT LIVING"

"Civilization has indeed forced upon us many difficulties in the conventions deemed best for the protection of society and they [these conventions] have been much abused," insisted Elida Evans, author of *A Psychological Study of*

Cancer (1926). In the scientific literature, authors listed a catalog of likely causes of cancer in the modern age, from tea and tobacco consumption to cosmetics ("paint used by girls") and even vermin. Through the first half of the twentieth century, cancer rates defined the gap between the civilized and the primitive, between men and women. The pattern was clear, wrote Evans: cancer's mortality rate had doubled in those places where lifestyle changes "lead people away from the natural way of living their own lives." She was quick to refute the argument linking dirt and cancer, noting, "but the cleanest and well-to-do are the victims while dirty savages over-run with vermin are comparatively free from it." Like most other observers, she pointed an accusing finger at the stresses of modern life, in which people's natural impulses and instincts collided with oppressive new demands and roles. Cancer was a disease of maladjustment to civilization. "We are told by doctors living and practicing in the wilds of Africa and Asia that carcinoma is rarely found among primitive tribes. It is generally conceded to be a disease of civilization," Evans wrote, echoing a potent truism of the time.[44]

For women, a principal anxiety revolved around fears that some earlier decision or some transgression of correct living had planted the seeds of cancer. As Elida Evans observed, the ASCC, the nation's premier anticancer organization, had put its full weight behind combating fear with a positive message "so that the public would not hide ostrich-like from its threatening dangers." Their message was relentless: avoid chronic irritation; recognize the danger signals; report suspicious moles, recurring sores, and lumps to doctors; embrace aggressive early operations. The ASCC also insisted that living right would avoid cancer.[45] "A few faint voices have been lifted that right living would prevent cancer," Evans wrote. "Undoubtedly true, but how is one to know what is right living?" Her lengthy interviews with cancer patients tried to separate the right and wrong of how they lived. Her subjects were mostly women but also included men, traveling diverse pathways through modern life and its diseases. She adorned her descriptions with the then-fashionable psychological theories of Carl Jung on personality, repression, and the psyche, and, like so many of her time, saw cancer as rooted in the individual's emotional and psychological maladjustment.

Cancer, Evans insisted, started with personal, intimate crises. One story about an unmarried woman showed vividly how maternal domestic tensions gave birth to disease. The woman, who was identified only as Mary, had made a career as a writer and had also worked as an artistic assistant for a man thirty years her senior. As she approached menopause, she realized that she might never have children herself. Disappointment followed, with financial losses from a new writing venture close behind. Following the failure of her own business, Mary was compelled to move in with another man and his wife, a critical move that Evans saw as a fatal regression to girlhood. "Nature does not allow us to disobey without a penalty," she opined. The woman, "as though trying to compensate for an inactive motherhood, where no use or growth was possible in the mammary gland . . . discovered a small nodule in her breast." Though Evans's interpretations based on Jungian theory were unique in their particulars, she echoed the general belief that unrealized maternity could be the genesis of cancer, and that "as the breast is visible and considered a beautiful evidence of motherhood, it is even more the seat of motherhood than the uterus." Her other case studies, chosen to illustrate her theory, followed suit, depicting mostly women (but also a few men) whose cancers were caused by inner psychic, biological, and role turmoil—jealousy, envy, desire, or unfulfilled longing.

These modern women differed much from their mother's generation, suggested Evans; but their newfound freedom was also their curse. For their mothers, corsets were the norm, larger families were common, suffrage was controversial, and propriety reigned. "The old-fashioned gentle lady, with her embroidery, many servants, and leisurely existence, is passing; the helpless female, depending entirely upon the prim and proper chaperon in youth, upon her husband, home and children in later years, has nearly passed," she wrote. But independence sowed seeds of disaster, for in modern women "it is frequently the reproductive instincts . . . which have failed to bring a satisfying fulfillment to the patient's desires." Cancer had other origins as well, she alleged: "it may be an absorbing business interest from which the patient has been suddenly and violently separated, it may be the patient has tried desperately to cling to an objective aim as to a life saver, and for some reason is unable to lead an independent, separate existence without clinging."[46]

Leading eugenicists such as the prolific Charles Davenport went a few steps further than Elida Evans, for in addition to arguing that reproductive and disease trends went hand in hand they insisted that new disorders threatened the future of white Americans. While American eugenics was notorious for its forced sterilization campaigns among the so-called unfit, the program of "positive eugenics" was equally concerned with improving the reproductive habits of white, middle-class families. In eugenics circles and beyond, there was little doubt that the susceptibility to cancer was inherited and also that modern lifestyles had increased the risk. "Just as we have [hereditary] strains of scholars, of military men, of lazy sots, so, too, we have strains of paupers, of sex offenders, of feeble-minded of other sorts, . . . [and] strains with a lack of resistance to tuberculosis, to cancer, to excessive nervous stress," Davenport wrote.[47] As historian Wendy Kline has observed, "in the eugenic vision of racial progress, the mother of tomorrow would save civilization from destruc- tion" by marrying wisely, embracing domesticity and reproduction, and avoiding diseases believed to be hereditary.[48] Within the eugenic mind-set, the apparent rise of cancer rates among white, middle-class populations was a par- ticular cause for alarm. "Nordic race leading the disease's sufferers," reported the *New York Times* in 1928, pointing to a British conference on cancer where one European expert found "the higher rate in London, as compared with New York, must be due . . . to the greater proportion of the Nordic type in London."[49] With such reports widespread, who could blame older stock Anglo-Americans if they believed that they—the Nordic type, the civilized, the higher classes—were singled out by this modern plague?

The focus on the "Nordic" type as cancer-prone illuminates the era's mind-set—with its complex assumptions about race typologies. A racial type was not defined merely by biology or skin color. The crucial factor in deter- mining cancer vulnerability, therefore, was not biology alone but a complex intermingling of nationality, history, geography, the "civilized" state of one's lifestyle and surroundings, and even one's sensibility. When authors spoke of the white race or of race suicide, the concept of "race" subsumed all these fac- tors—history, lifestyle, social context, geography, and biology. As such, races came in multiple varieties. While Frederick Hoffman, the chief statistician of the Prudential Life Insurance Company, could insist that "without exception, the general cancer mortality is higher for the white population than the Negro," he also believed that this situation could change.[50]

Metropolitan Life's Louis Dublin, an immigrant from Lithuania, divided the population his own way. He had grown up in New York's Lower East Side, and saw beyond the usual distinctions of Negro and white. His research found that Jewish men in the city (whom he indicated were mostly Russian by birth) experienced higher cancer rates than native-born Americans; the women of this group, however, were less likely to suffer cancer than the U.S. average.[51] Women of the "Irish" racial stock suffered the highest mortality of all—far higher than women of German stock, or than those classified as from "Eng- land, Scotland, and Wales." These, in his view, were the prominent "races" in New York City. Italians, he found, had the lowest cancer profile for both men and women. Such fine-grained ethnic categorizations (which were rather obvious groupings in early twentieth-century New York City) were not common in other studies. National studies, on the other hand, jettisoned such distinctions in favor of simpler terms like "colored" and "white." But in every context, it was assumed that "race" (broadly defined) intermingled with environment, history, lifestyle, biology, and modernization to shape the cancer rate.

At the birth of modern cancer awareness, biologists, health statisticians, surgeons, and many other authorities linked the racial health and reproductive capacities of white women (carriers of the nation's future) to the health of the country. As the Louisiana surgeon C. Jeff Miller insisted, white women's tendency to bear fewer children than African Americans and immigrants was tantamount to race suicide. He argued that there was "a possible connection between the rapid increase in the incidence of uterine cancer and the corresponding decrease in the bearing of children, since uterine and mammary cancer are increasing most rapidly in those countries in which race suicide is most prevalent." Such arguments saw disease as a mediating force in women's sexual independence and reproductive lives. The woman who was married "but who at the same time repeatedly avoid[ed] childbearing [was] misusing her organs, and [was] not functioning physiologically," Miller observed. By contrast, "the virgin . . . even though she does not bear children is not misfunctioning," he added. Miller admitted that his characterization might be wrong. "Diametrically opposed to this view is the long accepted theory that cancer of the cervix develops because women have had children," he noted. Yet, whatever the theory, white women were marked as being most vulnerable to this deadly scourge.[52]

The class overtones in cancer awareness promotions and publicity were often as stark as the racial ones, with authorities insisting that the middle-class and well-to-do might be saved where, by contrast, lower-class whites would perish. "Among the more ignorant women of the laboring classes," wrote one observer in 1927, "cancer of the womb is almost never diagnosed in time to cure."[53] "It is the purpose of the propaganda organized by the medical professions to banish this ignorance [about cancer]," wrote physician David Riesman in a 1935 *Hygeia* article. Such cancer patients should not look "on the disease as something loathsome, perhaps as contagious, as something of which to be ashamed." Rather, cancer "is a disease like any other, and in no sense need the patient be ashamed of it."[54] But for these lower classes, it was said that ignorance, lack of education, filth, and failures to recognize unusual discharges from the womb made awareness difficult to build. This sealed the demise of many poor and working-class women. Indeed, across the white class line (according to opinion prevailing at that time), cancer followed a different logic depending on the class status of the patient. For working-class women, bearing too many children was linked to higher rates of cervical and uterine cancers. In other words, these women faced a different and additional challenge than that faced by well-to-do white women: too frequent childbirth, too little medical care during delivery, too much damage to the uterus, and too little attention to sexual hygiene. White vulnerability, it was believed, came in several forms, depending on one's social status.[55]

BUILDING AWARENESS AND FIGHTING STIGMA: THE EARLY YEARS

Because the toll of cancer apparently fell disproportionately on women, the first awareness campaigns sought to change feminine beliefs, behaviors, and coping styles in the face of oppressive stigma. "There is no class of chronic disease, not even tuberculosis, in which the unfortunate receives so little human consideration and tenderness as does the one with advanced cancer," wrote Dr. LeRoy Broun in the *American Journal of Nursing* in 1925. The revulsion and "personal dread" when people witnessed a cancer patient with their "peculiarly unpleasant odor surrounding the patients, often dries up the springs of human sympathy, and denies the patient those small comforting attentions and acts that go such a distance in smoothing the rough road . . . they are traveling," wrote Broun. If it fell on women to be disproportionately victimized by the disease, reasoned Broun, then it also fell on women (as mothers looking after loved ones and as nurses) to carry the burden of caring for cancer sufferers. In his view, "the great body of women who add so much to the recovery of the sick have it in their power to save lives by keeping in mind the indications of the earliest commencing of cancer and by insisting that such conditions when brought to their attention should be thoroughly looked into *at once*."[56]

The genius of this era's cancer awareness script was the relentless dissemination of poignant scripts and believable dramas to speak to these vulnerable women, to counsel to their inner anxieties, to encourage them to maintain their sense of propriety and discretion even amid public revulsion, and to help them navigate this treacherous terrain between disgust and action, between fear and bravery. One 1933 story told in *Hygeia* from the perspective of a cancer survivor captures the struggle at the core of cancer awareness: the challenge of talking about one's experiences with a stigmatized disease and of unearthing repressed fears while remaining outwardly controlled. Longtime friends (and now women with families), Margaret, Nan, Caroline, and the female narrator of the story routinely gather for tea, card games, and conversations: "Some days we talked gardens . . . If we felt like playing bridge, we played . . . More often we discussed antiques." On one day, however, the card table is pushed to the side, and talk turned to another friend who had, quite suddenly, taken sick and, just as suddenly, died. "Tilly Pearson dead!" gasps the author. "I didn't even know she was ill." The cause is breast cancer, but none of the bridge group had any inkling about the problem. "She never told anyone about it," declares Caroline, "or even sent for a doctor until a week or so before she died. Then, of course, it was too late to do anything." Each woman responds differently. Nan's mother had died from breast cancer when Nan was just a girl, and she had long nurtured her own fears that it would hit her next. Margaret, on the other hand, is repulsed by the whole conversation. "Stop being morbid," she pleads, trying to change the topic. But while the banter swirls and sorrow intensifies, the author confesses to her readers (but not to her friends) her own secret. "These three had been my bridesmaids. Margaret and I lived in the same sorority . . . But they didn't know that, under the new green wool dress I was wearing . . . that afternoon, high up on my breast was plainly visible a two-inch incision, where nine years ago . . . a tumor had been removed."[57] In its staging and dramatization, the story takes readers into the vexed cancer psychology of this group of women. The 1920s and 1930s produced many such popular portraits and essays in which readers saw their own fears acted out, and thus began grappling with their tensions between secrecy and openness, and with the "reign of terror" inside themselves.

Leading women through these fears became a key motif in the discourse of cancer awareness, for cancer was widely understood to produce a horrible end that should be avoided at all costs. For many, to be diagnosed with cancer was to be sentenced to death, and to become figuratively dead. Everything about the disease connoted death. "The foul odors," wrote Shields Warren in 1927, "so distressing and so commonly associated with advanced cancer are due not to the tumor itself but to the action of bacteria living on dead tissue."[58] When cases were confirmed, the disease was often already advanced. Survival talk was a hopeless charade. The gruesome imagery of cancer wards could be shocking, but their sights and smells were well known, particularly since most deaths occurred at home, rather than in clinical settings. Gottfried Benn, for example, a German physician-poet, revealed a world that few wished to discuss publicly. A doctor, walking among the all-but-dead bodies, noted:

> Here this row is disintegrated wombs. And this row is disintegrated breast. Bed stinks by bed . . . They do not take much nourishment. Their backs are sore. You see the flies. Sometimes the nurses wash them. As one washes benches.[59]

In less shocking prose, Dr. William Preble of Boston described the case of a Mrs. Barry to Richard Cabot in 1919. Her "discharge from the bladder was very foul," he wrote. In such accounts, cancer was a noxious form of suffering, its taint bordering on contagious. As LeRoy Broun noted in 1925, "the necrotic odor [the smell of dying tissue] of the discharges in advanced cases is so persistent, even after several washings of the hands, that for one's comfort it is well to use gloves . . . [even more so because] these discharges are teeming with streptococci."[60]

The graphic sense of "foulness" stigmatized sufferers and distressed those nearby, making cancer all the more a hush-hush disease. The death process was so awful and foul that euphemisms and duplicity were more or less the norm. Although Mrs. Barry's doctor "wash[ed] the bladder out several times and the urine would not be foul immediately after washing," the horrid odor always returned, Preble wrote to Cabot, as she "went steadily downhill and died." Even then, there was speculation about whether the case was truly cancer.[61] Such tortured private accounts rarely made it into public reading, and often such ambiguous cases never appeared in cancer statistics.[62] Doctor and patient saw cancer as a graphic, fetid decline where lingering questions of diagnosis endured even beyond death.[63] As physician William Woglom acknowledged, doctors often shunned recording "cancer" as the cause of death for fear of offending family sensibilities. As a result, the statistical "records are vitiated [suspect, corrupted, and debased] by a curious reluctance on the part of surviving relatives to have cancer appear on the death certificate."[64] As one 1925 public official noted, "Pressure is not infrequently brought upon physicians to induce them to hide the existence of cancer, because of the implication of hereditary taint or wrong-doing or both." Often, the attending physicians recorded "pneumonia" or some other such common cause of death.[65] Concealment was both a social desire and a professional norm.

Although disgust, fear, and concealment were major impediments to cancer awareness, teaching middle-class women to talk publicly without squeamishness or a sense of immodesty about these stigmatized issues became a hallmark of the movement. At the birth of cancer awareness, then, it fell on middle-class women to become exemplars of a new awareness: to show how to control fears, how to wrestle with revulsion and disgust, and how to tie middle-class maternal sensibilities to the survival of family and of the race. Advocates and authors became increasingly sophisticated about representing the battle against cancer in terms that these women understood.

THE INTIMATE PSYCHOLOGY OF AWARENESS

Given the vexing problem of cancer's stigma, few patients publicized their plight or stepped out of the shadows to challenge the firmly held popular and professional truisms about the foul and deadly disease. It was largely in fictional and popular secondhand accounts, then—in novels, short stories, newspaper accounts, and magazine dramatizations—that the voices and interior life of cancer victims were heard and seen, and where tensions over the ambiguity of diagnosis, the disease's social profile, and the stigma of a gruesome death sentence became visible. In these accounts, we see the specificity, psychological tailoring, and intimacy of cancer awareness.

Imaginative fictional dramatizations of cancer patients revealed the possibilities and limits of cancer awareness, often doing so more powerfully than the moralizing appeals of cancer crusaders. W. H. Auden's dark 1938 poem "Miss Gee" presents us with a quintessential portrait of a cancer victim. Auden wrote, "Childless women get it. / And men when they retire; / It's as if there had to be some outlet / For their foiled creative fire." In the ballad, Miss Gee, whose lips were thin and small, her shoulders sloping, and having "no bust at all," had never married. Childless and living alone, she privately dreamed of being the Queen of France while going everywhere "with her clothes buttoned up to her neck." When "she passed by loving couples, she turned her head away," but the logic of her own repressed life brought her one day to Doctor Thomas. He "looked her over" and said, "why didn't you come before?"

These literary representations of cancer left out the physical unpleasantness of the experience; in this and other ways, they exemplified the standard script presenting cancer as a bane to well-to-do women whose lives in privileged social settings made them uniquely vulnerable. In language more sympathetic than Auden's, authors of respectable literary works also imagined how cancer entered women's lives. The fictional character of Eve in Mary Hastings Bradley's 1937 novel *Pattern of Three* represented the efforts of society women to balance discretion and diagnosis. Allan Updegraff's *Whatever We Do* revolved around the European travels of Bobbie and George Parson of Missouri, in an adventure set in the wake of the world war and "complicated by the danger—so the doctors in Paris said—of cancer." In this cancer story, "death cast . . . a shadow over the carnival spirit" of the Roaring Twenties.[66] Alice Woods's *Gilded Caravan* portrayed an expatriate husband returning home to the United States to cope with his wife's death from cancer, and Raymond Weaver's *Black Valley* also featured a wife "dying quietly and bravely of cancer."[67] Such novels delved deeper than statisticians and doctors ever could into the emotional trauma and the sense of privilege, blame, responsibility, and discreet concealment that shadowed women with the disease.

In Bradley's novel *Pattern of Three*, cancer could best be dramatized in the context of Chicago high society, a culture in which discretion ruled. Eve, the centerpiece of the novel, is a product of that society. At age thirty-nine, she is sensitive about her fading youth and lost beauty, and is threatened by a younger woman's affection for her husband, Dick. However, rather than face the truth about Dick's affair or about herself, she denies it. This denial, Bradley writes, would be her undoing. "For a long time, [Eve] kept the door shut against all admission; her instinct for self-defense had been subtle and expert with shifts, excuses." Eve believes, wrongly, that "her seeming innocence of disaster would be her immunity against it." Wasn't this denial the crux of the problem for many such victims? These traits—for instance, her coiled defensive posture—haunt her through the amicable divorce. And when illness befalls Eve, these traits again appeared. "You mean you're ill?" Dick asked late in the day. "Not ill. I don't feel a thing. But there's something growing—one of those breast things." When he learns that Eve had sensed these symptoms for some time but failed to seek medical help, Dick is aghast. "'And you waited?' . . . His voice was harsh . . . 'that's folly. You shouldn't have waited an instant.'" Later, as the seriousness of the matter sinks in, he inquires, "why don't you let people know? . . . Your friends . . ." But even as he speaks, Eve has risen from her chair, drawn her fur around her shoulders, and voiced her era's all-too-common refrain about cancer: "Not a word, please, to anyone," she warns.[68]

Eve illustrates how women of her social station traveled through the gray zones of cancer awareness, from suspicion to diagnosis and treatment. The surgeons act aggressively and preemptively to remove the entire breast at the elite Mayo Clinic in Rochester, Minnesota. Eve later reports casually to Dick, "it was just a little lump . . . they rather overdid it, I think, taking so much away." Throughout, she remains nonchalant, denying to Dick and to herself the seriousness of these events. The pattern of self-denial and self-deception continues. And not surprisingly, at the dramatic culmination of *Patterns of Three*, cancer returns. "Now the thing has come back—lower down," Eve admits to Dick, confessing that she understood well the gravity of her condition. Yet, as Eve's euphemistic phrasing of her internal cancer ("lower down") suggests, new ambiguities emerge during the treatment and follow-up phases. This time around, the doctors (as was their custom in terminal cases) keep the truth from her: "The doctor tried to tell me that this new trouble may be something else, independent of the other, something like gall stones, but I know better . . . I had too much experience with Aunt Margaret not to know what to expect . . . I know this is the end . . . I shall get weaker and weaker and have to be dosed for the pain. . . . Aunt Margaret went slowly. My case may be quicker."[69] For some women of this generation, like Eve, knowledge of the cancer signs had become commonplace.

Bradley's story, read alongside the contemporaneous medical writing that we have been reviewing, illustrates how half-truths and coded references swirled everywhere around the cancer-aware woman of the early twentieth century. Cancer awareness carried an underlying paradox: specialists preached about the warning signs and novelists dramatized awareness, but once a patient was declared inoperable, such discussions often ceased. Families were informed; patients were not. Awareness ended at death's door—or as soon as the prognosis was terminal. In 1912, for example, Dr. Henry Prescott wrote to Richard Cabot about a forty-two-year-old woman. "I am referring to you Mrs. James Graham . . . for whom an operation seemed unwarranted," as her ailment was too far along in its fatal course. "It seems to me she shows signs of lung involvement . . . [there was also] loss of appetite, nausea . . ." Prescott was "anxious to have another opinion," however, and sent the young woman, unaware of Dr. Prescott's prognosis, to Cabot. The letter to Cabot came with a clear warning: "Mrs. Graham has been told the tumor is benign."[70] For all their talk of awareness, doctors felt no obligation to divulge the truth under these circumstances, believing it would only cause further anguish. If families feared being stigmatized by the diagnosis, doctors too pushed for suppressing information. As one public health article reported, "secrecy is often encouraged by the physicians . . . [who] hide from their patient the fact that he has cancer, lest he become despondent at the thought that he must inevitably succumb to it."[71]

Cancer awareness, then, paradoxically involved a strong measure of concealment and deceit in the name of benevolence and medical paternalism, particularly when the prognosis was dire. Days before Jane Addams's death in 1935, her nephew James wrote to his brother, "they do not want Aunt Jane to know . . . Dr. Britten and Alice Hamilton think she will be much more comfortable if she is not informed . . . Britten thinks she may have six months, but it is very unlikely; more probably two." In case the message was missed, James concluded, "I repeat, they do not want anybody except Mrs. Bowen and us to know this."[72] This was a doctor-patient relationship that many women could see right through, but it was a charade that physicians supported and that many families gravely tolerated.

Meanwhile, women faced their own challenges in cancer awareness. Should they be discreetly vigilant, or ashamed? If the disease struck them, was it their fault? Did their choices of how many children to bear or whether to breast-feed invite the attack? The early twentieth-century campaigns hinged on this notion that cancer was a special concern of the patrician female sailing through dangerous waters. It was women—married and also unmarried, middle-class and well-to-do—who had the most at stake, according to prevailing wisdom; and it was their sensibilities that were placed at the center of awareness discussions. Surrounded by a vexing array of claims and counterclaims, stigma and blame, suffering and hope, silence and hyperbole, opinion and guesswork, they were warned to avoid the unscrupulous salesmen and hucksters of the latest cancer cures. They were also counseled to maintain faith in real experts and in coming scientific cures. And, most important of all, they were told of their ability to protect themselves through the choices they made. Men, by comparison, enjoyed different outlets for their restless sexuality, dodging their own distinct perils. "Men," Elida Evans had speculated in *A Psychological Study of Cancer*, "denied their natural functions either from a frigid wife, or some really legitimate reason, seek satisfaction for existence and pleasure in food, and cancer of the stomach is most common with them."[73]

Edith Wharton's 1933 short story "Diagnosis" dramatized this gender disparity in an imaginative narrative about the psychological trauma caused by a mistaken cancer diagnosis. Her patient is a man—well-off but also fearful. Paul Dorrance, who has "built his easy, affluent, successful life," has not been feeling well, and calls on his family doctor. After the consultation, he finds a piece of paper that had fallen from the doctor's pocket upon which another patient's diagnosis was written. Believing that the diagnosis is his own, Dorrance is shocked and filled with "pity for all the blind gropers like himself . . . who thought themselves alive, as he had, and suddenly found themselves dead."[74] He slowly reconciles himself to his fate, deciding to change his life. His wife, who knows the truth about Dorrance's lack of cancer (but, in a manipulative twist, prefers her new, "dying" husband to his former self), keeps her own counsel. Wharton's "Diagnosis" offers a telling insight into the anxieties, beliefs, and intimate maneuvering surrounding the cancer diagnosis. In part, it highlights the then-prevalent belief that to have cancer was to be already dead. But it also highlights the levels of personal duplicity surrounding the stigmatized disorder. Surely, Wharton used the common script about cancer as a woman's disease imaginatively and ironically—as a comment on the era's gendered assumptions, silences, and assumptions about cancer death. As the story reveals, society's well-off men, like their wives and daughters, also feared cancer, and they too worried whether the disease was a consequence of prosperity, aging, and longer life. Yet the numbers and sweeping public imagery of the time suggested that the toll fell disproportionately on women.

According to the cancer awareness script, these modern women, although vulnerable, possessed a fortunate hidden advantage—a set of personal qualities that transformed mere awareness into prevention and survival. Truly modern women, it was believed, had the intellectual capacity to appreciate the difference between superstition and reality. They possessed the insight and self-control to overcome their fears. They were socially and economically positioned to embrace early detection, early surgery, cancer prevention, and the nuances of right living. They were told that their education was the key to their health awareness, and in this way they learned that they held their fate in their own hands.

The crucial difference between these women and so-called primitives was the modern woman's capacity for introspection, self-knowledge, and readjustment. Primitives and savages had neither the modern cancer-causing dangers to dodge, nor the inner capacity to address the new situation. All people, Elida Evans alleged, had primal fears and superstitions. But, she continued, showing traces of Jungian thought, primitive people "actually live the myth and symbol. Born in the collective unconscious as we all are, they never leave it, while we are supposed to educate ourselves out of its power." Even if cancer rates ran high in the world of savages, Evans would not have expected campaigns to take root. "The primitives are the children of humanity, but without the will of civilized children." Such assumptions about risk, vulnerability, privilege, progress, class, and good breeding were widespread in the 1920s, hovering in the background of conversation about cancer and its victims. Evans acknowledged, for example, that her own interest in the topic began after she witnessed the divergent fate of two women battling cancer: "each loved life and people and beauty," but "there was one noticeable difference: the woman who lived had conquered herself. The woman who died was unyielding, and a victim of the complexes within her."[75]

Cancer discussions from the 1910s into the 1940s placed these questions of health psychology, self-control, and preemptive action squarely into the foreground for the so-called vulnerable women. It wasn't that experts ignored cancer rates in black women, new immigrants, men, and "uncivilized peoples," but the topic (when taken up) lacked any attention to this inner life of health awareness. Any effort to promote cancer awareness in these other groups paled in significance next to pressing concerns about communicating to well-to-do white women about the rising rates. Contemporary cancer statistics supported this view that some were more vulnerable than others. (One typical report from Maryland in 1926, for example, found that for African Americans the leading causes of death were tuberculosis, heart disease, cerebral hemorrhage, with cancer "tenth as a cause of death of Negroes"; for whites, by contrast, cancer was in fourth place after heart disease, kidney disease, and cerebral hemorrhage.[76]) But even more than the numbers, ideology offered support for this standard view that well-to-do white women were more susceptible. Although cancer rates in black women were known to be high, the ASCC and public health agencies aimed their message at the women deemed most capable—emotionally, intellectually, and financially—of acting on the warnings. As one specialist said in the late 1930s, expressing quite clearly the tilt of the anticancer campaign at that time, cancer was "a public health problem peculiarly adapted to the needs and attitudes of educated women."[77] Women who pursued nontraditional career tracks were also at higher risk. "Other factors being equal," commented *Newsweek* in 1940, "cancer of the breast is more common among professional women who bear an average of 2.8 children than among the wives of unskilled laborers who usually have four or five offspring."[78] Experts did not tailor these messages for a generalized audience. Almost all experts agreed that "old stock" (i.e., Anglo) American women were squarely in the path of the storm, and they tailored their awareness efforts to the intimate concerns of those at greatest risk.

At its inception, cancer awareness defined a stark and intimate line of color, gender, and cultural belief, with whites apparently living in a cancer-prone world and blacks supposedly living in a zone of relative immunity. This line was almost entirely modeled on the larger black-white divide. (In 1920, 10 percent of the U.S. population was African American, and 89.7 percent was classified as white, with Asians and American Indians making up only 0.2 percent each.)[79] The black-white racial line was also a regional line, for in 1920, 85 percent of black people lived in the southern states. In the minds of most authorities, cancer was not set apart from this broader story of race—it was a crucial feature, a by-product, of how race and difference were understood in America.

Cancer and cancer awareness followed this racial logic. African Americans lived in a world where infectious disease mortality prevailed, whereas the white and well-to-do lived in a world where cancer was a rising nemesis that dictated their heightened sensitivity to body, behavior, and the perils of modern life. In the minds of doctors, scientists, and public health officials, the differences in their health challenges could not be any starker. Given this racial divide, it is little wonder that, as historian Kristen Gardner found, "early detection [and] cancer education targeted a white and middle-class audience."[80] There was no room here for the involvement of African Americans. Public health itself was a segregated enterprise, and the health problems of "the negro" bore little resemblance to the health challenges of well-to-do whites.[81]

There were some, of course, who dissented from this orthodox view, insisting that the true health challenges of black folk were impossible to see accurately, for they were concealed behind the obscuring shadows of segregation. Louis Dublin, with an eye for ethnic nuances as we have seen earlier, acknowledged that the supposed racial gap in cancer (the apparent tilt toward whites) was not quite what it seemed to be. "The white female rate is only slightly higher than that for colored females," he wrote as early as 1919.[82] And as such experts actually examined the health status of African Americans more closely, their views on health across the color line would inevitably become more nuanced. As one Morehouse College sociologist astutely observed twenty years later, "white people who control the mechanics necessary for health improvement have shown alarming indifference to the health of 'America's Tenth Man.'"[83]

For most learned professionals, however, cancer also defined the gender line, with women being vulnerable and men less prone. In a race- and gender-conscious era sensitive to the reality of the color line, a primary conceit in cancer control by the 1930s was the belief that educated, civilized, and intelligent women, who learned to be comfortable with intimate conversations about their bodies, had the power to manage their fears, reduce their vulnerabilities, and control their destinies.[84] "Armed with intelligence and enlightenment," Baltimore's Joseph Colt Bloodgood insisted in 1933, "it is hoped that women soon will banish false modesty, which has in the past been in large measure responsible for the lack of advance in the control of cancer of cervix of the womb."[85] Women who fit this profile internalized the cancer awareness message, and by the late 1930s their clubs had combined forces with the ASCC to create the Women's Field Army, dedicated to spreading cancer awareness. Before 1937, such clubs occupied themselves with teas and cookies, gardening, bridge, and cookbooks. With the creation of the Field Army, breast self-examination films and other public efforts became their focus.[86] Men (regardless of race) and nonwhite women (in whom cancer rates also ran high) fell below the radar of this early cancer awareness movement.

Although most cancer specialists by the 1920s acknowledged that black women's cancer mortality was rising alongside white women's, black women lived just beyond the zone of professional cancer awareness, figuring not at all in the emerging discussions over detection and self-awareness. In his short paper on "the special problems of the colored woman," New Orleans surgeon C. Jeff Miller insisted that "the safeguarding of the health of the Negro [was] anything but an easy task, for the fight is not against disease, but against physical, mental, and moral inferiority, against ignorance and superstition, against poverty and filth."[87] The fight in the South was against a particular group of problems: tuberculosis, malaria, infant death, syphilis, and all kinds of infectious diseases. As most experts saw it, the world was divided between the *civilized* environments and peoples (where cancer rates were high and rising, and where the latest radium therapy was within reach) and *primitive* places (where deaths from infectious diseases still ran high and where cancer patients seemed few in number). "At least in civilized countries," wrote Louisiana's Jeff Miller, "as one writer puts it, every person saved from death in youth is one more potential victim for cancer in old age." Even with all these uncertainties in view, he insisted, "the fact still remains that part of the increase is real . . . Statistics are notoriously unreliable, but these figures permit of no argument."[88] Such health authorities also knew that epidemiological patterns changed, that cancer was a moving target, and that entrenched truths about race and disease were always evolving. Frederick Hoffman, chief statistician at Prudential Life Insurance (as Louis Dublin was at Metropolitan Life), insisted in 1937, for example, that "when uncivilized peoples (Arabs, Negroes) become civilized, the death rate from cancer reaches the average for civilized people."[89] Thus, although most authorities agreed that there was more cancer in the "white" world than in the "colored" world, and that civilized women needed to be particularly watchful for signs of disease and degeneration, they also believed the balance of disease and society might well be shifting.

VULNERABLE WOMEN AND
THE BIRTH OF CANCER AWARENESS

Cancer consciousness came to many white middle-class women in early twentieth-century America through images in magazines such as *Hygeia* (the American Medical Association's popular health magazine first published in 1923). For more than a half century, the cancer awareness script encouraged these women to tread the line between irrational fear and blind ignorance, to talk openly with other women about the disease, and to protect themselves by maintaining well-balanced maternal and reproductive lives. With diagnoses among such women increasing, many experts perceived this group as uniquely vulnerable and portrayed cancer as a bane of the "civilized" woman.

In bold strokes, *Hygeia*'s 1938 article "I Am Not Afraid of Cancer" was one among many portraits of changing awareness. Four friends sit around the coffee table reflecting in different ways on the death of a friend from cancer. One, repelled by the issue, wishes to avoid the conversation altogether; others are somber and hushed. But the main character admits (to readers, though not to her friends): "These three had been my bridesmaids. Margaret and I lived in the same sorority. But they didn't know that, under the new green wool dress I was wearing that afternoon . . . high up on my breast was plainly visible a two-inch incision, where nine years ago . . . a tumor had been removed." Such accounts vividly captured the fear and stigma associated with cancer, filtered through the lens of middle-class women's sensibilities.

Courtesy of the American Medical Association

Epidemiological studies and health statistics confirmed the view that while women suffered most, mortality among white men was advancing fast, although colored male mortality appeared to be strikingly low. Gender and biological assumptions played a prominent role in explanations of these trends. As physicians such as Francis C. Wood insisted, "Unfortunately, cancer afflicts women in a very much larger proportion than it does men, for the simple reason that there are two organs in women in which cancer frequently occurs that raise the percentage—the breast and the womb" (1927, *The Woman Citizen*).

2

PRIMITIVE'S PROGRESS

From the opening years of the twentieth century, medical experts promoted a compelling theory of black cancer immunity; at the same time, they bemoaned that "the Negro" was slowly leaving this primitive, cancer-free paradise. In his 1913 cancer treatise *The Monster Malady*, the American vegetarian guru and well-known eugenicist J. Harvey Kellogg argued, "in Africa, in his savage state, the Negro is almost wholly free from this scourge." Even in America "the Negro . . . still retains to a considerable degree his natural immunity," Kellogg insisted; but modern life was eroding this native-born protection, dealing a new hand to the racial group. "The Negro" was in transition—a fact readily observable in "the statistics of a number of our cities." In Kellogg's view, a perspective widely shared by experts across a spectrum, cancer was a white disease, linked to white prosperity and civilized habits, that victimized "the Negro" only when he became affluent enough to "adopt the habits of his white brother and . . . other luxuries of the white man."[1] This explained why cancer among the "well-to-do Negro living in northern cities" was on the rise. The British author J. Ellis Barker echoed the refrain thirteen years later: "Now, when they live like white men, they die freely from cancer."[2]

Widespread and influential, such theories sculpted a public image of African Americans as a primitive type. When cancer experts characterized cancer across the color line, they did not speak about the inner psychological fears, anxieties, and traumas that so dominated their discussions of white women. Their reading of the numbers promoted another type of epidemiological awareness. There was no intimate talk of the crises of modern womanhood, personal fears and modesty, or the importance of moving beyond a stigmatized image of disease—hallmarks of the new cancer awareness campaigns. Instead, black Americans were seen as members of a migrating horde. Experts saw a teeming and monolithic mass of humanity moving from country life to cities at a rapid clip, adopting new behaviors associated with whiteness and bringing new health challenges. The experts' own awareness mirrored widely held views on the differences between black and white Americans, for the color line was defined not only by skin color alone but also by presumed differences in social setting, sensibility, group behavior, and intellectual capacity. Using the racial language of the day, public health and medical scholars described the cancer problem in black America in bold strokes, seeing a multitude of primitives in transition. For most authors the Negro question in cancer was therefore not a simple biological puzzle; it was a complex sociocultural mystery in which specific forces in black life were driving the rise of disease.

Although American biologists, physicians, surgeons, and laymen might differ slightly from one another, they had become jointly captivated by the romantic idea of the savage Negro's ecological transformation. They saw civilization as a powerful, noxious force in black life during the Jim Crow era, and they wove this dramatic racial narrative deeply into the era's cancer discourse. In his book *Cancer: Its Origins, Its Development, and Its Self-Perpetuation* (1931), New York surgeon Willy Meyer argued that primitive cultures "in the familiar character of their restful unchanging surroundings" knew little cancer because their lives "would almost seem to be on a par with the fish of the ocean, the life of which is spent in placid indifference in the never changing salt solution and its always equal temperature." Life in the "natural," supposedly worry-free South with its agricultural lifestyle and languid pace was said to offer African Americans protection from cancer. According to Meyer, "prolonged worry is almost unknown among [such primitive peoples] . . . and [they are absent] of nervous and psychic strain . . . which is the bane of modern civilized man."[3] Just as fish did not suffer cancer, so also people who existed in "placid waters," free from the stresses of modern life, were immune to the disease. Like Meyer, Elida Evans also opined about lower rates among African Americans in her 1926 *Psychological Study of Cancer* (1926) mentioned in chapter 1. In particular, she speculated about the absence of skin cancer among blacks: "As the race is not afflicted with perversions, their skin serves only its natural function," she concluded. People unadorned by modern cosmetics, without vanity, anxiety, and stress, and who maintained natural habits suffered less cancer—so went the prevailing theory. Primitive people allowed instinct to guide them; they lived as their bodies, their basic wants, and their innate tendencies dictated. "It should be remembered," ran the common refrain, "that cancer is mostly a product of civilization."[4]

Once these disease truisms took shape early in the twentieth century, they became entrenched in professional and popular thought and difficult to overturn; indeed, it would take massive social and demographic change for experts to stop singing from this old script. Mass migration, economic depression, and the shifting professional recognition of cancer revealed new realities even as it reinforced the focus on the black masses. Migration swelled urban hospitals, put stress on public health programs, and created crises of indigent care, infant mortality, and elder care. The influx of people to cities gradually changed the face of cancer. Setting aside civilization theory, experts slowly saw that new kinds of logic were shaping health trends in general and cancer trends in particular. A new kind of awareness of the disease was dawning—shaped by a growing patchwork of cancer registries in states and cancer surveillance in cities and by the federal government's efforts at detection through the U.S. Public Health Service.

A distinct minority of cancer scholars had always questioned the race and civilization hypothesis.[5] Writing in *Social Forces* about trends in 1920s Harlem, for example, physician Ira Reid regarded as mysterious the "phenomenal" increase of the incidence of cancer in blacks from 1900 to 1925, a 120.5 percent rise compared to a 62.7 percent increase in whites: "How much of this cancer is due to more exact diagnosis, better reporting, and to the increased length of life of the Negro is an interesting and complex problem," and worthy of deeper study.[6] To many observers, the era's demographic shifts provided the crucial context for interpreting cancer trends. The nationally known journalist and critic H. L. Mencken decried the demographic shifts in his beloved city of Baltimore, "inundated by several waves of low-grade immigrants, all American-born." First had come industrial workers; then, "set in motion by the depression, came a rush of negro yokels from Virginia, the Carolinas and beyond." Next came "a movement of anthropoid mountain whites from Appalachia," he railed, all of them making "heavy demands on the Johns Hopkins" Hospital. Their presence, Mencken claimed, reduced the living standard of black Baltimore, dragging down those African Americans who had pulled themselves up before the "influx of shiftless and unclean barbarians from the Southern swamps."[7] This movement, as we shall see, spawned new theories of disease while still supporting the characterization of black Americans as a monolithic and threatening force.

To most authorities, cancer was an allegory about some of the most pressing questions of their day: the fate of black people as they moved toward the urban North, the question of immigration, the changing racial character of the U.S. population, and the so-called competition between "the races."[8] Were black Americans destined for extinction, experts asked? Were they making progress only to begin "dying like white men"? Were black Americans standing on the brink of a new age when rising cancer death rates would be their downfall? Were they not better off staying in the South, where their rural brethren lived protected from these ravages of the white man? Would their supposed "immunity" be eroded in unforgiving northern environments?[9] Or would black immunity give them a survival advantage in the numerical struggle with whites? Such questions, buttressed by shaky statistics and by the era's fascination with savagery and civilization, defined early epidemiological awareness about black Americans and cancer. As experts in Baltimore, Harlem, Detroit, Nashville, and cities across the nation took stock of the surging masses, it seemed to them increasingly implausible that fundamentally different innate vulnerabilities explained black and white cancer mortality differences. In the epidemiological imagination, these old truths were fading away, and new theories of race and disease took shape.

LOSING IMMUNITY IN THE MODERN WORLD

Cancer mirrored the color line—so most scholars contended. But they also could see that cancer—a disease defined by biology, environment, history, and profound social differences—was changing. "In his own environment," wrote one author in the *Washington Post* in 1924, "the negro may be immune, but in the United States he is not."[10] "All over the world," bemoaned another writer in 1929, the "diet and habits of the white man is deteriorating these robust races wherever contact is effected between them, and the process of degeneration goes on till finally the physique of the native and his liability to diseases become identical with that of the people among whom his lot is cast."[11] The theme would be recycled in later decades for other groups coming to

America—Jews, Italians, Vietnamese (as discussed in chapter 6), and so on. They had left behind unimaginable poverty, Old World diets, and antique beliefs, but in becoming modern, urban, and civilized Americans, they were becoming prone to cancer.

Many authors saw the American South as a middle zone for black men and women, a geographical space that was not quite primitive Africa but also not fully civilized America. Below the Mason-Dixon Line, they contended, cancer rates in heavily rural lands of cotton, tobacco, sugar, and livestock were naturally lower than in the North, but not as low as in native Africa.[12] "In South Carolina," one writer noted, "the crude rate among white people was 41, among the negroes, 25 . . . Statistics show that the negro is far less susceptible than the white man."[13] In southern cities like Birmingham, Alabama, John Harvey Kellogg claimed, the death rate among whites (112.9 per 100,000) was twice the rate for "colored" people (47.9).[14] The gap between white women and black men was particularly stark. In 1919, Metropolitan Life's Louis Dublin had found that while the white female death rate was 88.4 per 100,000, the rate for "colored men" was less than half of that, 31.0.[15]

As black people headed north, Kellogg insisted, the cancer situation seemed to reverse itself. In St. Louis, the colored cancer rate had inched past the white rate—83.3 for colored, to 81.3 for whites. In Evansville, Indiana, the gap was even larger—83.3 colored to 71.1 white. And three hundred miles north of St. Louis in the heart of Chicago, said Kellogg, the colored rate had raced ahead of the white rate, 91.4 to 72.1. A diet specialist obsessed with the loss of healthy lifestyles, Kellogg wedded these cancer statistics to the up-from-prim-itivism theory that would have a long career. Cancer variations could only "be explained by change of habits, chiefly in relation to diet and out-of-door life, which the Negro makes in moving from a southern plantation to a northern city."[16] Even the black physician Louis T. Wright embraced the "civilization" thesis.[17] And sociologist James Reinhardt seized on the rising cancer rates to prove that theories of innate racial difference and biological inferiority were flawed, for "the cancer rate appears . . . to rise with advances in social and cultural conditions."[18] Cancer, in short, sprang upon these people like a maraud-ing bandit as they moved north. Go north, the prevailing awareness script warned, and cancer would surely follow.

But how much did these theorists and self-styled experts really know about health and disease in the South, where the data was notoriously sparse and unreliable? Writing in 1928 on the "health of the negro," Louis Dublin acknowledged the limits of diagnostic and statistical knowledge of the black health condition: "my reliance will be on the materials collected for many years by the Metropolitan Life Insurance Company . . . [which] now insures . . . close to 2.5 million Negroes." Proud of this data, Dublin admitted nevertheless that "the conditions which prevail in the rural South, where a large proportion of the Negroes still live, are . . . not closely reflected by the insurance experience."[19] Intelligent observers had well-founded doubts about the many silences and gaps in the numbers. "Is the death rate from cancer among Negroes less than it is among whites?" wondered Walter F. Willcox in 1917.[20] Though it *appeared* to be so, the data were so unreliable and so erratically collected that "no great weight can be given to them . . . My own belief," Willcox concluded, is "that much, if not all, of the difference is due to differences in the accuracy of diagnosis."[21] In the absence of reliable information, tales of immunity flourished even among careful statisticians like Dublin, who speculated that "the Negro in America has clearly been outside of a normal environment [i.e., Africa]. Just as it has proved difficult for white men to live in the tropics, so have Negroes struggled to adapt themselves to the rigors of our northern country with its variety of parasitic organisms to which they have little or no immunity."[22] For African Americans, who lived as Dublin said beyond the margins of "the insurance experience," and who were only now migrating into areas where cancer diagnosis was more common, these stories of lost immunity thrived—a by-product not of rising cancer rates per se, but of migration, rising visibility, and health surveillance.

How cancer crossed the color line became, in part, the story of how black Americans migrated slowly into "the insurance experience" so that their health conditions could become diagnosed and statistically known. In this era, insurance and data collection played critical roles in scientific awareness, determining which groups' health problems were visible and which remained shrouded in mystery. As James Marquis, journalist and historian of Metropolitan Life, acknowledged, black Americans "a few years out of slavery" had once been seen as a promising new market for life insurance. For the first generation of former slaves, "Prudential issued policies on colored lives at the same rate as whites." Metropolitan Life did likewise; but "by 1881 . . . the fact that Negro lives were subject to a much greater mortality than whites had become apparent."[23] From the insurance perspective, these people who died at earlier ages were bad insurance risks—they paid less in premiums over their lives than longer-living policyholders. As a result, Frederick Hoffman of Prudential Life Insurance had infamously predicted in the 1890s that "in the struggle for supremacy the black race is not holding its own" because of heavier infectious disease mortality: "its extreme liability to consumption [tuberculosis] alone," he claimed, "would suffice to seal its fate."[24] In this view, which gained credibility because of the authority and breadth of insurance records, the Negro was doomed. By the late nineteenth century, Metropolitan Life and its sister company Prudential had begun charging black Americans higher premiums, a move they defended as "dictated by actuarial findings . . . [but] misconstrued as racial discrimination."[25] This calculation naturally skewed life insurance data by reducing the representation of black policy holders. Thus, there was a circular, self-reinforcing logic at work—for the data of Met Life and Prudential disproportionately tracked the experiences of the financially better-off policyholders, leaving the larger story of life and death across the color line in the shadows.

Theoretically, personal accounts of the black cancer experience might have been able to fill some of the gaps of awareness created by skewed insurance records, paltry evidence from state-by-state mortality surveys, and ideological fascination with "the horde." But personalized narratives of cancer in black America are nearly impossible to find. So, in the literary annals, the fictional character of Ollie Weaver, a creation of award-winning North Carolina short-story writer and playwright Paul Green in a collection of stories of small-town southern life under the title *Wide Fields*, represented a rare type. An unusual fictional cancer patient for any era, Ollie was a particular standout in the late 1920s for three reasons: Ollie was a southerner, he was male, and he was African American, a tenant farmer. Every statistician knew that such individuals ranked far below white women, black women, and white men among those who were cancer prone.[26] Yet the fictional 1920s story of Ollie Weaver is revealing. Hired to clear land by Old Man Murchison, a white property owner, Ollie works hard with his mule Old Tom, spurred on by the promise that he can keep the profits of what he grows for three years. Ollie's tragedy and his cancer begin, however, on a dark day when Old Tom breaks away and tramples his son, Chick. "Then it was that the sky grew dark and all was bitterness and woe." It is here that Ollie's cancer starts, in much the same way that it was said to begin for others—from tragic disappointment, maladjustment, trauma, and loss.[27]

Cancer puts Ollie into a tragic spiral. In the wake of Chick's death, a sustained lethargy overtakes the once-hardy farmer, and it is hard for him to say whether it is rheumatism, heartache, headache, backache, or laziness that plagues him. "I'm getting lazy and no' count, I reckon," he says. "I feel bad all the time." In reality, it is a cancer that has quietly set in, Green tells his readers, though Ollie remains unaware that a "sentence of death" has been passed.[28] Seven medicines, plasters, poultices, and teas later, at the age of thirty-two, Ollie is taken by a kind neighboring landlord up to Raleigh to see a specialist. There, after a quick examination, he learns, "you've got a tumor or something, and it'll have to be taken out." Hearing the word "tumor" "he remembered again the sufferings of old Yen Yarborough with his cancer, and the horror of old Miss Minty's agony and death." A surgery is planned, though it is unclear who will pay the cost. A short while into the operation, however, the surgeon discovers that the tumor is extensive and inoperable, and withdraws. Ollie's wife, Lettie, is told the truth, but Ollie is not. Neighbors gradually learn that "it was too far gone. And so they sewed him back up. And poor fellow, he thinks he's going to get well."[29] Ollie only discovers the truth by accident, near the end of his slow demise and silent suffering.

The message of Ollie's demise was not lost on one reviewer of *Wide Fields* who, years later, praised the book's "balanced collection of tales," noting that "the same things happen to white and black alike and the author is wise enough to know that there are good and bad people everywhere and in all races."[30] In Green's telling, Ollie's life and death by cancer is a metaphor for life and death across the color line, and a commentary on shared experiences. That cancer had come at all to a black man, thereby drawing attention to the particularities of his life and intimate struggles, was the remarkable feature of the fictional story. As Louis Dublin had put it, black men were certainly outside "the insurance experience," beyond the data collection regime of the time. Green, one critic noted, "made no distinction between the traveling fiction and the actual or embroidered incident."[31] The portrait of Ollie's cancer stands out starkly against what epidemiologists believed to be the demographic norm. And Green's writing reflected something else: an egalitarian ideal—cancer as an equal opportunity disease—that would not gain wide currency until the 1950s.[32]

A NEW DEAL IN HEALTH AWARENESS

The economic turmoil of the 1920s and the Depression era sensitized experts to health as a migration problem. (Even before the Great Depression, the 1920s was a difficult economic time for farmers.) The Depression era redistributed the African-American population, as great waves of migrants moved from southern farms to northern cities in search of work.[33] Especially amidst depression, it became clear that health and disease were linked to the loss of work, the rural-to-urban migration, and the changing American political economy. Calls for government relief grew. As African Americans found their way to urban hospitals and as researchers found their way into the remote reaches of the country where men like Ollie worked, the insurance statistics of Dublin and Hoffman began to seem limited and biased, unsuited for tracking the modern health dilemma. The movement of people created instability and conflict.[34] But for cancer experts, population movement also complicated the tracking of health trends.

Among the nation's small but growing coterie of government health officials in the 1920s and 1930s, a new kind of cancer awareness took shape. "One-third to one-half of all dependency can be traced to the economic effects of illness," wrote the tireless social reformer Grace Abbott, who had helped in establishing the Social Security Administration.[35] In progressive federal agencies designed to address Depression-era economic insecurity, men such as Harold Dorn of the U.S. Public Health Service (PHS) saw health as an element in the political economy.[36] Other state and federal agencies also documented the health challenges that came in the wake of economic turmoil. As the chief statistician of the PHS, Edgar Sydenstricker, saw it, hard times meant taking the "broader view that the state is responsible for the health of the people—not merely for community conditions such as sanitation, pure water and foods, and the control of infectious disease, but also for the early diagnosis of certain diseases and impairments, the prevention of infant and maternal mortality . . . education of the individual in the principles of personal hygiene . . . tuberculosis, cancer, and orthopedic defects."[37] It was obvious to those in charge of New Deal agencies that "illness is one of the major causes of economic insecurity which threatens people of small means in good times as in bad."[38] Indeed, cancer (as one of the most notorious chronic and degenerative diseases) had become "an element in [the] social security" of the nation. Calls grew heated for a government institute dedicated to finding a cure. As with polio, for example, cancer was said to absorb "a relatively larger proportion of the services of private and clinic physicians than do the acutely ill."[39] Surgeon General Thomas Parran Jr. worried over these trends. He also puzzled over the "development of the health consciousness of the Negro," while others commented that illness and migration had also "created the need for comparative data on illness among Negroes in urban areas."[40] In the midst of America's economic doldrums, government experts acknowledged that there was a pressing need for reliable information on disease incidence, severity, and duration on both sides of the color line.

Building institutions such as the National Cancer Institute (NCI) to remedy gaps in knowledge and unevenness in care took on urgency. Hospitals had become magnets for migrants, and, as one researcher saw it in 1932, "the increasing hospitalization of recent years has attracted many rural and small village residents to the larger, better-equipped urban centers for medical treatment."[41] "In the 30th Ward of Philadelphia," argued Samuel Jackson Holmes in his treatise *The Negro's Struggle for Survival* (1937), "where there are exceptional hospital advantages for Negro children and where special attention has been given to the instruction of Negro mothers, infant mortality . . . has been reduced below that of whites."[42] Yet a 1935 survey by J. W. Schereschewsky in seldom-studied Georgia found that "there is no organized cancer treatment clinic in Columbus."[43] Nor did "organized facilities exist in Albany[, Georgia, which] seems to be a municipal center for a radius of about thirty or forty miles . . . The city lacks both a radiologist and a pathologist."[44]

To rectify unevenness in resources and health data, reform-minded health officials like Schereschewsky insisted that building cancer clinics in nonmetropolitan areas was essential. In La Grange, Georgia, he found, "the only facilities for treating cancer . . . are those at the disposition of Dr. Enoch Callaway, who is both a surgeon and a radiologist . . . He does practically all the radium treatment for cancer in a radius of thirty miles" with "100 milligrams of radium and a model 200 K.V. deep therapy machine."[45] The color line was clearly evident in towns like Athens, which possessed "the Clarke County Hospital of sixty-five beds, of which six are for colored."[46] And in Savannah, Schereschewsky observed, although "Dr. W. H. Myers, a leading surgeon . . . manifested great interest in the possibility of establishing a regularly organized cancer clinic," he admitted "that it would be necessary, because of the local conditions, to establish two clinics, one for white and one for colored."[47] Such surveys exposed deep structural barriers to medical care. The Public Works Administration, for example, had recently built a thirty-bed, "thoroughly modern" hospital in the remote town of Toccoa, Georgia, but the area lacked adequate roads for potential patients to get there. The town, wrote Schereschewsky, was "too near the state border, and also not sufficiently accessible . . . to be considered as a possible location for a cancer treatment center at this time."[48]

The notion of innate racial cancer disparities began to seem increasingly implausible to public health leaders in New Deal America, especially in the face of mounting evidence of organizational, economic, and social disparities. They also saw Jim Crow's shadow over the health care system. Grappling with the problem of uneven access to care for cancer, for example, Georgia legislators passed their own modest "State Cancer Control Act" in 1937, setting aside "$50,000 . . . annually for two years to aid indigent cancer patients" deprived of cancer care.[49] As the state became more involved in such efforts, its board of health turned to women (on both sides of the color line) to spur cancer awareness. As Florence Hunt, president of the Georgia Federation of Colored Women's Clubs, saw it, "the state Federation of White Women is doing the field work in the districts in which they live." Her hope was to "organize the State Federation of Colored Women's Clubs to carry on this work among our own people."[50] Funds for these efforts were always scarce, and more and more experts understood that the vagaries of racial segregation and health care budgets, rather than biological differences among the races, defined the line between life and death with cancer.[51]

By 1936, researchers like Harold Dorn—aware of how movement, mobility, and institution building was changing the picture of cancer—had brought this broad-minded disease outlook into an expanding PHS, joining "the cohorts of social scientists recruited for national service during the administration of Franklin D. Roosevelt."[52] Other states besides Georgia had become active in tracking cancer trends. In 1935, for example, Connecticut, home to many national insurance companies, had pioneered in creating a division of cancer research within its health department, the first statewide cancer registry in the nation.[53] A patchwork of such state registries slowly took shape, each with limited data and incomplete coverage in its state. At the national level, "systematic surveys of cancer incidence, morbidity, and mortality were organized to elucidate problems of cancer pathogenesis," one participant in the effort later recalled. And with the creation of the National Cancer Institute (NCI) and an expanding PHS, in 1937 "a gigantic pioneering one-year study of the National Institutes of Health (NIH) [of cancer mortality rates] in ten metropolitan areas" was organized.[54] As a result of these Depression-era projects, populations that had previously received little attention in health studies came into view.[55] Cancer was coming to be more easily detected in the urban hospitals and in public health studies. But whether urban living was itself increasing the cancer rates, whether urban living was selectively victimizing the rising black urban population, or whether urban living merely increased *awareness* of the disease, these questions required deeper study.

More than ever, cancer seemed to be a social disease since access to health institutions, physician training, and the wealth or poverty of patients made the difference between life and death. As the southern physician Isidore Cohn put it, "it would hardly be fair to compare end results [i.e., cancer treatment outcomes], morbidity, and mortality, from a well organized institution with those obtained by the occasional operator [a surgeon] who has only indifferent equipment and associate personnel." Moreover, some patients came to the hospital in dramatically worse conditions than others, which also affected survival differences. "The character of the clientele is a factor which must be reckoned with," Cohn insisted, "if data which are to be presented are to be of value." The New Orleans surgeon insisted that "the more highly intelligent, the better the financial status of the individual, and the proximity to institutions where skilled management of the case can be obtained are factors which though intangible cause marked variations in end results." "Statistics," he concluded, "to be comparable must share the same type of patients and with the disease at relatively the same period in its development."[56]

TRUTHS IN TRANSITION: THE JEWS AND CANCER ABROAD

While the American puzzle of race and cancer was painted in black and white, the European counterpart of the race and cancer problem featured Jews at its center. Yet here, too, mass mobility unsettled old truths. And once again, old group stereotypes about race proved hard to outgrow. Analyzing this parallel case is instructive, for it illustrates how other societies' racial assumptions were also being revised during the same decades.

For Maurice Sorsby, a young surgeon at the London Jewish Hospital, the race problem in cancer was not a black-white American dilemma, but a European paradox—one in which Jews played the central role. In the early 1930s, experts on both continents saw cancer as a complex sociological puzzle that was unfolding amidst economic crisis and racial turmoil. For years, the thirty-two-year-old surgeon had heard both that Jews were prone to cancer *and* that they were less vulnerable. Sorsby regarded both as facile truisms that sprung up around flawed statistics, breathing life into racist claims of intransigent Jewish differences. Cancer had much company. "Quite a series of diseases have been claimed at some time or other, as disorders to which Jews are either specially prone or particularly immune," Sorsby noted. On one side, experts compiled a long list "regarded as specifically Jewish" afflictions, from Tay-Sachs to

Buerger's disease. On the other side, "it [had] been claimed that chronic infections, such as tuberculosis and syphilis, seldom affect Jews." Cancer occupied "a position peculiarly its own" among "these ill-substantiated claims for a racial factor" because "until quite recently, Jews were held by some to be practically immune; yet statistics were not lacking to prove not only an equal but excessive incidence."[57] Which was true? Were Jews immune or especially vulnerable to cancer? Sorsby looked to the statistics of ten European cities, among them Amsterdam, Budapest, Leningrad, Warsaw, and Lodz, for an answer. His book, *Cancer and Race*, was not widely influential at the time. Yet Sorsby's study reveals him to be a sophisticated skeptic battling against the old truisms and foreshadowing changes to come in both epidemiological analysis, cancer stereotyping, and characterizations of Jewish people.

As the Nazis rose to power in Germany, the notion of Jewish cancer immunity (running parallel to the idea of black immunity) had become "a thesis with which no clinician could have any patience," Sorsby wrote. "It is a far cry now from the days of 1890 when . . . W. S. Bainbridge could show a case of sarcoma in a Jewish girl as a pathological curiosity."[58] Opinion on the Jews had changed just as it had for "the Negro." By the 1920s, the public health statistics of major cities undermined the old truths, but only partly.[59] The problem was that the statistics were confusing. The cancer mortality data from cities across Europe were particularly inconsistent on the topic of the Jews. Sorsby did not reject entirely the notion of Jews as a "racial" breed apart, for "not only are they a race of considerable purity of stock, but by their ubiquitous presence they supply the interesting phenomenon of a racial unit subjected to widely-differing geographical influences."[60] The question was whether their racial difference explained cancer differences—or whether other factors were at play. Sorsby's lengthy study took readers across Europe city by city to consider the statistics and different stories coming out of Vienna, London, Warsaw, and so on.

In some European cities the cancer mortality rate among Jews was higher than the rest of the population; in others, it was lower. One reason for the mortality divergence from one city to another, Sorsby insisted, was the failure to think comparatively, to account for mobility trends, or to think critically about the numbers. "There is," he insisted, "one difficulty specific to statistical studies concerning Jews, for Jews being a wandering race do not lend themselves very well to statistical examination." Moreover, Sorsby argued that the mobility of young Jews and the relative immobility of the old explained the wildly varying claims about Jewish susceptibility and immunity, creating havoc in disease awareness in Europe as in America. "The younger element tend to migrate from established settlements, leaving behind them an elderly Jewish population, so that an artificially high death rate and an apparent high cancer mortality may arise. On the other hand, a new community with its influx of young Jews will tend to show a low total mortality and a low cancer death rate." In the era before systematic age-adjustment was standard practice in analyzing mortality data, such differences in the relative age of populations could be misleading—causing one place to have low rates, and others to have higher ones. "Such influences as these may explain why cancer has been claimed both as a specific Jewish disease and as a disease to which Jews are practically immune," the London surgeon concluded.[61]

Taking on facile racial theorizing, Sorsby insisted that a thorough assessment of populations, going city by city, proved that "there is certainly no evidence of any Jewish immunity to cancer, [and] little [evidence] that Jews are more prone to cancer." "There is a fairly close approximation of the rate for the Jews to that of the non-Jews of the various cities studied," he observed. Thus, "in Amsterdam and Budapest [rates for both groups were generally higher because] there are more people of the cancer age in the Jewish population." And "particularly in Vienna, the rate for Jews is decidedly higher."[62] Considering the increasingly obvious geographical variation in the United States, the Public Health Service's Mary Gover had also noted the curious effects of migration on statistics, commenting that "among colored males, the recorded rate for all forms of cancer is slightly more than twice as high in the North as it is in the South . . . Among colored females . . . the rate . . . is one-and-a-half times as high in the North as in the South."[63]

Foreshadowing theories that would take root two decades later, Sorsby focused on a striking anomaly: Jewish women did enjoy "a remarkably lower rate of uterine cancer" and cervical cancer than did non-Jews. This type of cancer, therefore, warranted closer scrutiny. For Sorsby, behavior and custom rather than *race biology* per se held the key. Like most experts, he believed "it is clear that married life in some form or other is the usual soil from which uterine cancer springs." But why would the linkage between marriage and cancer be different for Jewish women? It was possible that Jewish communities had larger proportions of unmarried women, he speculated—but "even a superficial acquaintance with the Jewish masses dispels the idea." Could it be that Jewish women experienced lesser trauma during childbirth (since another widespread theory implicated birth trauma as a cause of such cancers)? Sorsby found "no evidence . . . that Jewish women are subject to less trauma than their non-Jewish sisters . . . nor any cause for belief that their pelves are wider and Jewish foetal heads smaller, thus obviating difficult labours." The answer to the puzzle of low cervical/uterine cancer was behavior, the surgeon insisted: it was the "regulated sexual life" of Jewish women that "might be a favourable factor in the avoidance of this disease." This regulated sexual life stemmed from Jewish religious observance. "The Mosaic Code, with its insistence on local cleanliness and abstention from sexual intercourse during the presence of a blood-stained discharge," imposed clear restrictions on marital relations and also imposed limits on the resumption of sexual activity after childbirth, the surgeon claimed. The ritual bath [the mikvah] made "Jewish women obeying ritual laws . . . cleaner in body than the masses of non-Jewish women." It was these religious codes and rituals that guided Jewish women, Sorsby believed, and protected them when other women fell to cancer.[64]

Writing at the same time when Aryan race theories abounded and the Jewish question took on enormous political significance, Sorsby pushed aside the fatuous theories of Jewish immunity and susceptibility to focus instead on the complexities of migration and aging, cross-city differences, and customs and rites. But his account of the Jewish cervical cancer gap also put a decidedly behaviorist spin on the "lower incidence of uterine cancer among Jewish women." In Budapest, where the uterine cancer rate had climbed for the general population from 1924 to 1927 but remained low among Jews, Sorsby was quick to point to "the ever-increasing lack of observance of the ritual code by Jewish women."[65] In many ways, the idea echoed familiar teachings about the relationship of Jewish scripture to health.[66] The novel twist was Sorsby's focus on cancer. For him, Jewish law taught women to inspect their bodies during menstruation, for "the appearance of discharges [was] a cause for inquiry as to its nature, and a woman with a blood-stained discharge is theologically 'unclean.'" In writing *Cancer and Race*, he hoped to move European understandings of Jews beyond crass racial stereotypes and demonization to suggest that, indeed, much could be learned from the Jews. Low uterine and cervical cancer rates were a "lasting achievement of the Mosaic code that has taught Jewish women that vaginal discharges are essentially pathological and avoidable."[67]

Sorsby's analysis highlights how researchers were looking behind prevailing racial truisms in Europe and in America, scrutinizing epidemiological "facts" with a critical eye, and getting to the social causes of so-called racial differences. When he read Sorsby's account, the American Society for the Control of Cancer's Clarence Cook Little called it a "very interesting study" and accepted the likely influence of "environmental factors in the lives of Jewish women." He made no mention of Sorsby's focus on Jewish behavior or religion as cancer protection. But Little and other scientists of this era would never entirely abandon the notion of racial differences and innate biological immunities. Writing in 1934, Little concluded that "the possibility of the existence of a racial factor cannot . . . as yet be considered eliminated."[68] As Sorsby himself saw the situation, Jews were indeed a "race," but they were no more biologically prone or susceptible than other "races" to cancer. They were an uprooted, stateless people under siege throughout Europe, equal in almost every way, yet protected by religious tradition from the ravages of this one form of cancer. In both Europe and America (where Sorsby eventually migrated), there were a handful of such researchers who interpreted the statistical data in this critical and careful fashion, not as the final word on race and cancer but as the beginning of a social mystery in which the vagaries of population migration were of critical importance.[69]

BLACK ADVANTAGE? DISEASE IN THE STRUGGLE FOR RACIAL SUPREMACY

If the Englishman Maurice Sorsby saw cancer as an emblem of the Jewish woman's protection by Mosaic law, the California biologist Samuel Jackson Holmes saw cancer as the stage for American racial conflict, a fight in which blacks held a hidden advantage over whites. Like many scientists writing on the cancer question, Holmes worried over the shocking inadequacy of the statistical evidence. Even with improvements in the registration of cancer deaths in many states, "many uncertainties are involved . . . on account of the incomplete registration of deaths in the Negro population."[70] But this did not stop such experts from dissecting the numbers, or reading them as part of a grand ecological struggle between blacks and whites for supremacy.[71]

Samuel Jackson Holmes was well into his sixties when he decided in 1936 that cancer trends carried lessons for the future of the nation, and like many before him he saw the disease as a parable about racial survival. There was "no way of avoiding the conclusion that biologically Negroes and whites in the United States are rivals for the possession of a common territory," the biologist wrote. "The victories won through high fertility or a low death rate are just as fatal to the losing competitor as a war of extermination."[72] In this view, diseases like cancer were not merely problems of individual suffering; they were an arena in which blacks and whites and other groups battled for supremacy.

And in this warfare black people had a clear upper hand, argued Holmes in a 1937 book, *The Negro's Struggle for Survival: A Study in Human Ecology*. In his view, the trends showed how "the whites have done much to help their meeker brethren to inherit the earth."[73] Statistics on cancer trends were a bad omen for whites in the "competition between the races," he concluded.[74]

By the mid-1930s most experts—Holmes included—understood that the official statistics on cancer mortality, although numerous, were built on weak foundations. "If we interpret the statistics as their face value," he had observed in an essay in the *Journal of Negro Education*, "we must conclude that the Negroes are relatively free from cancer, but cancer statistics are notoriously deceptive."[75] The challenge of accounting for black mortality was by now well established. "Cancer appears to be less prevalent in the colored population," he insisted in another article, only because "deaths are not so likely to be diagnosed as due to this cause as in the whites."[76] Southerners, rural citizens, and men with internal cancers (including those in the urban North) died in larger numbers without their diagnosis ever becoming official. "Undoubtedly," Holmes noted, "difference in the accuracy of diagnosis in our white and colored populations have some effect upon our statistics on cancer death rates." Comparing mortality across lines of race was also tricky, Holmes asserted, because black people lied: "Negroes beyond middle age tend to overstate their age," and these "troublesome problems of relative mendacity" skewed even the most earnest calculations. He acknowledged, "I have long puzzled over how greatly this . . . [fact] would affect the accuracy of age specific mortality rates." Writing in the *American Journal of Cancer*, he concluded that "the rates for the colored population are less reliable than those for the whites because they are based upon much fewer cases, and there is a considerable degree of fluctuation due to chance."[77]

The nation's weak system of data collection distorted awareness in a bizarre fashion, Holmes scoffed: "Every student of cancer statistics knows that improvement in the accuracy of diagnosing the true cause of death has led to a statistical increase in mortality from cancer."[78] The whole enterprise of diagnosing cancer, tracking deaths, and keeping population records accurately in this highly mobile society was fraught with peril, he argued. Even the Census had come under attack for systematically undercounting African Americans, and if any population were undercounted it would artificially skew the death rates.[79] In 1920 the Census had shown "colored" Americans failing to reproduce at the same pace as whites; but the next Census in 1930 showed a healthy rebound. "If the returns of the 1930 census are substantially correct," Holmes wrote skeptically in 1936, "we must face the possibility that the Negro population has taken a new lease on life." If such population gains were real, he worried that "the Negro problem, instead of decreasing in relative importance, may become more serious in the years to come," and predictions about the future health of the race would have to be revisited.[80]

Holmes believed that a new analytical strategy offered better insights on which groups were truly surviving or suffering from disease—and his findings unsettled old truisms about the relative immunity of African Americans. He divided races into their age subgroups and found that each subgroup had peculiar age-specific cancer vulnerabilities. No group was entirely immune or prone to cancer. "If we break up our populations in five-year age groups" (comparing deaths across races for ages one to five, six to ten, eleven to fifteen, and so on), "we find some curious facts," observed Holmes. Up to age forty-five, there were no marked differences between white and colored men in cancer deaths. But after age forty-five, "cancer mortality in the white male becomes increasingly higher . . . two to three times as great." The situation was reversed for women; death rates for colored women exceeded whites "in the age groups from 20 up to about age 60, after which the mortality of white females becomes increasingly preponderant . . . about double the rate for colored females." In short, white men and white women were more susceptible to cancer in later years than "colored" people. But at younger ages, these differences were nonexistent, or even slightly reversed. Among all types of cancer, the only exception was uterine cancer, where younger black women saw higher death rates; for this category, Holmes argued that health practices ("the greater neglect of uterine traumas associated with childbirth") rather than race in itself explained higher death rates.[81]

What did these trends mean for predictions of racial survival and extinction? Using this data, Holmes revisited Frederick Hoffman's dire prediction in 1896 of a coming black extinction. Cancer trends, Holmes insisted, did reflect a struggle for survival of the fittest, a war between blacks and whites. But the lessons were muddled. Looking at the overall higher white mortality, he noted, one might wrongly believe that the disease rates "would favor the vital prospects of the colored population." But white deaths were usually at advanced age, and therefore (in Holmes's view) inconsequential with regard to the future reproduction of the race. The death of elderly women who no longer bore children or raised families made no difference in numerical supremacy. "From the standpoint of the biological struggle for existence," he wrote, "it matters relatively little what becomes of people after they no longer contribute to the natural increase of their kind." On the contrary, it was "the deaths occurring in the reproductive period of life [that] are relatively more numerous in the colored than in the whites" that told of the lasting impact of cancer death rates.[82] Thus, "if one should ask how cancer mortality affects the struggle for numerical supremacy between whites and blacks," he suggested, "the answer which seems immediately to suggest itself would probably be wrong."[83] Cancer *was* more a white disease—this was true—but Holmes believed that because of its graver impact on younger African-American women, in the grand scheme of things the disease would hinder the growth of the black population more than it would the white population.[84]

But in the grand struggle for ecological and racial dominance, cancer was only one actor among many, Holmes wrote. "The white race has often proved to be a deadly scourge to native peoples with whom it has mingled," he found, but that was in the past. Times had changed, new diseases had appeared, and these previous "untoward effects" had abated.[85] The new truth would only be found by sorting through his reorganized data, paring away the confounding factors of migration and immigration, accounting for the Census's unreliability, considering the age-related death rate, and taking rates of racial reproduction into account; only then could the truth of race and cancer be revealed.[86] Rejecting stale truisms about black inferiority, he insisted that while "it seems not unlikely that the Negro suffers from some handicaps of this kind [for example, high mortality due to allegedly small lung capacity] . . . on the other hand, he is favored by some partial immunities which probably constitute a valuable permanent asset." Holmes concluded that taking all diseases into account, the notion "that the Negro is 'constitutionally inferior' to the whites, as was formerly asserted by some writers, is a conclusion devoid of adequate foundation."[87]

Most expert observers knew by heart the long list of afflictions that "discriminate against the black man," weakening them numerically, Holmes wrote, such as tuberculosis, pneumonia, heart disease, venereal disease, measles and diphtheria, homicide, and infant mortality; but on the whole, black people remained fit. These major diseases killed not because of innate biological factors, but "because the black man lives in a social and economic environment largely dominated by the whites."[88] Even in tuberculosis, where death rates for African Americans continued to be "about three to five times greater than the white," Holmes suspected that the numbers were skewed because of the "racial difference in the recognition or admission of disability or differences in the completeness of enumeration of illness."[89] By the mid-1930s, the accumulating evidence suggested that former predictions of an impending demise of the black race due to disease had been grossly exaggerated. "With the possible exception of his greater proneness to tuberculosis and the acute respiratory infections," Holmes concluded, "[the black man] is, on the whole, probably a better animal than the white man."[90] Other experts, like M. O. Bousfield of the African American–owned Supreme Life Insurance company, cheered that the old truisms were in decline, and that "the question of racial susceptibility of the Negro . . . [once] of constant interest to persons working in this field . . . is becoming less and less an issue. Other more important factors exist for solution."[91]

Looking at cancer trends alongside other disease and population trends, Holmes not only rejected the idea of innate black inferiority but also concluded that the news was ultimately worse for whites than blacks. In the end, the eugenics-minded Holmes concluded his cancer study professing sympathy for the black peoples' struggles in their competition with whites: "They may be less well adapted than the white man to live in a cold climate, but their fate will not be decided by death rates alone." Indeed the secret black advantage, Holmes said, was that the black birth rate continued to exceed that of whites, while the death gap was narrowing. If these trends continued, he insisted, "their net rate of natural increase may come to equal, if not exceed, that of their white competitors." Yes, economic stress, social disadvantages, and health hardships created many mortality problems for blacks, but so too, he insisted, did prosperity—which amounted to a kind of curse for whites and blacks both.

Overall, Holmes concluded paradoxically, "the fact that the Negroes occupy an economic and social status inferior to that of the whites will probably be a positive biological advantage." Conversely, prosperity "if carried beyond rather modest limits . . . is commonly a prelude to extinction."[92] He also believed that the passage of immigration restriction laws in the 1920s had given the black population another leg up, with "the war period [giving] a great impetus to the industrial employment of the Negroes," and the U.S.'s "exclusion of the immigrant created the Negro's opportunity" by removing this other source of competition.[93] The PHS's Harold Dorn, however, disputed the notion that "competition between foreign-born whites and Negroes [had ever] been strong enough to be of importance in restraining fertility."[94]

As health statistics and epidemiology matured as a field and its practitioners debated these issues, researchers such as Samuel Jackson Holmes and Harold Dorn increasingly seized the reins of the race and cancer discussion away from the likes of Frederick Hoffman and the insurance experts. For Holmes, the rigid racial truisms about the primitives' immunity that were current at the dawn of the century would not hold as new data was accumulated, dissected, and analyzed. Cancer, he suggested, did not draw such a sharp line between blacks and whites as many had believed—this new truth became apparent by considering the vulnerabilities of age cohorts. No biological immunity protected African Americans. But even though Holmes rejected some old truisms, he held on to others. He continued to believe that cancer had different implications for blacks and whites—seeing them as two monolithic racial groups that, he believed, would always be in sharp conflict with each other for resources, for numerical supremacy, for ecological dominance, and for survival.

By the late 1930s, mass migration and economic turmoil had unsettled the epidemiological awareness of the era, making the social determinants of health differences stunningly obvious. Experts in the growing, diversifying cancer field handled questions of Negro racial immunity with more subtlety and skepticism than in earlier decades. Although observers like the African-American physician William McKinney might insist in the black press that "cancer is a white man's disease . . . it is rarely, if ever developed among native [i.e., African] Negroes," most experts approached this assumption with caution.

Not only were disease statistics changing rapidly, but the emerging contradictions across types of cancers and within populations were turning old racial truisms on their head. Cervical cancer and "cancers of the female genital system," for example, increasingly stood apart from the other types, the only example where black mortality was "higher than in the white population."[95] Holmes had found this type was "more prevalent in Negroes than in whites in every age group, but more especially in younger women."[96] So heavy was the toll that high cervical cancer mortality alone swung the race-cancer calculus, "outweigh[ing] the relatively low Negro rate for other kinds of cancer" and making "the total cancer mortality of females in the child-bearing period higher in the colored than in the white population."[97] Increasingly in this new research environment, each type of cancer seemed to tell its own racial narrative. Physicians (both black and white) insisted that in cervical cancer it was not "race" per se, but the failure to repair uterine damage after birth and the lack of obstetrical care that was killing women.[98] "They are notoriously rare in women who have not borne children," Holmes noted, and "less adequate care after childbirth . . . [such as] the neglect of lacerations and other injuries, would naturally tend to cause more uterine cancer among Negro women."[99]

In the context of widespread economic dislocation and distress, experts were also more inclined to question the alleged biological uniformity of racial groups, or the notion of group immunity. "I do not believe that there is such a thing as *absolute* racial immunity to any disease," Louis Dublin wrote in 1937.[100] Race was as much a moving biological and social target as was disease. "The factor of the 'crossing' of the white and Negro bloods also beclouds the issue [of immunity]," Dublin admitted, "since the mulatto, the octoroon, etc., have both white and Negro blood, although they are classified as 'colored.'"[101] This critical awareness of race-mixing and racial ambiguity (which was a potent backdrop to American segregation) only surfaced occasionally in the epidemiological imagination. As New Orleans surgeon Isidore Cohn concluded in 1941, "after fifteen years of continuous observation of the cancer trend throughout the world, I have become convinced of the utter futility of drawing useful conclusions from general cancer death rate."[102] He did believe that racial biology remained a potent force, but insisted that biological race was more complex than it had ever been because "the Negro population of America is no longer a pure race."[103] Only occasionally would other experts follow suit, acknowledging that blacks (and whites, for that matter) were both malleable groups with multiple ancestries and ever-changing patterns of intermarriage. Cohn's views on biological and social transformation offered a new spin on the notion of "blacks becoming whites." His views also signaled that racial thinking was evolving again. Certainly, Americans' antagonism toward the virulent Aryan racial ideology of the Nazis contributed to skepticism about simplistic racial thinking. Moreover, the growing threat of fascism reminded experts such as C. C. Little of the ASCC that cancer similarities were just as socially important as differences, and that the disease carried other lessons for democratic thinking that transcended racial ideology. "For some years," he noted in his 1939 book *Civilization Against Cancer*, "we have been spending most of our time and energy in a blind and ineffective struggle for individual, group, class, creed and race preference." "In our absorption," he continued, "we have forgotten that the real enemies of mankind are common to all men."[104]

For the growing number of scholars working in an expanding U.S. government system in a nation then at the brink of joining in a world war, cancer trends provided an opportunity for a new discussion—of commonalities across groups, demographic changes, migration trends, population aging, behaviors and customs, and the changing political economy of African-American life. "The fact that an aging population must suffer a rising mortality from cancer, elementary though it may be, has often been overlooked in discussions on the relative frequency of cancer among different people," one observer noted in 1943, his bland tone a far cry from the hyperbole of race and cancer talk in the 1920s. The writer added, "those who assert, for example, that cancer is rare among Negroes, Egyptian peasants, and certain natives of India . . . forget entirely that these people die at an early age and so escape the chance of developing it."[105] Epidemiological and clinical awareness of health across the color line was changing. As two Nashville physicians insisted in 1940, the increase in cancer "diagnosed in Negroes is made possible by the better preparation to recognize the disease as well as by the greater clinical interest now taken in the Negro people" who were themselves "becoming more cancer conscious."[106]

Despite these important changes, we can see that the era's cancer discourse continued to draw heavily on a deep American fascination with the black multitude living "far out in the dark unsavory marginal regions of American life."[107] "The Southern Negro was believed to be sensitive and gentle," wrote another commentator named Helene Margaret in 1932. Blacks had become geographically and economically mobile, but "we are still taught to believe that behind these conventions of civilization is the savage . . ."[108] Health experts were not immune from this style of thinking. "In the general population, and more especially in the rural sections," wrote Louis Dublin in 1937, "the diabetes death rate has always run much higher among the whites than for the Negroes . . . [but] even if the more or less carefree rural Negro is more immune than the white man, it now appears that in urban surroundings the Negro is subject to much sickness and high mortality from this disease."[109] Such experts used diabetes, cancer, and other modern maladies in microcosm to tell the story of black transformation. Even if African Americans "marry, accumulate their little fortunes, and submit to the conventions of modern life," continued Helene Margaret, "it is because America wants to look upon the Negro in this way that she had been remarkably receptive to the savage myth." She concluded, "America prefers to bear her colored population like a cancer, and take an unhealthy delight in familiarity with the disease."[110]

Entrenched beliefs about the primitive's group encounter with civilization would continue to influence ideas on racial character and disease even today as discussed in chapter 6. For Holmes writing in the 1930s, cancer remained a measure of racial fitness. In 1935, however, public health scholar Milton

Rosenau observed that "cancer seems to be more a disease of civilization than of racial stocks. The evidence here, however, is somewhat conflicting."[111] Isidore Cohn in turn clung to the old notions of racial biology, observing that "cancer is practically never met with among strictly primitive types not in close contact with civilization," while acknowledging that the American Negro had come a long way from this kind of primitivism.[112] In this style of thinking, African Americans were not distinguished for their inner lives, their psyches, or their social anxieties—they were most notable for being an undifferentiated horde that was neither primitive nor civilized, a people without a well-developed individuality whose collective health would continue to be affected by their hybrid nature.[113] Decades would pass before this fascination for black people as a monolithic, yet evolving, primitive type would change.

SAVAGE IMMUNITIES AND THE
NEW DEAL IN AFRICAN-AMERICAN HEALTH

From the 1910s into the 1940s, experts developed the theory that cancer was the bane of civilized mankind and that black Americans were less vulnerable—perhaps because of their origins in so-called primitive environments or their supposedly carefree American life-styles. New York surgeon Willy Meyer insisted in 1931, for example, that primitive people, "in the familiar character of their restful unchanging surroundings," knew little cancer because their lives "would almost seem to be on a par with the fish of the ocean, the life of which is spent in placid indifference in the never-changing salt solution and its always equal temperature." Such experts built robust theories linking cancer to racial difference that reflected the inter-mingling of ideology and science in theories of cancer causation.

Museum of Vertebrate Zoology, University of California, Berkeley. Photograph by Oliver P. Pearson.

The American biologist and eugenicist Samuel Jackson Holmes (1868–1964) (above) portrayed white–black cancer trends both as an epidemiological puzzle and as part of a larger struggle for racial supremacy, with the black man enjoying a distinct advantage. Writing in the *American Journal of Cancer* and in his 1937 book, *The Negro's Struggle for Survival: A Study of Human Ecology*, he observed: "If we interpret the statistics at their face value, we must conclude that the Negroes are relatively free from cancer." Yet he also acknowledged that epidemiology could lie: "Cancer statistics are notoriously deceptive."

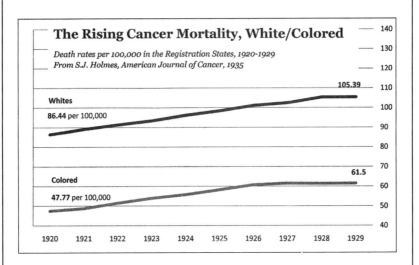

The Rising Cancer Mortality, White/Colored

Death rates per 100,000 in the Registration States, 1920-1929
From S.J. Holmes, American Journal of Cancer, 1935

Whites
86.44 per 100,000
105.39

Colored
47.77 per 100,000
61.5

1920 1921 1922 1923 1924 1925 1926 1927 1928 1929

140
130
120
110
100
90
80
70
60
50
40

Photo by
W. Eugene Smith/
Time Life Pictures/
Getty Images

How cancer crossed the color line in America became, in large part, the story of changing epidemiological awareness. There was black migration into areas where cancer surveillance was growing; the New Deal era and World War II produced an expansion of public health nursing; and cultural and public health awareness of these "other Americans" grew. (Pictured above: public health nurse Maude Callen, from a profile in *Life* magazine, 1951.)

3

THE FEMININE MYSTIQUE OF SELF-EXAMINATION

The character of Mary Scott in the 1950 Hollywood film *No Sad Songs for Me* was emblematic of postwar biases and contradictions in cancer awareness. On one side of the contradiction there was a new desire for openness and telling intimate truths about the stigmatized disease; but on the other side there was also a willingness to perpetuate old tropes of the white woman as the victim at the center of the storm and to foster other deceptions.[1] In the person of Mary Scott (played by Margaret Sullavan), a decades-old stereotype of the cancer patient as white, female, and psychologically self-aware prospered even in the face of statistical trends to the contrary. As historian Kristen Gardner has noted, "cancer awareness programs targeted privileged white, educated, and middle-class women . . . and the narrative and images portrayed in . . . publications reflected the dominant American culture of a white and middle-class population."[2] In the late 1930s, an aggressive cohort of middle-aged white women, organized as the Women's Field Army (with "more than 160,000 enlisted in the movement"), had become active in the anticancer effort.[3] Few nonwhite women's groups were invited to participate in "sounding the bugle call . . . to mobilize . . . in waging war on this dread disease."[4] Mary Scott transported this color contrast from the women's magazines, advice columns, and novels onto the silver screen—and she popularized the new cancer fighter in bold strokes. Film proved to be a powerful vehicle for shaping public awareness of cancer, and in 1950, even as *No Sad Songs* came to local theaters, the National Cancer Institute and the American Cancer Society (having changed its name from the ASCC five years earlier) also turned to motion pictures "to show women themselves, the basic facts about breast cancer and a simple method of periodic self-inspection of the breast."[5]

Like the magazine stories and the iconic posters preaching cancer awareness, *No Sad Songs* offered a sanitized vision of health awareness. The film catered to mainstream majority ideals about propriety and self-control, often by erasing uncomfortable truths and unpleasant complexity.[6] The character of Mary Scott—appealingly frank without being macabre—was manufactured by Hollywood for middle-of-the-road appeal. More than anything else it revealed, this character reflected how Cold War–era public anxieties about women on the home front, personal vigilance, and domestic security were widely broadcast and how they influenced public views on the disease. "As a gentle young wife and mother who is suddenly and shockingly told by her doctor that she is dying of cancer and that she has but a few more months to live, Miss Sullavan plays with such sincerity, such dignity and restraint that the morbid and tearful situation . . . is cloaked in gallantry," wrote Bosley Crowther in his glowing *New York Times* review of the new film.[7] That the plot of *No Sad Songs for Me* could have been embraced for its "realism" offers insight into what passed for cancer awareness and cinematic realism in 1950. Yet this was not the only reaction to the film: "At the risk of seeming callous," wrote the *Chicago Tribune* reviewer, "I must say this film struck me as moving but premeditated, as skilful but superficial, as tearful but not entirely truthful."[8] For other critics, like one *Los Angeles Times* writer, *No Sad Songs* was remarkable for its "grim realism and soul-searching," the film being one among a new crop of "dramas about the physically handicapped . . . about the sick . . . [and] about racial prejudice . . ."; yet the skeptical reviewer also cautioned readers that "what was disturbing about all this was that people were likely to believe it, to confuse the theatrical representation with the real thing."[9]

What can such a path-breaking cinematic production tell us about cancer awareness and the color line in postwar America? Of course it is not at all surprising that popular, melodramatic films such as *No Sad Songs* featured white characters. As observed by Daniel Bernardi, editor of *Classic Hollywood, Classic Whiteness*, Hollywood produced white identity through its choice of images, stories, and aesthetics, and through its portraits of "perseverance, community, insight, and passion." Actors of color or those defined by ethnicity were relegated to secondary roles, if that. Bernardi notes that "a color line defined by whiteness directed the trajectory of the Hollywood style," although for many observers, then and now, "seeing this refraction of race is as difficult as seeing whiteness itself."[10] This was not a whiteness discourse that made explicit appeals to civilization versus primitivism, to white reproduction rates, or to race suicide, as were seen in earlier decades. This was a new notion of whiteness that made more nuanced appeals to civility and domestic suburban virtues, doing so in cinematic grandeur and through mainstream mass media productions. In this new context, figures such as Mary Scott—representing self-awareness and perseverance—emerged to take 1950s Americans into a complex new zone of cancer beliefs. They sketched out the psychic costs of going public with one's disease; they articulated new doctor-patient tensions; and they became the leading edge of a new movement for breast self-examination and self-awareness. Images of figures like Mary Scott appeared on cancer awareness posters, in the news, in popular magazines, and on the silver screen. They represented, as the historian Elaine Tyler May has written, a cultural ideal of "domestic containment" and embodied the taming of potentially dangerous social forces by the ideals and values associated with the white suburban home.[11] If wartime and postwar foreign threats called for a brave citizenry, then cancer called similarly for psychological strength, truth-telling, and vigilance—and women like Mary Scott assumed lead roles in the drama, safeguarding themselves, their families, and the nation. "Race," then, operated on two levels in popular cancer awareness: people of color were conspicuous by their absence; and whiteness became the frame through which discussions of self-examination, bravery, vigilance, going public, and truth-telling would take place.

Mary Scott was carefully crafted in the mold of the American soldier—and the war ushered her onto the national stage as the faithful brave wife and disease fighter; she was also part of a continuing battle against the public shame and stigma associated with patients.[12] The producer Buddy Adler had first approached Irene Dunne to play the starring role of Mary Scott, but he had been bluntly rejected, both by Dunne and then by Claudette Colbert.[13] He knew that cancer remained stigmatized and that the film would push against the boundaries of that stigma, but Adler "was surprised when the first two actresses to whom he showed the script . . . turned down the part, flat." " 'I was afraid I would get it [cancer],' one of them said," to which Adler responded, "Tush and nonsense." Five other actresses, including Joan Crawford and Rosalind Russell, apparently were also unwilling to play the cancer victim.[14] When

Adler asked Margaret Sullavan to consider the role, however, her response was refreshing and frank: "When do I start?"[15] Sullavan saw Mary Scott not as a cancer victim but as "a dramatic study of fortitude."[16]

But was the film a welcome dose of postwar "realism" telling a long-hidden truth about a stigmatized disease, or was it an entertaining charade delicately sanitized for mass consumption? "The recent campaign to educate the American layman about cancer has undoubtedly made him more 'cancer conscious,' " noted two Philadelphia surgeons in 1953. As more people came out of the shadows as cancer victims, personalized and cinematic health appeals provoked admiration but also raised concern. On the positive side, wrote the surgeons, "leaders of the campaign . . . have given wide publicity to the symptoms and signs of cancer to encourage the public to seek medical advice early."[17] But they feared that cancer awareness books, motion pictures put out by the National Cancer Institute, news articles, and optimistic early detection posters were also doing damage.[18] "The common people are educated on cancer and other medical conditions to the extent that cancerphobia, poliophobia, and many other psychological disorders exist," they said regretfully. "This is an evil . . . one of the greatest seen in practice today." Information was fine, but protecting the patient from knowing all of the morbid details was also imperative. "Can we inform the layman up to a point and still keep him from recognizing a positive diagnosis?" they wondered.[19] It was into this new world of cancer awareness that women waded, and through the 1940s and 1950s, the ideals and contradictions of medical practice and white femininity would give rise to new notions of cancer awareness. Mary Scott, then, is merely a starting point for understanding how health sensibilities were crafted, and how the awareness of such women were idealized and projected into popular culture.

BRAVERY: CANCER SOLDIERS ON THE SILVER SCREEN

Looking back, it is hard to ignore the overwhelming weight of Cold War ideology on cancer discourse in the 1950s. The cancer awareness script referred to hidden enemies within, the need to "contain" damage, the importance of "surveillance" and "early detection," and always the virtue of soldiering on.[20] "It's cancer," Mary tells her husband when she finally confides the truth. "Nasty things that sneak up on one without warning. They must be of Japanese origin."[21] Nor could one miss the popular focus on self-control, illustrated by the rise of breast self-examination and the efforts to move women to the front lines in their own defense. The fusing together of health and military motifs was no accident. At this moment in the history of awareness, the idea of cancer gained sweeping popular currency as a threat not only to women but also to men, children (with the new focus on leukemia rates), and the American family. Mary Scott was one salvo in a new campaign that nurtured heightened fears of risk. It was women like her—white, middle-class, and resilient—who were targeted, who were told to blame themselves for any failure to detect cancer soon enough, who were counseled to trust the promising new treatments (cobalt bombs, other forms of radiation, radical surgery), to value the prognosis of doctors and specialists, and to exhibit a kind of stoic, cheerful optimism even in the face of death.[22]

Even before America entered World War II, the cancer "crusades" and "campaigns" used larger-than-life military motifs to mobilize the public to action. Metaphors of war infiltrated public health messages. And so it surprised no one in 1950 that Mary Scott's story was infused with images of war, patriotism, self-sacrifice, and the virtue of soldiering on. In Ruth Southard's 1944 novel of the same title on which the film was based, Mary learns of her diagnosis around the time of the bombing of Pearl Harbor, an event that famously shattered America's complacency and illusions of invulnerability. "Over three hundred soldiers reported killed . . . Over three hundred telegrams to the many nearest of kin," Mary thinks at the time. "For more than two years, all over the world, such telegrams had been going out, perhaps every minute, faster than babies were born. Now they were coming to them. It was their war, their front. No more would they listen complacently to news broadcasts."[23] At once her fate and the soldiers' merge and reflect upon each other. When Ruth Southard's book appeared, the message of domestic vigilance and mobilization had already grown loud and preachy. War saturated the medical talk of the period. U.S. Surgeon General Thomas Parran Jr. implored the public: "Our country needs all of us strong and able to do our part . . . Even though you don't punch the time clock at a war plant, illness in your family is certain to detract from the war effort in some way."[24] And one Miami physician remarked at a U.S. Senate hearing in 1946, "cancer killed 607,000 of our people between Pearl Harbor and VJ-day, more than twice as many as were killed by the Germans and Japs combined."[25] War defined the film in other ways. When Southard's book was made into a film, the producer of *No Sad Songs* told one reporter that his own wartime filmmaking for the military had given him "an advantage over Hollywood people who didn't help indoctrinate the ten million men in the services with a taste for realism." The war "marked the definite ascendancy of pictures" of the kind he envisioned making—films with "a more realistic approach to life," in contrast to the "merely romantic themes on which Hollywood has fattened."[26]

Mary represented a soldier on the suburban home front—a new paragon of understated beauty, modesty, self-control, and personalized sacrifice. Keeping her diagnosis to herself, Mary wonders in the novel: "What was the scourge of her own disease compared to this greater one of war? . . . For next spring she would be marching away—with victims of another battle. Her own body was unimportant in its present moribund state, but science would keep it alive to the last twitch, while healthy flesh was sent to be ripped by shells, destroyed by fire." Mary's sense of sacrifice extends to her family. Only gradually does she become aware of her husband Brad's interest in a woman named Roma, a recent war widow and a Czechoslovakian émigré whom he has hired to work in his small firm.[27] At first Mary nurses resentment about the flirtation. But then, confronting her own reality, Mary decides that Roma represents the best "hope for Brad's happiness and [her daughter] Polly's future" after she is gone, and she sets out to prepare Roma to take her place in the ill-fated family.[28] The drama of the story lies in how this quiet suburban woman sacrifices herself for a far greater good, and does so with stoicism and self-control.[29]

Frank talk was a vital weapon in confronting fear. In 1944, as injured soldiers came home from the war, Surgeon General Parran exhorted Americans to be "brutally frank" in their discussions of war wounds, mutilation, and recovery. "If we fail, we will only cause further wreckage in the lives of men who have suffered already," he asserted.[30] Mary, accordingly, is blunt, direct, and matter-of-fact in her relationship with her doctor, but the character's frankness was unbelievable, even to some sympathetic film critics. In Southard's book, the moment of diagnosis comes without flourish: "'Is it cancer?' she asked quietly." Her doctor, who is also a family friend and a bridge partner, nods. "'The symptoms are indisputable—so far advanced a layman could recognize them," he says to her plainly. "'I see,' she said mechanically. 'How—how long do I have?' 'Nine months at the most, I would say.' 'How long will I—be on my feet?' 'Six months, perhaps longer, depending on how you take care of yourself."[31] The film echoes this frankness. In a later encounter with her doctor in the film, she explains to him more wistfully, "Once in a while when I stop fighting it, I get a flash of . . . I guess you'd call it, philosophy. Suddenly I realize that what really matters isn't how long we live, but how. It's a strange and wonderful feeling. Does that make any sense?" The melodramatic portrait was, on one hand, "shattering conventions," as the *Los Angeles Times* noted, but on the other hand, it also kept cancer carefully scripted in order to garner popular acceptance.[32]

In several ways, however, Mary Scott's middle-class drama (with its focus on death and sacrifice) was out of step with the era's cultural trends, which stressed relentless optimism in the face of cancer and other illness. As one wartime essayist noted, "the patient herself is the first line of defense against cancer," and there was growing hope that fast action would prevent women from suffering Mary's fate.[33] There was a growing belief that surviving the disease involved heightened vigilance, self-surveillance, and early detection, and that those who spouted truisms such as "never trouble trouble 'til trouble troubles you" were misguided.[34] Against this backdrop of optimism, Southard's Mary Scott is a tragic figure. After first being told she has a serious condition, the doctor asks, "Why didn't you come to me sooner?" Mary responds forcefully, "There was nothing wrong with me . . . Just tired sometimes. Why?" "'Why!'" he retorts. "'A year, even six months ago, I might have been able to help you, but now . . .' He threw out his hands helplessly."[35] In this optimistic era, few would have read the novel or sat through the film without wondering whether Mary hadn't brought this fate upon herself, and whether early detection might have saved her. The war had itself brought many promising new weapons—radiation, chemical warfare, and nuclear tools—into the cancer fighting effort.[36] In 1943, C. C. Little had pledged that the conquest of disease was coming, and that it would involve an "island-hopping strategy rather than a single major victory."[37] Others preached that the word "inoperable" no longer meant "incurable," since "today a small but appreciable percentage of 'inoperable' cases can be salvaged" by "the pioneer radiologist" doing "a better job . . . with his weapons than the surgeon has been able to do with his."[38] More and more, the standard script of cancer awareness stressed how self-awareness could ensure survival—and in this sense Mary Scott stood apart from the optimistic trends.[39]

Dramatizing illness on the big screen presented another paradox of awareness, since Mary never becomes obviously infirm, disabled, dependent, or physically ailing in either the novel or the film. Southard's book never names the particular form of cancer Mary develops (lung, cervical, etc.). Facing death, Mary assures herself that "everything would flourish under Roma—Brad, Polly, and this house . . ." and it is only then that readers casually learn that "pain was stirring through her, tiny laps she knew would soon break over her in huge, relentless black waves . . . Her system was soaked with those little white pills, and they were bringing shorter and shorter relief."[40] Similarly, for all its talk of frankness and brutal honesty, the film was a charade (like the very image of self-contained, white, suburban life it portrayed). Graphic realities of suffering or death were nowhere in the film, and had no part in the era's cancer awareness paradigm. True, the film had opened a taboo topic for public conversation, but it remained silent about the dreaded realities of cancer, especially the clinical details. Some critics of the film were impressed with Mary Scott's effort, yet others scoffed. Bosley Crowther praised Margaret Sullavan for avoiding "the obvious pitfalls of mawkish sentiment," playing a role that could have been "distasteful and depressing, with fluent and elevated grace" and admirable "dignity and restraint."[41] But the *Chicago Tribune* reviewer quoted earlier saw Mary as "tearful but not entirely truthful."[42] Another critic, Richard Coe, characterized the earnest drama as a "fearful fraud."[43] But this was Hollywood after all. As Coe put it, while "she does complain near the end of her allotted 10 months of being tired . . . the script sneaks swiftly off the topic into the movies' well-loved sphere of Love and Another Woman."[44] On this topic, even Adler agreed: "It isn't even a picture about cancer. It's a picture about bravery, about how to live, about defying fears that can destroy lives quicker and even more thoroughly than a dread disease."[45]

The character of Mary Scott personified and brought to the big screen a cultural stereotype that had mass appeal, one that linked cancer to mothers and to their hopes and fears in safeguarding the home and family. Although experts and informed laymen knew that the disease was not confined to suburban women on one side of the color line, the imagery of the era reinforced the now-classic view of the disease as a penalty driven by these women's life choices. "Today the heaviest cancer burden is falling on women who have chosen wifehood and motherhood," stated an article in the *Ladies' Home Journal* in 1955, echoing the gendered cancer discourse whose roots had been laid down decades earlier. The incidence of cervical cancer was higher in these women, while (paradoxically) "breast cancer, the other major form concerned with the female organs, is found most frequently in women who have never been pregnant." What were women to do? According to one writer, cervical and breast cancers made up "43 percent of the entire cancer picture in American women, and in a number of other countries the proportion is considerably higher."[46] The threat of cancers boxed women like Mary Scott into a tight domestic corner, forcing them to navigate the tortuous terrain of maternity and reproduction.

For many women, cancer continued to be associated with dirtiness and shame, failures of hygiene, and implicit accusations of a tainted morality. "The most significant and characteristic concept held by our patients was that cancer was a disease of unclean origin," found two Harvard psychiatrists in a 1953 study at the Massachusetts General Hospital. That it was "a 'dirty disease,' 'unclean,' 'repellent,' [this] was repeated over and over again." The end-of-life stage of cancer—a topic that both the novel and film avoided at all costs—was particularly unpleasant. "In the end," said one fifty-year-old woman, "there is odor. Often there is deformity. People fear contagion. They don't like to be with cancer patients. Heart disease is not unclean. People don't object to being with those who have heart trouble."[47] As one cancer patient saw it in 1960, writing in the *Ladies' Home Journal*, "without exception the cancer patient is portrayed as a martyr, deeply suffering, but led at last through his troubles to realize the big things in life. All his trivialities are swept away, he appreciates the wonders of nature as never before, a change has come over his character . . . he has turned to God, and he keeps his temper. I think it is time we let down our hair and told the truth." Recoiling from this projected image, she concluded: "Frankly, if the truth were told, we embarrass our friends, and we often bore them."[48] All of these contradictions, both those truths embodied by the brave and vigilant Mary Scott and those evaded by her and by others, defined the new possibilities and limits of cancer awareness in this era.[49]

PATERNALISM AND DECEIT: A CHARADE FOR THE DYING

Cancer awareness in the 1950s was built upon a paradox, a new openness that, at the same time, was still woman-centered, sanitized, civil, and "in good taste." And this awareness was embedded in a trusting and paternalistic but also deceitful doctor-patient relationship.[50] In this era it was usually the dying patient who was kept in the dark about a terminal cancer, while the family knew the truth but played along with the doctor's tragic script. It was the doctor, not the patient, who controlled information and withheld the brutal truths in order to serve, safeguard, and protect. This was a not-so-secret rule that guided doctor-patient-family encounters.

The close links between the patient's health awareness and his or her trust in medical authority should not be taken for granted, nor should the linkage between trust, race, and identity. Commenting in 1947 on the relationship between "Negro soldiers of better than average attainment" and white doctors, psychiatrist Jerome Frank found that these soldiers harbored deep mistrust and resentments about mistreatment, attitudes shaped by the broader atmosphere of racial discrimination and by misunderstanding.[51] Conversely, Mary Scott's trust in her doctor reflected much about her class and race position. Cultural norms of the era dictated that such patients were portrayed as trusting the physician, working within this confiding relationship, and even tolerating medical paternalism. As women soldiered Americans into this fraught new territory of awareness, such assumptions about trust, benevolence, and authority were often in full view.

Lorna Doone Burks, an actual patient (also white) who chronicled her last months in the 1946 book *I Die Daily*, saw medical deception as an acceptable charade and self-deception as her own personal flaw. At first, her doctors were up-front about her diagnosis. The doctor "told me a piece of tissue would be removed for test purposes, and that I'd be X-rayed. He didn't evade the issue a bit. I had cancer, well along, fourth or fifth stage. He was so cheery about it that I wasn't even shocked." But as the disease and treatments progressed, Burks was told that her cancer had been successfully treated. "I had a check-up at San Diego . . . [in] September . . . 1944. No evidence of cancer was found. A miracle had occurred. I had been so far gone, yet modern science had rescued me. I was told to return, however, on December first. Between the first examination and the second, I was increasingly what our grandmothers called 'ailing.' I blamed it on my reaction to X-rays. Doctor Pyle had told me to expect unusual reactions." From there the duplicity grew, with scripted excuses for why she did not improve: the recovery was slow; another disorder was present; she was on the verge of taking a turn for the better, and so on, Burks wrote. "My cancer was so far advanced that my case was hopeless. Understand, nobody told me this. Instead, I was greeted on every side by the most cheery demeanors possible. Nurses, corpsmen [her husband was a marine lieutenant], doctors, vied with one another in keeping me cheerful." In most instances, the patient understood the game. As Burks noted, "they didn't know I had been around hospitals too much to be fooled."[52]

Burks accepted the paternalistic charade, and blamed herself in her post-humously published account. "I am not complaining about being kept in the dark," Burks wrote toward the end of her life. "Hadn't *I*, myself, kept myself in the dark for *years*? Simply by refusing to believe I could be ill, or that if I were I could 'whip' it myself, without going to some doctor I couldn't believe in anyway?"[53] By the time Burks began running the regular gauntlet of cheerful attendants on each visit to the hospital, she welcomed it as a gesture intended to protect and safeguard her sensibilities. According to prevailing opinion, physicians and surgeons were obliged to show a benevolent regard toward dying patients, always promising hope, thereby preventing the patient from knowing her true condition, becoming depressed, and hastening her own decline. Paternalism toward the hopeless patient was an idea with deep roots in cancer care, but one that some women had begun to question.

As these kinds of dilemmas of truth-telling took center stage in the 1950s and increasingly in the 1960s, cancer awareness entered a transitional era. Where hope and optimism for "cures" was high, physicians and lay observers began to ponder whether some patients had the capacity to handle the morbid realities of the disease. Determining which patients were equipped for such cancer awareness was no simple thing. Again, it was women who led the way in these discussions. As early as 1938, *Ladies' Home Journal* had asked its readers their opinion: "If you had an incurable disease, would you want your doctor to tell you that you were sure to die?" The question was "one of the oldest and most baffling . . . in all the history of medicine," debated by interns and by "bearded doctors at monthly meetings of their medical societies." What did the women of America think, the magazine wanted to know? Did their readers have the strength to face such an enemy? "It appears that the women of the United States have the courage to face even the fact of oncoming death," proclaimed the magazine: 60 percent had answered yes, while 40 percent "would prefer to remain in ignorance."[54] "Many arguments are presented for and against the telling the patient about his condition," and a new question—What type of "awareness" was appropriate for which type of patients?—increasingly became a topic of medical and social debate.[55]

A revolution in cancer care (radical surgery, chemotherapy, and new radiation treatments) brought new hope to patients and challenged the reign of medically orchestrated deceit. In this context, some physicians wondered whether the old deceitful charades could last. Testifying before a congressional health inquiry in 1953, the American Cancer Society's Charles Cameron explained that Americans were facing paradoxes driven by social progress and medical advances: "high living standards, high literacy rates, good nutrition, high quality, and general available medical care, reduce . . . deaths from infectious, contagious, and nutritional diseases and that leaves little to die from except cancer and heart disease."[56] Not only were demographic trends making cancer ever more common, but the machinery of cancer care was increasingly obvious to patients and expensive as well.[57] Hospitals paid handsomely for the high-priced technology: $30,000 for a cobalt machine for treating cancer, $20,000 to $50,000 for X-ray movie cameras.[58] And popular magazines like the *Saturday Evening Post* and *Reader's Digest* published accounts of famous patients benefiting from the new medicines. After reading such stories, for example, a desperately ill Ray Hosier of Birmingham, Alabama, could write to New Orleans cancer surgeon Alton Ochsner in 1955, "can you tell me what treatment or treatments Babe Dietrickson [sic], the famous woman golfer, used in curing her cancer. I am a patient of intestinal cancer . . . [now spread] to kidneys, lung and pelvis. In spite of all the doctors can do, I am not getting any better."[59] Such patients could not easily be deceived. They and their doctors attached great meaning and hope to novel treatments. "The rapid advances that are being made in the cure and control of cancer make an ostrich-like approach increasingly unreasonable," as one Hartford, Connecticut, doctor wrote in 1955.[60] His was one voice in a small but growing chorus calling for disclosure and openness.

But medical norms did not budge easily, and many doctors' reluctance on disclosure hinged on their dim view of the cancer patients' mental capacities or emotional strength. "Physicians frequently follow a policy of dissimulation in acquainting patients with the nature of a cancerous malady," acknowledged the noted surgeon Owen H. Wangensteen in 1950. Published in the pages of the journal *Surgery*, Wangensteen's was an unusually public defense of the patient's capacity to handle the truth. Instead of speaking the word "cancer," doctors and surgeons used terms like "neoplasm," "malignancy," and other euphemisms to convey the diagnosis, or they lied outright. "When Babe Ruth, colorful hero of baseball, died [in 1948], a well-known radio commentator said the nature of Ruth's illness had been so carefully hidden from him that he probably never knew he had cancer," Wangensteen wrote. A typical doctor, faced with a patient whom he deemed unable to handle the truth, hedged when asked for a prognosis.[61] Wangensteen called on his peers to start a "critical reexamination of what is accomplished by this artifice . . . this faithless fraud." But in defense of artifice, two fellow surgeons insisted that "the patient should not be told that his disease was cancer except in those uncommon instances in which his cooperation could be won by telling him the nature of the disease . . . [T]he mental shock of this sudden knowledge" alone was enough to throw patients into depression and sap their will to fight on.[62] Much of the doctor's decision about what to say, how to say it, and whom to trust with the knowledge hinged on his notions of patient aptitude, character, psychology, demeanor, and capacity.

Without question, then, different patients inhabited different worlds of cancer awareness—worlds created by their physicians, and also by cultural norms and familial practices. In the same year that Mary Scott came to the screen and Wangensteen called for openness, the popular press dramatized yet another shocking dilemma of truth-telling, awareness, and deception by covering the California case of John Guy Gilpatric's "mercy" killing of his wife Louise. At age fifty-two, Louise had been told by her doctor that "she had a breast tumor but, evidently in kindness, was told it was not malignant." According to standard practice, "Gilpatric was called in and told privately the tumor was malignant." The couple went home, and it was there that the distraught husband retrieved his .32-caliber pistol and shot his oblivious wife as an "act of mercy" before also killing himself.[63] In the news coverage, there was dramatic storytelling but very little analysis, commentary, or criticism of Gilpatric or of the physicians—as if to acknowledge that the underlying issues were beyond public debate and that readers tacitly understood the man's motives. There were also melodramatic euphemisms about "mercy bullets" and about Gilpatric's love and desire to avoid "seeing her suffer from cancer," suggesting that the many observers accepted the need for pretense, and understood the paternalism of both husband and physician.[64]

Clearly, American cancer awareness was deeply conflicted, with physicians themselves troubled by the blurred lines between benevolence and professional hubris and exploitation. "If I had a malignancy and some doctor did not tell me, I would be tempted to do something violent on the spot," said one patient interviewed in a 1949 North Carolina study. Yet, in another breath, the same person who promised violence if deceived also acknowledged, "To me the unknown is much more frightening than the known . . . Of course, personalities differ, but I would want to know the diagnosis, prognosis, and the rest." Beneath the veneer of the brave cancer fighter, then, conflicting passions stirred about the "lack of frankness on the part of some physicians." Another patient resented the idea that a doctor should even attempt to "gauge . . . the intelligence of the patient" when deciding on what to disclose about cancer. The interviewer herself believed that when doctors avoided frankness in favor of vague euphemisms, "there was a realism . . . missing from those who had been left in doubt." These "patients whose physicians had 'hedged' and skirted the issue of telling them the implications of the symptom or diagnosis" later believed that precious time had been wasted. Even so, the interviewer accepted that the "final judgment as to how much to tell the patient must, to be sure, rest with the physician, who takes into consideration the wishes of the immediate family."[65] Deception by physicians (often in the name of benevolence) was common, and carried diverse meanings for patients depending on the individual and group. A 1955 *Newsweek* survey asked "Should a patient be told he has cancer?" and found that men's and women's views followed cultural stereotypes: "Masculine replies made businesslike demands for a candid diagnosis in time to arrange personal and family affairs . . . [while] women expressed a desire for spiritual preparation for death." Other people who wanted to be told more were "conscious of the widespread cancer publicity, seemed determined to find a 'cure,'" the survey added.[66]

The rising public faith and trust in the promise of a cure (for example, the trend toward radical surgery) catalyzed debate about truth-telling, and again it was often middle-class white women who led the way into these discussions. Radical surgery raised a new specter: surgical "patients cured of cancer . . . but [also severely disfigured by] the methods necessary for cure have resulted in psychological invalidism," noted a 1952 *New York Times* article.[67] In an age of earlier cancer diagnosis and radical "disfiguring and mutilating" surgery, the idea of keeping cancer patients in the dark before they submitted to surgery was a profound paradox. If a patient went into surgery not knowing the grave diagnosis or the extent of disease, what kind of recovery could be expected after disfiguring surgery?[68] One recovering cancer patient, Marian Miller Kean, gave her account of mutilation, disfigurement, lost beauty, and loss of self-control in the pages of the *Saturday Evening Post* in 1954. Having lost part of her face in the operation, Kean acknowledged that "getting accustomed to a disfiguring wound is not one of the cancer patient's easier tasks. After the first really mutilating operation, which left an opening through my cheek into the area beside the nasal bones, it was five months before I would look at myself in the mirror."[69] But if she was a doctor, she confessed, "I would study my patient a long time before I would let him know the diagnosis is 'malignancy.' And in many cases I would never state it at all."[70] Such public accounts accepted the idea that paternalistic deceit was necessary to protect the patient's fragility and peace of mind. "In any event," Kean concluded, "I would urge every doctor to guard against giving away the secret that death is near or even create unintentionally that impression."[71]

But for every Marian Miller Kean whose awareness depended on a trusted physician, there was also an Edna Kaehele who regretted her doctors' benevolence. Both women (white, educated, in-control) give us insight into the inner life of the cancer patient, and the era's contradictions. Edna needed no protection, she insisted. "It has been six years since qualified cancer specialists gave me six months to live," she wrote in her 1952 book *Living with Cancer*. They had given her "six short months in which to wind up my small affairs and take final leave of the life and the people I had learned to love. I accepted their unhappy verdict and prepared as best I could to endure the unendurably bleak days until the end." But "fortunately," she recalled, "I have a sister who is a fighter—one who is eternally 'agin' [against] official pronouncements."[72] In spite of the grim expert prognosis, Kaehele hung on, and her survival spawned a maverick-like contrarian perspective. Fear, she now concluded, killed more people than cancer did: "'Six months,' he says, and in six months more or less the obliging patient lies down and dies, never having known he could do anything else. It is a form of modern-day voodooism, performed by medicine men in sterile white coats fearfully lacking in imagination." Kaehele also insisted that the increasingly aggressive therapy of the day debilitated the body and "lessened the flagging will to live"; and that cancer education had done as much harm as good—frequently serving "only to keep alive ancient fears."[73] It was women like Kaehele and Kean—white, middle-class, educated, assertive, and in control—who opened these windows on the inner world of the cancer patient, rising "above pain, despair, and hopelessness to a happy positive formula for living."[74]

The 1950s saw a spike in such personal accounts of people whose battles with cancer fascinated and troubled Americans. Before the decade was over there would also be famous men in this group (Secretary of State John Foster Dulles, actor Humphrey Bogart), although white women dominated the stage, giving insight into the new cancer psyche.[75] In 1953, Babe Didrickson Zaharias (the "Queen of Sport" and "Mrs. Golf") became the most prominent celebrity cancer fighter when she underwent a colostomy to "re-channel" the lower intestines.[76] Babe did not fit conventional stereotypes. As her biographer Susan Cayleff has noted, "she was southern, working-class, and ethnic; she was un-feminine, coarse, and loud," and, importantly, she was a closeted lesbian whose marriage to George Zaharias provided an elaborate front for her long-term relationship with her companion Betty Dodd.[77] At age forty, Babe Didrikson Zaharias found that her cancer called for a public act of another kind.[78] After her first treatments, she appeared to have beat back the disease, appearing at the White House with President Eisenhower to help raise twenty million dollars to help others in the fight.[79] Her physicians pronounced her to be sound, and soon she was competing and winning at golf again. "The real triumph," wrote Quentin Reynolds in a *Reader's Digest* article, "was her demonstration that she could come back after a serious cancer operation, not only to live a normal life but to become a champion in a sport that makes almost superhuman demands on the physical and temperamental resources of anyone who challenges it."[80] Twelve months later, however, Zaharias would find herself hospitalized again.[81]

When her condition worsened and "a new cancer appeared in 1955—a small lesion in the posterior of the pelvic girdle"—the news coverage mixed all of the classic cancer fighting motifs of the era with some of the grim realities.[82] Zaharias was said by her husband to have received the news of the cancer's return "unflinchingly," "like the mighty champion she has always been."[83] By November, she was fighting off pneumonia and undergoing X-ray treatment and a cordotomy (severing of spinal cord nerves) for pain relief.[84] By the time Zaharias's illness had reached its final stages in late 1956, the newspapers described the golfing legend as "America's No. 1 cancer victim . . . setting an example that will encourage and inspire countless others." "Privately," noted one observer, her doctors "marvel at her will and fortitude, and several now believe along with her that she will by sheer strength and determination weather immense assaults which would have consumed lesser spirits." Near the end, in September 1956, the writer Bob Considine penned glowingly, "The Texas girl has questioned her doctors closely on just what is the score, and she . . . had the stomach and heart to take their glum news and carefully weigh their airy optimism."[85] But this too was a charade, as biographer Cayleff noted. Babe in fact became deeply depressed after her second cancer. "When she got struck down the second time, I think that was emotionally disturbing to her," her companion and lover Betty Dodd recalled. "She'd hit balls off the beach in Galveston . . . at her home in Tampa . . . but her interest was just gone."[86] In September 1956, when President Eisenhower learned of Zaharias's death, he praised her for putting up "one of the kind of fights that inspire us all."[87]

Brave women like Zaharias and Kaehele were the popular face of cancer awareness in the 1950s, cast as the lead characters in this grim masquerade, helping the public to navigate through the minefield of truth, deception, and conflicted awareness. At most patients' bedsides, however, the anxious charade continued. Into the early 1960s, doctors still defended their evasions, but pressure was building for change. As one doctor commented bluntly in the *Ladies' Home Journal*, "To most people, intelligent or not, the word cancer means a death sentence." For this reason, he routinely withheld diagnostic information: "I do not tell them." Deception was what such patients expected from a benevolent, caring doctor, he argued: "*Cancer* is a fear word . . . so I may tell a patient that he has 'a bad type of tumor' or 'abnormal tissue growth,'" and then only "after he has absorbed the initial guarded information the reaction will be less profound if he finds out—by reading, or from a hospital or clinic where he goes for treatment—his illness is cancer."[88] For such doctors, truth was the enemy of hope.[89] But other caregivers insisted that keeping the patient in the dark—especially in an era championing cures and preaching awareness—only bred mistrust and resentment. "I always tell the truth," one physician countered. "In 40 years of practice I have had only two instances when the truth was not well received. You can create distrust in the profession and bitter loss of faith in the family if deception is practiced by anyone."[90] In 1962, advice columnist Ann Landers offered her own guidance on the topic: "It is a relief not to pretend." Landers continued, "I, personally, believe in the philosophy that truth begets strength and peace of mind. Lies breed fear and unrest."[91] Despite a cancer awareness movement that was now more than three decades old, the issue of whether or not to frankly disclose a lethal diagnosis remained raw and contentious. At stake was more than just deadly disease. The challenges of cancer awareness confronted Americans with deep questions of trust in authority, the limits of paternalism, and the differing emotional capacities of citizens when faced with torturous hardship.[92]

SELF-SURVEILLANCE: THE CULTURAL ORIGINS OF BREAST SELF-EXAMINATION

Whether or not these women were stalwart suburban mothers or path-breaking mavericks, were they truly up to the task of facing the morbid reality of cancer, let alone of detecting it themselves? As one doctor warned in 1944, "Speak of someone who has heart disease, or tuberculosis, and you will hear only the conventional manifestations of pity or sympathy, but let the conversation turn to a patient with cancer and you will see an expression suddenly frozen in horror."[93] But within a short space of years, cultural assumptions were shifting. Advances in diagnostic precision, media coverage, and the rise of breast self-examination (BSE) in particular forced such experts to rethink their presumptions about what kind of information certain sick people could bear and what kind of awareness was appropriate for whom.[94] "Our mothers would not say the word 'cancer,'" opined one *Ladies' Home Journal* writer in 1952. But the new cancer-aware woman was capable of confronting the enemy. "Women today have learned to say it, and now—if they do not 'look away'—women have in their own hands the most powerful weapon known for combating breast cancer."[95] The rise of BSE reflected a significant new direction in women's cancer awareness, the apogee of a belief in self-knowledge and self-surveillance as the woman's best protection. With the appealing idea of hands-on prevention, BSE took hold as a cultural ideal for middle-class white women. It achieved a larger-than-life profile on the 1950s silver screen as well, and also modestly breached the color line becoming a vehicle for communicating awareness to women of color.

The World War II experience, with the omnipresent news of death and destruction along with innumerable women entering the workforce to take up previously male occupations (think of Rosie the Riveter), helped some doctors see that supposedly demure and protected women were up to the task of managing their fears when confronting the dreaded disease. "More women die of mammary cancer annually than could possibly die from or be incapacitated by such forms of fright," one physician observed in 1945. Writing in the midst of war, he believed that they had the emotional strength to face the challenge. As he put it, it was "far more humane and sensible to allow each woman to face the reality of discovering a mass in the breast . . . than it is to allow her eventually to realize that she has an incurable disease." Holding up the wartime woman as an ideal, such doctors advocated that "all women over thirty years of age be taught to palpate their own breasts at least six times a year and report immediately to their physicians when a lump is felt."[96]

Buoyed by military metaphors, wartime ideals, and postwar anxieties about containment, BSE by the early 1950s emerged as the "front line of defense," concrete proof of how personal initiative and self-knowledge saved lives.[97] "Every woman had in her own hands the strongest defense known today against a dreaded enemy," proclaimed a 1952 article in *Ladies' Home Journal*.[98] Experts insisted that "a woman can find a small lump in her own breasts that most doctors would miss," and the NCI and ACS also got behind the effort with their own public service films aimed at spreading the word.[99] Posters were displayed prominently to capture the nuances of self-examination: the woman's proper attitude, the details of procedure, and the calm self-control necessary for finding a suspicious lump. The text accompanying much BSE education bluntly told women that every year 50,000 women developed breast cancer and half of them died within five years. And it made a bold claim: "if the woman herself were to discover the mass during the first month or two, surgery could save 80 per cent to 90 per cent of the proven cases."[100] Against the growing number of stories of cancer death, pressure mounted for women to monitor themselves. As in earlier decades, awareness was targeted toward white, educated women of means—women who, it was suggested, had the power in their hands to diagnose cancer, and the self-control to notify the doctor of early warning signs. "Between 80 and 90 percent of these deaths could be prevented," the ACS's Charles Cameron promised optimistically, "if women themselves recognized the early stages."[101]

The foundations for self-examination were laid not only in the war and in the home but also with an earlier innovation—the Pap smear for early detection of cervical cancer—that had recently reshaped the American women's discourse of early detection.[102] Since 1947, when Charles Cameron, the medical and scientific director of the American Cancer Society, had recruited Arthur Holleb to convince gynecologists and obstetricians of its value, the Pap smear, named for its developer, Dr. George N. Papanicolaou, had become a "household word."[103] At first, Holleb had encountered skepticism about a high rate of false positives and false negatives, and experts believed that it would be used only as a complement to cervical biopsy "but never to replace it."[104] But by the end of 1949, the test had become the new centerpiece of cancer awareness, with some 930 specialized cancer-detection centers around the country.[105] The Pap smear remained in the popular news, opening the doors to new thinking about the detection of "preinvasive lesions" as opposed to lesions that "never become clinically cancerous."[106] And by the mid-1950s, women learned from *Ladies' Home Journal* that "improvements in the [Papanicolaou] technique now make it possible to detect not only cervical cancer in the early stages, but conditions which, it is believed, may be precursors of cancer. This makes it possible to deal with a cancer before it is a cancer!"[107] Some physicians were even touting the possibility that a "home kit" would soon allow women to take their own vaginal specimens, easing the way to at-home detection of cervical cancer.[108] Such developments undergirded the movement for BSE. In 1950, a new film about the practice was premiered at the American Medical Association's annual meeting.

Self-examination was no mere professional innovation; it was a movement calling on each woman to readjust her attitude, to command her fears, to internalize a sense of personal risk, and to take self-control—or suffer the consequences. "[Each woman's] attitude is going to determine largely whether or not we will continue to have 15,000 and more deaths annually from this type of cancer," reported one author in 1945.[109] "It is her responsibility to watch for those signs of cancer which can be seen or felt by her, and to consult a competent physician immediately if she notes a cancer sign or symptom . . . she has no one to blame for the consequences but herself."[110] This postwar message was double-edged: it promoted self-awareness while also suggesting that women who contracted the disease had failed to protect themselves and their families. The BSE brought closer to home the old stigma that cancer was the result of the woman's failure of self-monitoring and self-control. "Self-control is a fetish with us," Lorna Doone Burks had written in her tragic 1946 memoir as she entered the last stages of illness. "We do not believe in losing our tempers, in being irritable, in feeling angry toward anyone; above all we do not believe in losing faith."[111] Into the 1950s, it was again middle-class, white women, focused on self-control and containment, who championed "self-inspection" and this double-edge awareness—qualities that, experts contended, marked the difference between women who died and those who lived.[112] Breast self-examination therefore emerged not as an objective practice that all women, regardless of rank, race, and class, could believe in—rather, it was closely aligned with particular ideals about blame, trust, self-control, moderation, and faith, all of which assumed a white, middle-class subject.

The archetypal cancer patient of the 1950s was the middle-class white woman who trusted and turned to medical doctors for guidance. This patient strove for the kind of self-monitoring reflected in the BSE. The ideal woman steeled herself amid gossiping friends and superstitious fears. "Gossip can be a killer," warned Dr. Paul Fluck in *Today's Health*.[113] The ideal woman remained vigilant about changes in her own body—the breast and the cervix of the uterus—and she acted promptly to tell authorities when something was amiss. She had fully internalized cancer awareness. She also understood that her responsibility was to her family. As one cancer patient wrote in the *Ladies' Home Journal* in 1947, when she shared her fears with her physician husband about a possible cancer diagnosis, he informed her matter-of-factly that "if it [was] malignant, [she would] have a radical removal of [her] breast. It's a tough operation, but I know you can take it."[114] Her comment to readers: "I tried not to disappoint him."[115] Such vigilance and forbearance pushed self-examination into the forefront of middle-class women's consciousness.

While this message drew upon a script primarily aimed at white women, the BSE message did slowly gain a wider circulation, an acknowledgment (as will be discussed in the next chapter) that cancer crossed the color line. When the new BSE motion picture was made available for public audiences in 1950, the African-American *New York Amsterdam News* urged "employers of large groups of women as well as women's organizations and social clubs" to show the fifteen-minute film. "If practiced monthly," commented the black press from New York to Atlanta, "physicians believe it will save thousands of lives."[116] "Attention Ladies, blared a 1952 advertisement in one Atlanta African-American newspaper, "The Life You Help to Save from Cancer May Be Your Own."[117] In line with this outreach, in 1956 the American Cancer Society named a black man, Monroe Dowling, as the organization's "national specialist in Negro affairs . . . to broaden the cancer control movement."[118] By the early 1960s, black newspapers in Pittsburgh, Harlem, Atlanta, and Chicago endorsed the BSE effort, stressing that avoiding cancer was a black women's personal responsibility.[119] One evening showing of the BSE film in Queens, in New York City, filled a theater with "night-shift workers from nearby plants in overalls" as well as housewives. There were good reasons for extending the message of cancer awareness, reported the *Chicago Defender* in 1960: "In the last 20 years, cure rates for uterine cancer have gone up twice as fast among white women as among Negro women."[120] The disparity in survival after diagnosis, the article suggested, hinged on early examination, availability, and awareness: "Many doctors believe this may be due in large part to the fact that a larger percentage of white women are taking advantage of the uterine examination."[121]

In the 1950s, race was not as explicit in American cancer discourse as it had been in earlier decades when cancer awareness was closely aligned with notions of white civilization, motherhood, and racial decline. Although the discourse of race in the 1950s was not always obvious, the racial features of cancer awareness were nonetheless linked intimately to white, middle-class women, their vigilance about domestic risks, their capacity for self-control, their modesty, and their trust in authority.

Given the ethnic makeup of middle-class audiences who consumed such messages and the Anglo-American tilt of Hollywood image-making, it is unsurprising that only white actresses (and especially those without visible traces of other ethnic heritage) such as Irene Dunne, Claudette Colbert, or Margaret Sullavan were asked to play the part of Mary Scott. Commenting on Hollywood's racial myopia, black novelist James Baldwin recalled that almost all the leading actresses "were white, and, even when they moved me (like Margaret Sullavan or Bette Davis or Carole Lombard) they moved me from that distance."[122] Who, then, given the cultural logic of cinema and race at the time, would have imagined casting, for example, Hattie McDaniel (known for her Oscar-winning performance as Scarlett O'Hara's Mammy in *Gone with the Wind*) as Mary Scott? It is not that such women did not suffer from the disease—indeed, two years later, McDaniel was "forced by illness to withdraw from the title role of radio's Beulah" (a popular housekeeper and cook role).[123] McDaniel died from cancer soon afterward at the age of fifty-seven.[124] Popular media and cinematic roles for such actresses followed familiar cultural conventions.[125] Although they were admired figures, McDaniel and Ethel Waters, for example, were "forced to be satisfied with playing the part of a servant in the 'homes' of supporting players."[126] As one motion picture insider explained in 1947, "Negroes have appeared in pictures as singers, dancers, and comedians," but there were lines that could not be crossed in the cinema and society. "Fur groups," he noted, once "objected to the showing of a Negro maid wearing a certain type of fur as injuring that business with white patrons."[127] The resulting Hollywood images rarely matched up with what James Baldwin knew of reality and rarely earned his trust as a viewer.[128] In the 1950s, Hollywood called upon "mainstream" stars in order to act out the manufactured "realism" of modern American life.[129] Even those with diverse national backgrounds—Archibald Leach, aka Cary Grant, or Rita Hayworth (born Margarita Carmen Cansino, a New Yorker of Spanish descent on her father's side and Irish-English on her mother's) were transformed according to the code of Hollywood. In much the same way, cancer too was cleaned up and recast for popular consumption.

Popular health awareness erased ethnicity, sanitized unpleasantness, and played down ethnic differences in favor of a generic, "de racialized" whiteness. When *Collier's* magazine in 1954 told the unusual story of Mrs. L., a woman in her thirties who died from a particularly virulent cervical cancer at the Johns Hopkins Hospital, it stripped away all ethnic references.[130] Today, we know this unnamed woman as Henrietta Lacks, whose story became remarkable when an inquisitive pathologist named George Gey noticed that her cells "grew remarkably fast and reproduced many times as rapidly as most normal living tissues."[131] Mrs. L.'s cells proliferated "like homesteaders swarming into the promised land" even outside of her body, unlike other cancer cells, which were usually short-lived when placed in scientific media (that is, in vitro).[132] The cells were "spreading like crabgrass," noted Margaret Gey, a surgical nurse and George Gey's wife.[133] Dr. Gey named the versatile and long-lasting culture "the HeLa strain" (using the letters of Mrs. L.'s first and last name, Henrietta Lacks), and "today the strain is used as a standard in tissue-culture studies" all over the world, noted *Collier's*.[134] "Thus, Mrs. L. has attained a degree of immortality she never dreamed of when she was alive, and her living tissue may yet play a role in conquering many diseases in addition to the cancer which killed her," the *Collier's* piece concluded. It was typical of the public face of cancer and the culture of the 1950s that *Collier's* did not mention one crucial fact about Mrs. L.: she was a poor African-American woman, recently migrated from Virginia to Baltimore before her untimely death, or that the gynecologist at Johns Hopkins (on first diagnosing her) had taken her "across the hall to the venereal disease clinic, thinking it might be a lesion caused by syphilis."[135] Nineteen-fifties cancer awareness avoided many such complex truths, choosing instead a thin, tempered, white, middle-class veneer—and pushing nuances of difference into the background.

If what passed for cancer "realism" in the 1950s was a charade, there were signs that many American doctors and patients saw through the game even as men and women played their accustomed roles. The producer of *No Sad Songs for Me*, Buddy Adler, noted that British censors (in considering the release of the film) expressed concern that the word "cancer"—which had never been mentioned before in a Hollywood production—would be uttered. Columbia Pictures, in the British release of the film, stripped out the offensive word. Americans would hear "cancer"; British audiences heard a Latin term instead, Adler said.[136] But, as the reviewer Bosley Crowther himself later admitted, the movie's mediocre run at the American box office was perhaps preordained by the topic. "Afflictions are not popular in films," he wrote seven years later. "Here we are," he continued, "a people who spend some $2 billion a year on medicines, heavens knows how much on doctors and delight in all kinds of ailment stories in the popular magazines . . . But break John Wayne's back in a film, as was done in 'The Wings of Eagles,' and see how disinterested are his fans. Give Margaret Sullavan cancer, as was done most touchingly in 'No Sad Songs for Me,' and see how politely she is shunned."[137]

The decade that began with the grim yet inspiring domestic narrative of Mary Scott's *No Sad Songs for Me* ended with another cancer story—a drama of diagnostic ambiguity, love, and family also set in a lily-white America. The film *The Young Doctors* (1961) was based on Arthur Hailey's deeply researched 1959 best-selling novel *Final Diagnosis* and his earlier 1957 television play *No Deadly Medicine*. It pitted a cantankerous old pathologist, Joe Pearson (Frederic March), against a young upstart pathologist just arriving to work in his lab, David Coleman (Ben Gazzara): these "harried men in white" would clash, in particular, over "the diagnosis of an ailing student nurse" named Cathy Hunt (Ina Balin) with a suspicious unhealed bruise on her knee.[138] Cancer was the question, and the drama centered on "the often simple, but sometimes agonizingly borderline, decision of whether a tumor is benign or malignant." As one reviewer describe it, "The surgeon's knife, the future of a limb, organ and life, await [the doctor's] judgment."[139] The fate of Cathy Hunt hung in the balance. Pearson diagnosed *osteogenic sarcoma*—bone cancer—and advised amputation, while the younger Coleman "wondered if the amputation to be performed tomorrow was necessary or not." As Hailey wrote in his novel, "Eventually, of course, they would know for sure. When the severed limb came down to the lab, dissection would show if the diagnosis of malignancy was right or wrong."[140]

Final Diagnosis spotlighted the uncertainty at the heart of medical and patient awareness. Surgeons, "who found surgery a convenient and profitable remedy for any female pain" judging from the "unnatural number of hysterectomies, and in too many cases healthy, normal uteri," could sometimes be too quick to operate. Doctors were unsure. "In such instances," wrote Hailey, "euphemisms in diagnosis like 'chronic myometritis' or 'fibrosis of uterus' were resorted to as a smoke screen to cover up the pathology report on the removed tissue." In Hailey's novel, the cancer (and the amputation of Cathy Hunt's leg) would end her chances of marrying the young Doctor Coleman, who recoils with pity: "In a flood of imagination he had seen situations the two of them might meet together . . . He had seen himself dive through surf, or lie on a beach near-naked in the sun, but with [her] dressed decorously, sharing none of it because a prosthesis was ugly when exposed and, if removed, she would become a grotesque, immobile freak—an object for pitying and averted eyes." As the doctor turns away from the cancer patient with a final good-bye, "she tried to answer, but her self-control had been taxed too long."[141] The film ends more happily, and through it all, fictional characters like Cathy Hunt are paragons of self-control.[142]

The years of World War II and the Cold War catapulted these images of the cancer fighter (white heroines and heroes on the home front and the silver screen) into American popular consciousness. The graphic realities of wartime death, tragedy, disability, rehabilitation, sacrifice, survival, and personal responsibility all helped to bring cancer out of the shadows into a new prominence as a more intimately depicted personal topic than ever before. But by 1960, realism took another turn. Cancer patients' true testimonies (rather than film dramatizations) were increasingly prominent: their psyches were now on display for popular entertainment, education, and consumption.

THE FEMININE MYSTIQUE OF DETECTION AND SELF-SURVEILLANCE

In the post–World War II years, cancer became the second-leading cause of American mortality, and new media (from diagnostic x-ray imaging to the cinema) opened new possibilities in disease detection. In the 1950s, improvements in cancer detection, from the Pap smear to the x-ray and breast self-examination (BSE) to radiation and chemotherapy, were rapidly altering expert and lay perceptions about when cancers started, how they could be detected, how to treat them, and which populations were most vulnerable. Here again, white women played a prominent role in moving Americans into this new zone of cancer beliefs. She embodied new ideals of self-surveillance, of controlled anxiety, and of "soldiering on" even in the face of death. These values were projected onto women on the silver screen (as in the film *No Sad Songs for Me),* broadcast in breast self-examination educational films, and woven into Cold War health awareness imagery.

Photo by Allan Grant/
Time Life Pictures/
Getty Images

BSE emerged as the "front line of defense," casting white women in the role of empowered victims and encouraging them to use personal initiative and self-knowledge to save their own lives. The medium of film became the vehicle for teaching women about and promoting BSE (pictured in *Life* magazine, 1953, opposite page, top)—a new trend in how women internalized their risk and their powers of self-protection. "Every woman had in her own hands the strongest defense known today against a dreaded enemy," proclaimed a 1952 article in *Ladies Home Journal.*

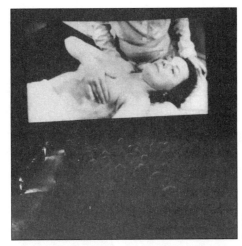

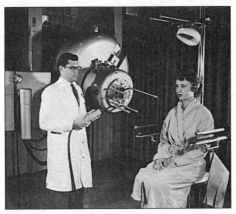

Cancer had a similar image in Hollywood. When the producer, Buddy Adler, asked Margaret Sullavan (opposite) to consider the role of a cancer victim in *Sing No Sad Songs for Me,* her response was refreshing and frank: "When do I start?" She saw the lead character, Mary Scott, as "a dramatic study of fortitude," crafted in the mold of the American soldier and reflecting Cold War American ideals. What appealed to Sullavan was the film's focus on a simple housewife's extraordinary, "almost superhuman courage" in a fight to save her life and to safeguard her endangered family.

4

HOW THE OTHER HALF DIES

In the annals of disease awareness, Harriet Wilson, an African-American woman, offers an unusually personalized portrait of cancer across the color line: a woman whose situation was written about with intimate poignancy, in contrast with the stereotypes of the Negro and cancer so common in the first half of the twentieth century. Mrs. Wilson's story was told by North Carolina public health student Rosemary Kent in the late 1940s. As she conducted her interviews with white women, African-American women, and white men (black men were not included in the study), Kent paid close attention to their cancer beliefs and the social context of the patients themselves. She was convinced that when all factors were considered, cancer knew no color line. Among such health workers, a new egalitarian assumption was emerging, holding that cancer was biologically neutral, an equal opportunity killer. Kent insisted that "the real goal" of cancer awareness "is the people . . . all the people. How can they be reached? How convinced? By whom? What forces and influences, what information and attitudes determine their behavior with respect to the cancer problem?"[1] An emerging epidemiological awareness suggested that any mortality differences across the population could be explained by social disparities, and women like Harriet Wilson seemed to prove the point.

Even as the intimate lives of white women continued to be at the epicenter of American cancer anxieties, old truisms of race, civilization, gender, and cancer were falling. The old racial thinking with its heavy emphasis on biological difference seemed much too closely allied with Nazi ideologies of racial inferiority and superiority—the contentious terrain upon which so much blood had recently been spilled.[2] Within Rosemary Kent's archive of interviews, Harriet Wilson's story stood out as a profile not of biological difference but of the social hardships shaping the patient's travails and accounting for mortality differences. Wilson was thirty-eight years old, divorced, and remarried and had lost her only child to illness. She worked in a tobacco factory, attended church groups, and turned to Christian publications like *Healing Waters*, the *Sunday School Times*, the *Baptist Reformer*, and *Herald of Hope* to help her navigate life's challenges. She also enjoyed listening to radio dramas about health matters. Wilson had a persistent health problem (a "pain in the side and a [vaginal] discharge").[3] Some people in the Carolina Piedmont region relied too much on gossip and home remedies, Kent commented. But Harriet Wilson was a reasonable woman, turning to reliable newspapers, magazines, doctors, and radio programs for information, and finally using this information to make a stand for her own health.

To Kent, Harriet Wilson's poignant case personified the new cancer divide, in which access to timely diagnosis and competent care defined the line between life and death. At first, "she went to a Negro physician" who described the discharge as "coming from a weak ovary," and she consented to an operation for "a tumor of the stomach," echoing common euphemisms of the time. Even after the operation, however, discharges continued. The physician recommended a round of "electric treatments" (likely X-ray or radium therapy) to which Wilson consented, still unaware of the true nature of her ailment. These treatments were "continued 'off and on every month or so for three years,'" but as her symptoms continued, Wilson's frustration mounted. Only after she read a column in the morning newspaper titled "What the Doctor Says" did she muster the strength to confront her doctor. "The column . . . described her symptoms—[a feeling of fullness in the abdomen] and discharge, sometimes bloody," and she returned to her doctor's office to ask bluntly, "Do I have a cancer?" At first, he denied it, but then he reluctantly agreed to examine her again and "took 'some flesh' [to send] to a laboratory." When the new report arrived, Wilson's doctor discovered "that he was dealing with a malignancy" and recommended an operation, but by this point Wilson's confidence in him was gone. She angrily refused his advice; they argued, and she left his office. Her refusal of a new operation had two origins. First, "she had in the past heard people say that if you 'cut for cancer, it will never heal up but will spread all over'"; second, she believed "that he had not told her his suspicions, and she did not, to use her words, 'like that *holding out* on his part.'" Not only was Wilson sensitive about medical duplicity, but she resented the doctor's condescension.[4]

Focusing not on race biology or stereotypes but on factors such as patient psychology, education, and social status, Kent also offered Harriet Wilson as a case study of how a persevering patient could find good cancer care despite poorly trained doctors, a flawed health care system, social inequality, and even the "bossiness" of the anticancer campaigns. "'People sometimes resent a person's talking to them or 'bossing' them,' she said. 'Put things in the paper for folks to read.'" Wilson's case, Kent asserted, echoed "the reaction of one of several patients who became dissatisfied with the medical treatment they were receiving, suspicious of their true condition, and who took steps to rectify the matter." Instead of doctors condescending to patients, Kent believed, more attention needed to be paid to how they came to believe what they did, where they got their information and views, how their views and awareness changed, and why. She saw Wilson as an independent-minded woman, a "dissenter" who regarded cancer experts suspiciously. Her common sense and good reason prevailed despite poor education and inferior medical advice. Kent believed that such sketches told a broader truth: "differences between races on health experiences and health practices were insignificant," except for the fact that black women more frequently had experiences like Wilson's, reported more "failure of other treatment and pain," and voiced greater skepticism about the information they received. For Rosemary Kent, Mrs. Wilson's struggle was not a crisis of race biology; rather, it was a lens into a situation where medical awareness was as confounded as patient awareness.[5]

With attention to such social difficulties coming into view, decades-old theories about black immunity, white women's vulnerability, and the protection afforded to primitive peoples were eroding, allowing a new epidemiological awareness to emerge. Epidemiologists, doctors, and scientists across a growing number of specialties in the 1950s began questioning the meaning of racial categories as never before. Did these categories reveal or obscure true differences? "The more we learn about the [cancer] situation among Negroes in America or Africa and the people of Indonesia, Asia, etc.," wrote the sixty-two-year-old scholar Sigismund Peller in 1952, "the less probable it becomes that one race is essentially more or less disposed toward cancer in general than is another race."[6] Peller, a Jewish émigré from Europe then residing in New York City and a noted researcher working on the margins of the U.S. cancer establishment, was busily reassessing race and cancer. He was not alone. Just as Rosemary Kent's public health thesis had done, Paul Steiner's *Cancer: Race and Geography* (1954) and Isaac Berenblum's *Science Versus Cancer* (1946) provoked readers to rethink "the *racial* approach to the problem of . . . human cancer."[7] "We know that there are separate races of mankind (even if these are not 'pure' in the genetic sense)," argued Berenblum, "and we have noted . . . how the relative frequencies of particular cancers tend to vary in different parts of the world." "More attention has been paid to this problem [of race and cancer] than almost any other," he commented, but "the results have on the whole been disappointing."[8]

Those who studied cancer in the 1940s and 1950s seized on new examples like that of Mrs. Wilson to turn attention to cultural customs, practices (from smoking and sex to diet), and social hardships rather than to rigid, old-style notions of racial stocks in order to produce new narratives about cancer trends across populations. For the first time in over a century, the "nonwhite" population was booming, "a departure from the long-standing trend toward a declining proportion of nonwhites which began in 1810 and continued uninterrupted up to 1930."[9] Cancer awareness was refracted through these wartime realities, postwar readjustments, and emerging epidemiological anomalies. New cancer curiosities gained wide attention: the Jewish cervical cancer paradox; the apparent links between men, smoking, and rising lung cancer deaths; the question of women's sex behavior and cervical cancer; and the apparently distinctive trends among Mexican Americans and other minority groups. Depending on how one defined "race" and depending on which cancer one studied, each curiosity produced its own racial narratives.[10]

Prewar epidemiological ideas were being revised by attention not only to newly visible groups but also to newly prominent types of cancer like leukemia and lung cancer. Looking at these emerging disease trends in the postwar era, few believed that biological difference or "race" as traditionally understood accounted for such shifts. While popular culture continued to revolve around the idea of cancer as a white woman's disease, medical commentators with an eye on its many anomalies began recasting the disease as a complicated egalitarian pathology that knew no color line. They looked at cancers across the color line for lessons about society and social difference, and built a new credo for a new era. "Cancer strikes persons of all races, creeds, and ideologies," insisted one 1947 newspaper editorial in Hartford, Connecticut. "Neither prince nor pauper, capitalist nor communist, is immune. In the fight against it, all men are on an equal basis."[11] Old "truths" were surely wrong. Meanwhile, another possibility emerged afresh: that access to novel therapies from radiation to chemotherapy to surgery and to expanding cancer facilities also defined the line between those who lived and died.

PAUL STEINER AND THE "RACIAL GEOGRAPHY" OF LOS ANGELES

Regardless of what had been said in previous decades, or what the numbers suggested, cancer was imagined anew by postwar epidemiology and medicine. "It is often said that cancer is a great democrat," the African-American radiologist John Moseley asserted in the *New York Amsterdam News*. "It does not discriminate because of race, creed, sex or age."[12] In the 1950s, many epidemiologists and medical scientists concurred with this view; cancer was the great equalizer. At the same time that cancer was being considered an "equalizer," the intellectual pull toward medical specialization led specialists in a number of fields, from lung pathology to gynecology, and from urologists to hematology, to theorize about cancers affecting different body parts and to conclude that there was no single, unifying logic of race and cancer. Rather, each type of cancer in each region of the body seemed to tell its own tale of ethnic custom, behavior, social interactions, and survival, and each region of the country also seemed to tell its own stories of race and disease.[13]

Caught up in this fertile moment of scientific, epidemiological, and cultural transition, pathologist Paul Steiner's 1954 book *Cancer: Race and Geography* offered a portrait of a multi-racial city. Based on autopsy records from the Los Angeles County Hospital (LACH), Steiner's study took aim at old truths. Faced with significant variations in cancer rates both within and among groups, Steiner began his study doubting that any single race theory could explain cancer trends.[14] Between 1940 and 1950, the "nonwhite" population in California more than doubled from just over 300,000 to almost 640,000.[15] Los Angeles, at the center of this demographic shift, was an impressive cultural crossroads that included populations of not only European-descended whites and African Americans but also people of Mexican, Chinese, Japanese, and Filipino descent. Nor was the white population homogeneous. Within Los Angeles there lived significant numbers of white ethnic groups (particularly

Jews and Italian Americans) who might not have been considered "white" even a generation earlier.

Steiner was attracted to oddities in cancer rates among the city's different racial and ethnic groups. "Cancer of the nasopharynx appears to be extraordinarily prevalent in South China," Steiner wrote, yet the rate was low in Chinese Americans. He therefore wondered, "Do second and third generation foreign-born (e.g., San Francisco–born) Southern Chinese lose this high frequency? If they do, what is its cause in China and why was the tumor frequency reduced in America?" Similar to the Chinese-American case, Steiner found that "the Afro-American has lost the high frequency of primary carcinoma of the liver that prevails in many native Africans." "Apparently he has escaped its cause," he concluded, gesturing vaguely to the impact of diet or environment. Cancer tradeoffs also worked the other way, however. Regarding the former African, he wrote: "Unfortunately, he has simultaneously acquired gastric cancer in the high frequency that prevails in the United States. In neither example are the causes for the changes yet fully known." And then there was the puzzling Mexican case. Steiner noted that while lung cancer in American whites tilted more heavily toward men, "the Mexican woman, in the Los Angeles area at least, has nearly the same . . . prevalence of lung cancer as do Mexican and Caucasoid males."[16] Such divergent trends posed a conundrum both for racial theories of cancer and for making straightforward links between modernity and cancer.

In Steiner's view, national trends were misleading, and it was increasingly "necessary . . . to use small, well-defined geographical units" like Los Angeles to truly understand disease trends "lest the statistical differences cancel each other out if these regions are combined." Each city and town also had its peculiar population and age distribution, its ethnic mix, its own migration trends, its trends in diets, cultures, and lifestyles, and its own environment—all of which created striking cancer differences. Specialists like Steiner also knew that wherever there were hospital services, diagnosis was more likely and cancer rates were therefore higher than in places that had poor health care and inadequate health surveillance. If one only looked at national figures, Steiner insisted, important variations remained hidden. It also made little sense to speak of cancer as if it were a single disease. His study of mortality trends at LACH covered no fewer than twenty-seven discrete cancers. Like each city, each type of cancer also followed its own logic, Steiner insisted. Skin cancer was a case in point. "In the United States," Steiner remarked, "the higher incidence . . . in southern states has long been known. The recent survey of cancer in ten cities by the National Cancer Institute reports sizable differences in many other tumors."[17]

For the earnest Steiner, Los Angeles was a complex laboratory where no fewer than six "races" resided: Caucasoids, Mexicans, Japanese, Chinese, Negroids, and Filipinos. Aware that many would look askance at his choices— separating Chinese from Japanese, and naming Mexicans a "race"—he noted: "The comment is frequently heard that there are no 'pure races,'" and some had even alleged that "studies involving the use of race or racial stocks are not justified." True, he admitted, there was no racial purity in Los Angeles, or anywhere for that matter. But his concern was not purity, he insisted. It was whether "large differences exist" across groups.[18] Steiner's choice of racial categories thus reflected a paradox, for while he rejected the older notion of black cancer immunity, he embraced other outdated practices of racial classification. To such scholars, categories were vital; it would be impossible to describe differences without them. Steiner understood that "race" was an imperfect term. Yet he also understood the truth of what anthropologist Franz Boas had written in 1937: "no matter how weak the case for racial purity may be, we understand its social appeal in our society."[19] The social appeal of race talk could not be ignored. Thus, Steiner accepted these categories on a contingent basis, not because they were scientific but because (as he put it) they represented the "near-popular" view of race. "The newsboy on the corner has no difficulty in most instances in distinguishing between the three main racial stocks here studied, and neither shall we," he opined. "No pretense is made that this is a precise genetical study."[20] The newsboy's categories were not science, but they were good enough for Steiner. Thus began his study of cancer and race in Los Angeles.

Steiner's detailed tally of cancer trends in Los Angeles over the thirty years from the 1920s through the 1940s used these categories, and the data itself revealed how the city's population makeup had shifted. "The Negroids" in this study, he noted, were "Afro-Americans who migrated to this area usually after a sojourn of variable length in eastern and southern states." When the data was first collected in the 1920s, this group's numbers were small, but its proportion "increased after the advent of World War II because of heavy migration into this area," doubling dramatically in the 1940s. Shipbuilding jobs, factory work, and other economic opportunities had pulled southern blacks westward into Los Angeles, and by the endpoint of the study 6.3 percent of the autopsies at LACH (2,236 cases) were "Negroids." By 1952, African Americans constituted the largest "nonwhite" group in the state (owing to the fact that people of Mexican descent were then classified as white, at least in the U.S. Census).

"In comparing the Negroids of Los Angeles and Africa," Steiner noted, migration had produced a mixed bag of good health and new disease challenges. "It appears that in the migrant there has been an increase in gastric, pulmonic, and gall bladder cancer and a decrease in skin and liver cancers," he observed. Were African Americans in Los Angeles more or less vulnerable to cancer than other groups in the city? Steiner found that L.A.'s blacks had higher death rates in only two areas—ovary and soft tissue carcinoma in females. But in seven other areas (stomach, large intestine, mammary glands, skin, and larynx and intracranial tumors and malignant lymphatic diseases), "Caucasoids" outstripped blacks. Not content merely to map this diversity, Steiner, like so many of his predecessors, speculated that "these changes in the Afro-American appear to be the result of change in the environment following migration." In the end, however, he concluded that overall "cancer frequency is less in the Negroid than in the Caucasoid." In the aggregate, cancer in Los Angeles remained more of a white than a black disease.[21]

Tracking cancer rates in the Mexicans of Los Angeles posed another kind of puzzle for Steiner, since this group was a hard "race" to classify. "Obviously, this group is racially heterogeneous," he concluded, "containing both Caucasoid and Mexican and American Indian elements, the latter probably greatly predominating." Mexicans did not fit easily onto the Caucasoid, Negroid, Mongoloid racial grid, and they defied the standard logic of categorization. A particularly large population in Los Angeles, people of Mexican origin accounted for 17.4 percent of the cases (6,150 in all), and had three times more autopsies at LACH than the Negroid population. Again, popular meanings of race overcame the scientific nuances. *Mexican* "is used in the regional popular sense for want of a better term," Steiner explained. "The term . . . has no exact anthropological, ethnological, nationalistic, or citizenship significance." In other words, people of Mexican descent blurred into each of the other categories; what made them separate was not biological coherence but the fact of Spanish descent among these "immigrants from Mexico and their descendants."[22] Not surprisingly, cancer patterns ran the spectrum among the city's Mexican Americans. In eleven types of cancers, there were no Mexican-white differences. Five types of tumors were more frequent in them than in Caucasoids—lung (female), larynx (female), gallbladder (female), bone tumors (males) and chorioepithelioma; and nine types of tumors were less frequent.[23] What to make of these patterns Steiner could not say. These patterns did not lend themselves to facile generalities.

The Asians of Los Angeles posed yet another type of racial ambiguity, for they, like the Mexican population, were an obvious amalgam of diverse groups. "The Mongoloid stock," Steiner commented, included three subgroups in the county hospital autopsy records: Chinese and Japanese ("which pose no problem in classification"), and Filipino, "which is usually regarded as predominantly a Mongoloid basic stock mixed with other strains to form a Malayan people to which Caucasoid elements have been added."[24] The Chinese and Japanese were a mixture of immigrants and first- and second-generation immigrant descendants, while most of the Filipinos were immigrants themselves. What he called the "Mongoloid stock" (a somewhat out-of-date racial term, interchangeable with "Asiatic" and "Oriental" in the 1940s) was, in fact, a complex amalgam.[25] Despite the vast internal complexity among so-called Mongoloids, Steiner was ready to speculate about their cancer rates. But when lumped into one group, these Mongoloids made up merely 1.1 percent of the hospital's autopsy cases (392) over the thirty-year study.[26] Hence, he concluded, few meaningful generalizations could be made from such a small sample.

If the pathologist Steiner had been as consistent with his racial logic as he was with his cancer typologies, he would have regarded the category Caucasoid as also problematic—a racial group made up of many ethnicities (diverse European nationalities, as well as Mexicans on occasion). But Steiner held on to it for purely practical reasons. Caucasoid, as he saw it, was the group "representing the mixture of European races and stocks," and "in individual cases the ethnic origins are unknown," but "because of the subsequent mixing, attempts to subdivide the Caucasoids for separate analysis would probably be futile, and it was not attempted." According to Steiner, it was simply too hard to differentiate the different racial stocks and ethnic subgroups that made up the Caucasoid group. Steiner's unwillingness to disaggregate "white" into ethnic parts in 1950s Los Angeles stood in marked contrast to Louis Dublin's Metropolitan Life Insurance studies from 1922 New York, where the Irish, Italians, Russian Jews, and Negroes all warranted their own population groupings. But in the intervening years, an Irish man might have moved west, married an Italian woman, and raised children in Los Angeles who thought of themselves as "white" in the city. In a society where racial and ethnicity identities and categories could change every generation, the prevalence of cancer rates in the "Irish" would fade from view, becoming less observable as groups intermarried and migrated. In Los Angeles, "white" became the benchmark for comparisons because, as Steiner put it, "they are the largest group and because more data on them are available in the literature for comparison than in the other races."[27] Caucasoid, then, had a very different racial logic than Mongoloid or Mexican or Negroid. It was used, if not because of biological accuracy then because it was convenient. Regardless of the ethnic composition of the white population, one could point to a highly usable category and compare white rates from one city or region to the next and to other groups—ignoring internal complexities.

Steiner's strange racial typologies, then, provide us insight into the cultural and political assumptions shaping race categories. With its sometimes tortured rationales, Steiner's study illustrates how practitioners, hailing from such diverse fields as statistics, pathology, surgery, epidemiology, insurance, biology, and medicine, were conscious of the flawed racial categories with which they worked, but were willing to promote them nevertheless. Many also understood the high stakes of classification. These classifications, so central in biological thinking, the law, and the public policy, were an unstable bedrock justifying social difference and supporting the American color line. In 1930, for example, the U.S. Census had pronounced that "practically all Mexican laborers are of a racial mixture difficult to classify," and that "in order to obtain separate figures for this racial group, it has been decided that all persons born in Mexico, or having parents born in Mexico, who are not definitely white, Negro, Indian, Chinese, or Japanese, should be returned as Mexican."[28] In 1940, however, the Census defined Mexican Americans as "white." The stakes of classification were increasingly obvious. As Ariela Gross has noted, throughout the period, lawyers in places like Texas had been fighting Jim Crow barriers on behalf of Mexicans as well as African Americans, with the result that growing numbers of Texas Mexicans referred to themselves as "white" as a strategy for overcoming the effects of racial segregation.[29] By 1960, the bedrock had shifted again when the Census instructed classifiers: "Puerto Ricans, Mexicans, and other persons of Latin-American descent—These are not racial descriptions. Mark 'White' for such persons unless they are definitely of Negro, Indian, or other nonwhite race."[30]

These oddly shifting practices of classification created many uncertainties. Some cancer specialists saw the obvious difficulty with racial categories, especially when it came to Mexicans and other "nonwhite" groups. Did white rates include Mexicans? Who, in fact, were the nonwhites? The once-firm truths of race and cancer were being revised by the unsettling process of categorization. "While Mexicans are classified as whites in vital statistics and census returns,"

William Haenszel wrote in 1961, "the designation is not strictly accurate, since biologically they represent a mixture of white and Indian blood."[31] Of course, what was true for Mexicans was equally true for all other categories—white, Negro, Asian, and so on. But experts, forging ahead, usually ignored these questions, insisting that biological integrity was not necessary to justify comparisons. As long as categories like "Mexican" had social or popular or political meaning, they would be useful. But another worry was that these idiosyncratic categories undermined comparisons between eras, across regions, and between nations. Increasingly in the postwar era, forthright scholars like Steiner acknowledged that their classifications made little biological sense. Yet classify he did. In the end, Steiner's sober assessment of Los Angeles' racial and disease anomalies was emblematic of the time. Cancer, he said, represented a complexity that defied easy categorization: "Unfortunately, our minds are not yet prepared to understand the information Nature is revealing by these and other exhibits."[32]

THE NONWHITE EXPERIENCE . . . THROUGH WHITE EYES

Nothing better exemplifies the confusion surrounding population and racial health than the invention and spread of the new population category "nonwhite"—intended to chronicle the nation's emerging diversity at mid-century. Paul Steiner was not alone in worrying over the proper categorization of cancer in Los Angeles. With a growing diversity of cancer types and American populations at risk, specialists of various kinds were noticing a perplexing array of new trends. Cancer rates were literally all over the map. The global ironies and cancer anomalies were numerous. "Cancer of the penis never occurs in Orthodox Jews, yet it is frequent among the inhabitants of Indo-China," observed the American Cancer Society's Charles Cameron in his best-selling 1956 book *The Truth About Cancer*. He added, "In parts of India, Malaya, and the Dutch East Indies, cancer of the inner surface of the cheek is very common, but it is comparatively rare elsewhere. Cancer of the bladder is a good deal more prevalent in Egypt than it is in Europe. Cancer of the liver is unusual in the United States, but among the Bantus of South Africa it is a serious problem." In America, each region and group stared into a different face of this menace. "Cancer of the skin is about three times more frequent in Texas and Arizona than it is in Maine and Vermont . . . Cancer of the cervix occurs only about one-fifth to one-tenth as often in Jewish females as in non-Jewish white females, and the rate of deaths from this cause among southern Negro women is about twice as high as it is among white females of the northern United States . . ." White Americans faced their own threats since "breast cancer is the commonest major form of the disease among white women in England and the United States, but it is comparatively rare in Japan." Nor could men escape. "Men in Denmark are more than twice as likely to suffer from cancer of the stomach as men in New York state," Cameron asserted.[33]

The dilemma of epidemiology in America was how to track trends in an increasingly diverse nation, where *nonwhites* were growing in the population. They were 10.5 percent of the U.S. population in 1950, and 11.2 percent in 1960.[34] But first, experts had to contend with the question of who were these *nonwhite* people? In a comprehensive 1955 U.S. Public Health Service report on *Morbidity from Cancer in the United States*, Harold Dorn and Sidney Cutler wrote, "[the] use of the term 'nonwhite' follows Census bureau practice. It refers to all persons who are not definitely white, so that it includes Negroes, Chinese, Japanese, and American Indians, as well as persons of mixed white and nonwhite ancestry."[35] (Notably, the Census did not include people of Hispanic background in the group.) These groups, noted the economist and statistician Paul Coe, were growing faster than whites, both because of the decline of white immigration and also because of "a higher rate of natural increase in the nonwhite than in the white population."[36] If categories like white and nonwhite lacked internal logic, they were nevertheless useful to epidemiologists. One goal of epidemiology was to compare patterns across the cities and states—to compare trends in Dallas with Iowa City, for example, or Atlanta with New York, and California with Mississippi. In pursuit of this goal, epidemiologists of the 1950s followed the Census in dividing the American population into "whites" and "nonwhites," and tracking trends in each group. It was a perverse strategy for tracking health, and the strange invention of "nonwhite" in the 1950s would have sweeping implications for decades to come.

"Nonwhite" incorporated different people, from different parts of the world, into one population box. A catchall term for all those who were not Caucasoid, the term illustrated the strange new logic of race in an era now attuned to diversity, yet blinded to the internal diversity of this "other" part of America. As epidemiologists Dorn and Cutler noted, when the term was first used, it was no more than a proxy for Negro: "More than 96 percent of the nonwhite population in the cities included in this study were classed as Negro by the Census bureau," they wrote in 1955, "so that the terms 'Negro' and 'nonwhite' are used interchangeably in this report."[37] In certain contexts the term "nonwhite" seemed reasonable, but, usually, comparing nonwhite populations from different parts of the country made no sense at all.[38] In 1956 rural and urban Iowa, for example, National Cancer Institute researchers noted that "the population of Iowa is predominantly white; only 41 nonwhite residents [out of 14,834 residents under cancer care] were reported . . . in 1950. Therefore," the study noted, "no attempt has been made to present material by race in this report."[39] But Iowa was not like Texas. In 1950 Dallas, the *nonwhite* population was 13 percent of the city and consisted almost entirely of "persons of Mexican birth or heritage who were not definitely Indian," as well as people not "of other nonwhite races [that] were classified as white."[40] Yet, even this characterization concealed hidden complexities. At least 1.5 percent of Dallas's white population had Spanish surnames, indicating Mexican heritage.[41] The actual composition of nonwhite American populations therefore varied widely from place to place. Not only did the term lack biological meaning but also it lacked comparability across regions, and its utility would decline with each passing year as the African-American proportion of nonwhites diminished.

Even at the time, authorities seemed to realize that the term *nonwhite* represented a perverse lumping of obviously diverse groups into a convenient new category; no one argued for it as a biological classification.[42] Indeed, the very point was to draw attention away from race as biology and toward commonalities in the social circumstances of nonwhites. In city after city in the late 1940s and early 1950s, the white–nonwhite cancer gaps were seen as driven by differences in social status and access to medical care.[43] In 1947 Louisiana, for example, the nonwhite male incidence was reported to have increased at a stunning rate (59 percent) "compared with a 12 per cent rise for white males." What accounted for the divergence? Perhaps, noted the Public Health Service author of the Louisiana report, it "may be an indication of improvement in medical care and diagnosis for this segment of the New Orleans population, rather than representing a real increase." Despite this nonwhite increase, cancer in Louisiana remained mostly a white disease, with cancer incidence still outpacing nonwhite incidence by 69 percent.[44] In Birmingham, Alabama, too, "the incidence rate for white persons remained about twice as high for nonwhite persons."[45] In Pittsburgh, the story was different, however. Here the term *colored* was used as a synonym for African-American. Moreover, the colored/white gap still made white men more vulnerable than colored men, while for women the gap had all but disappeared. As the Pittsburgh study noted, "the ratio of colored to white rate is 0.72 [a 38 percent gap] for males and 0.94 for females [thus, closer to parity]."[46] "It is unlikely," speculated the Pittsburgh study's author, "that colored persons are actually less susceptible to cancer. The lower rates, especially for colored males, are probably a reflection of less adequate medical care. It is likely that a large proportion of colored males with cancer do not receive any medical care for that condition."[47]

Arguably, the anomalous term *nonwhite* shifted the impulses of epidemiology away from biologizing race and toward the analysis of social difference. In 1947 Atlanta, white/nonwhite trends revealed that even though cancer incidence had a white face, the face of cancer death was increasingly nonwhite. The Public Health Service (PHS) study found that whites in Atlanta were being diagnosed with cancer at earlier stages than colored people. In whites, more cancers were coming out of the diagnostic shadows when the patient was still alive, so that only 5.2 percent of white male cancers could be labeled as "undiscovered until death," having killed patients without ever being diagnosed by a doctor. In white women, the number of such undiscovered cancers was smaller—only 2.4 percent. By contrast, cancers across the color line remained more hidden and undiagnosed. In the colored population (most of whom would have been African American), 5.7 percent of female cancers (twice the percentage of whites) went undiscovered until death. In nonwhite men, the percentage of such cases never diagnosed was 17.8.[48] This was an astonishing finding—nearly one in five nonwhite men with cancer became known to the Atlanta health care system only after they had died. Moreover, 58 percent of the cancers in white males were being found when the disease was localized; in nonwhite men, finding localized cancers was far rarer: only 14 percent of the cases.[49] These emerging disparities between whites and nonwhites drew attention away from race biology and toward the mortality gap.

The invention of the *nonwhite* category reflected a problematic moment in cancer epidemiology—at once signaling the recognition of common experiences among people of color while also engaging in a chauvinistic kind of "othering" in which categorizers imagined that whites were a unitary group and that all others were alike in not being white. In this white-centered worldview, differences among nonwhites mattered less than the fact of their nonwhiteness. It was an ill-conceived attempt to corral diverse peoples into a convenient, artificial, epidemiological category. One implication of the use of nonwhite was that through the 1950s and 1960s the experiences of African Americans, Asian Americans, Mexican Americans, and others would be difficult to track in detail. Even though the *white/nonwhite* paradigm did not make sense in many places (Paul Steiner's Los Angeles, New York, Dallas, Puerto Rico, or the soon-to-be states of Alaska and Hawaii), by using it researchers created new truths about national disease trends. One study (of fertility trends in Puerto Rico) explained that "although the island's population is quite mixed, varying from pure Negro in some cases to pure Caucasian in others, a distinction has traditionally been made in the censuses between white and non-white."[50]

The nonwhite fascination thrived in epidemiologists' imaginations not because of its biological acuity but because of its professional utility. As in the case of Steiner's categories, health scholars used these vague terms to discern emerging disparities and to compare trends across locales; but using *nonwhite* also created a troublesome and anomalous depiction of cancer trends. In the end, the designation "nonwhite" actually created an unhelpful binary that obscured experts' ability to see what was, in fact, a shifting array of colors and color lines.

SEX BEHAVIOR, CERVICAL CANCER, AND THE JEWISH ANOMALY

If Paul Steiner was a transitional racial thinker caught between pre- and post-war ideologies, and if the *nonwhite* category reflected the ideologies of an unsettled racial era, then the case of cancer and the Jews—neither colored nor white, according to some—was another of the era's transitional and curious developments. As historian Karen Brodkin has noted, "by the late 1940s, not only did economic and social barriers to Jewish aspirations fall away but the United States, perhaps in part from guilt about having barred Jews fleeing the Nazis, perhaps in part from a . . . greater horror of the Holocaust, became positively philo-Semitic in its embrace of Jewish culture." Jewish intellectuals and entertainers like Milton Berle, Sid Caesar, and Jack Benny, she noted, "were even more widely visible because they were in the arts and the new medium of television."[51] The old mystery of cancer and the Jews that Englishman Maurice Sorsby had seen in 1931 reemerged, given new meaning in the postwar milieu.[52] Once regarded as a separate racial group but now on their way to becoming "white," Jewish people's experiences with cancer became another lens through which racial ideologies evolved.

In this context, a new epidemiological mystery—why cervical cancer appeared to spare Jewish women—provoked authorities to ponder the Jewish situation in America. The case defied easy categorization, spawning new theories of difference. Writing from Mount Sinai Hospital in the heart of Jewish New York, three physicians observed that even though Jewish women outnumbered non-Jewish women by three to one in the hospital records (36,759 to 12,648), there had been only seven cases of cervical cancer among the Jewish women in the hospital but three times as many among non-Jews. Cervical cancer "was nine times more frequent in the non-Jewish group as compared with the Jewish group of women."[53] British authors like Isaac Berenblum in 1946 and Ernest Kennaway in 1948 had noted the anomaly a few years before; and Americans like Albert Rothman and Ernest Wynder in the early 1950s documented it in their clinics. All of these researchers, like Sorsby before them, had a goal; they had emerged from the war intent on taking up the old problem of Jews and cancer, seeing it as a testament not about Jews as a "race" but about their ethnic customs and social situation.[54] "The reasons for this [low cervical cancer rate] have been postulated by many, but proved by none," wrote the Mount Sinai doctors.[55] "Several hypotheses have been advanced to explain the low incidence," noted Sigismund Peller, among them "sex hygiene, less gonorrhea and syphilis, circumcision, lack of balanitis [inflammation of the head of the penis] in the male partners, and 'racial' peculiarity."[56] The anomalous case of Jewish women reflected two other trends: the increasing diversity of cancer theories at midcentury, as each cancer seemed to spawn its own theories, and the new focus on Jewish ethnic (rather than racial) behavior and custom as driving forces in this health difference.[57] At the same time, the case continued a long history of situating women, sexuality, and behavior at the center of the cancer debate.

In an era when the Alfred Kinsey reports on American sex customs captivated a wide audience, the titillating science and sociology of sex attracted much professional attention. Kinsey's 1948 report on the sex behavior of American men had "put a fairly difficult scientific report high on the list of best sellers," and public interest in the sex survey remained high when the sequel on women appeared in 1953.[58] Kinsey defended the absence of blacks in these studies of white Americans' sex lives by pointing to the "considerable difficulty in securing sex histories of upper educational and social levels of Negroes."[59] Sociologist Charles Spurgeon Johnson saw the irony of the exclusion: "nearly one half [of white women] were not virgins when they took their marriage vows" and "one in four . . . were unfaithful at least once after taking those vows," and these "purportedly scientific revelations of the sex habits of American white women now approximate many of the popular myths about Negro women."[60] Yet, the study contained no data to speak to these myths. The study had other blind spots. As journalist Doris Blake noted, it ignored "those who belong to devoutly Jewish or Catholic groups, rural groups, and those in the laboring classes."[61] These absences aside, the reports awakened general and scientific interest in the sex question. Physicians and specialists, who had long speculated on the role of sex in cervical cancer, now ventured where Kinsey had not gone—conducting medical surveys of patients' sex behaviors and white/nonwhite disparities.[62] It was in this context, then, that the Jewish cervical cancer anomaly drew attention as a model of how the intimate link between sex and disease could be broken.

The private sex lives of Jewish women became a professional curiosity, a useful lens for new thinking about these old problems of cancer and sex behavior and for generating new theories of disease and identity. Indeed, what began as an anomalous case laid the basis for constructing general truths. The question here was not "race," argued Isaac Berenblum. As he put it, in Jewish populations "some degree of intermarriage with the people of the country in which they have settled" ruled out any simplistic "conclusions based on any supposition of racial purity." Rather than defining Jews through some notion of biological essence, Berenblum described them as a social group "who are dispersed all over the world . . . [and] like other migrating people, have a tendency to maintain at least some of their customs in their wanderings." Yet the cervical cancer anomaly was evident not only in New York but also around the world. With a few exceptions, Berenblum noted, "the cancer incidence of the Jews tends to reflect very closely the pattern of their surroundings," with only cervical cancer and penile cancer standing out as striking exceptions.[63] Sigismund Peller was more expansive, noting, "it is now common knowledge that white Gentile woman have two to three times as high an incidence of cancer of the genital organs as Jewish women. The difference is especially marked with regard to cancer of the cervix."[64] For an increasingly cancer-conscious world, the case put a spotlight on Jewish rituals of hygiene, particular sexual practices, and whatever else Jews could teach their postwar fellow Americans about cancer avoidance.

Like Maurice Sorsby twenty years earlier, these authors saw Jewish sex behavior as a virtue that translated into good health. The atmosphere of the 1950s was more receptive to this message than the 1930s had been. The Talmud strictly prohibited sexual intercourse during and immediately after the woman's menstrual period: it was this practice based in religious observance that was the key to safeguarding women, Ernest Kennaway noted.[65] Writing in

1951, three Mount Sinai gynecologists echoed the notion (now entering the mainstream of the specialty) that "the limitation of cohabitation [sexual relations] during the menstrual period as imposed by Mosaic laws is an important factor in limiting irritation and subsequent carcinoma of the cervix in the Jewess." Even the recent rise in Jewish cervical cancer rates supported this idea, since according to these gynecologists it was evident that "the Jewish women of today do not adhere as meticulously to the Mosaic laws as they did at the turn of the century." But the Jewish anomaly also supported other theories, for example the idea that "the factor of hereditary immunity probably plays a role."[66]

Race biology, then, had not entirely disappeared from the debate on such disparities. Indeed, some authors still pondered whether Jews were a race or an ethnic group. Writing in the *New England Journal of Medicine*, two physicians speculated that in Russian Jews, who were "less deracinated [that is, more of an inbred population] than almost any other immigrant group from the European diaspora," cancer rates were higher. These authors contended, however, that it was not race but sex norms and religious observance that played the key roles. Among the Russian Jews, "strict observance of ritual prohibitions is largely a matter of individual conscience, and," in these cultures, "concupiscence [i.e., sexual desire or lust] frequently prevails over scriptural injunction."[67] Cancer as they saw it was driven by the higher degrees of individual freedom, lower levels of religious observance, and a culture condoning of sexual lust. Among European Jews, they argued, religious adherence and sexual restraint had become keys to cancer avoidance.

These new "truths" about the Jews and cervical cancer took on wider significance, influencing broader theories of cancer causation. By 1953, "the rareness of cervical carcinoma in Jewish women," the low rates among virgins, and the sexual virtue of such groups had become widely known in medicine and epidemiology—filling the pages of major medical journals, entering mainstream popular media, and offering many authorities the opportunity to moralize on women's ideal sex lives.[68] Jewish scholars like Peller and the physicians at Mount Sinai pressed this new awareness onto the cancer professions. Jews, defined here as a model minority, were healthy by custom and by adherence to religious tradition, not by biological immunity. Some doctors even believed that, given the rarity of cervical cancer in Jewish women, a surgeon treating uterine cancer in a Jewish woman need not remove the cervix as a precaution—as he would certainly do in other women. "Many advocates of the total operation will, when performing a hysterectomy on a Jewish woman, allow the cervix to remain because of the alleged rarity of cancer of the uterine cervix in the Jewess," noted three New York physicians in 1951.[69] The risk of a total hysterectomy, such practitioners argued, was "not warranted in this ethnic group."

Nor were Jewish women alone as exemplars of how to avoid the disease through right living. Among the nuns under his care, insisted cancer specialist Ernest Wynder, although some "of these consecrated virgins" did develop breast cancer and cancer of the uterus, "there had not been a single case of cervical cancer!"[70] In explaining these patterns, Wynder—who like Sigismund Peller had escaped Nazi persecution in the late 1930s—shunned race theory.[71] In a "Kinsey-like survey" in Los Angeles in 1953, such researchers confirmed that, after looking closely at the sex habits of 1,000 women, "half with cervical cancer and half without, in order to determine differences in sexual partners, frequency of sexual intercourse, [and] hygiene habits," it was indeed their behaviors and social situation (not biological/racial differences) that endangered women. Choices such as early marriage, "low economic status, divorce, separation from husbands and widowhood seem to have some relationship to the disease," the researchers concluded.[72]

In the 1950s, then, in Steiner's Los Angeles study, in the case of nonwhites, and in the Jewish example, new vistas in cancer and racial discourse opened. Old-fashioned racial biology positing a timeless Jewish people (a perspective closely allied with Nazism and scientific racism) was in full retreat while new forms of racial thinking were beginning to emerge. "The modern Jew," insisted medical scientists in a 1952 *Lancet* article, "is not necessarily a close racial relation of the people of the Bible some 3,000 years ago." In fact, Jews represented different lineages (the Central and Eastern European strains, the Spanish and Mediterranean groups, and the "Oriental Jews of Asia Minor and Arabia"), scientists argued, and any discussion of the group as a "race" also needed to consider the periodic "influx of non-Semitic blood into the Jewish community."[73] As authors like Berenblum insisted, human populations were complex. The genetic constitution of mankind was so mixed that this old language of "race" no longer explained difference in the compelling way it once had.

In a striking twist, the new theories on cervical cancer also drew men into the picture—implicating Jewish men in halting the disease in Jewish women. The possibility of "the carcinogenic action of smegma," had been raised in the late 1940s in *Science* magazine, implicating men in women's cancer.[74] Did poor penile hygiene give women cancer? Did "the practice of circumcision of the Jewish male" protect Jewish women from cancer?[75] If smegma was cancer-causing, then cervical cancer (which had long stood out from other cancers because of purported associations with sexually transmitted disease) could be linked to the "personal cleanliness" and sex practices not of women, but of men. Viewing cancer through this lens, Ernest Wynder's 1954 study of 1,900 women in twelve hospitals across four states asked them about marriage, marital partners, sexual intercourse, pregnancies, abortions, miscarriages, and other intimate matters. His findings confirmed many of the emerging truisms. "A woman whose husband is uncircumcised runs 2½ times as great a risk of cervical cancer as a woman, married only once, whose husband has been circumcised," he found.[76] As *Time* magazine reported the findings, circumcision had become a leading wedge in protecting women: "the fact that 85 percent of the boy babies in U.S. private hospitals nowadays are circumcised, regardless of the parents' religious beliefs, may be an important factor in reducing cancer of the uterine cervix (neck of the womb) in years to come."[77] By 1957, it was well established that circumcision also ensured men's health. As the British scholar Kenneway argued, "the fact is now well established that cancer of the penis . . . has never been found, with one exception, in anyone circumcised by the Jewish method"; moreover, "the low incidence of cancer of the cervix in Jewish women is now established by so great a quantity of evidence . . . from many different countries that we can take it as settled."[78]

If Jews were a "model minority" in cancer prevention, researchers saw African Americans as a worrisome example of how sexual customs and circumstances produced high cervical cancer rates. Black women were cast as sexually promiscuous, unhygienic, and ignorant—a dangerous combination.[79] Income, it was believed, played a role as well; a national conference in 1949 reported "a higher incidence [of cervical cancer] in lower income groups, perhaps due to a combination of diet, the trauma of multiple births and poor obstetrical care, and possibly some racial influence." Comparing Jewish and African-American rates, some experts obsessed about sexual practices.[80] Yet other scholars warned against linking cervical cancer too closely to marriage and sex, since "cancer of the cervix may develop irrespective of virginity or parity [the number of children borne]."[81] Others wondered whether "injuries sustained in childbirth" were the key, or whether other as-yet-unstudied habits of daily life held an answer.[82] Cervical cancer—in whatever group—brought researchers into a new thicket of speculation about intimate lives and sexual matters across the color line.

CANCER AS DEMOCRATIC DISEASE

Buttressed by numerous examples across the color line, medical theory in the 1950s took a sharp behaviorist turn. Experts, looking through the lens of cervical cancer, argued that "extrinsic factors, rather than biological variations, are responsible for the racial differences."[83] Cancer theories were also beginning to fragment, with each cancer type following its own logic and generating its own theories of race, of ethnicity, and of modern life's health risks. The forces driving the fragmentation of cancer theory were many: medical specialization drawing attention to the specificity of each cancer type; the slow retreat of older racial typologies; and the rising profile of cervical and lung cancer, which emphasized the role of behavior in disease. Scientific consensus solidified around the view that "cancers," of which there were a multiplying variety, were not all the same disease. Testifying before a congressional inquiry in 1953, Charles Cameron of the American Cancer Society remarked that "it is tremendously important to understand how many diseases we are actually talking about when we use the word 'cancer.'" There were "more kinds of cancer than there were other diseases combined," he insisted. Moreover, he said, "if we take one kind of cancer, cancer of the breast, we still have an enormously complicated problem because there is not 1 kind of cancer of the breast, but there are 6 or 8 general kinds." Cameron even turned the old trope of cancer as a disease of civilization upside down, insisting that "it is not civilization that causes cancer, it is simply that civilization produces the new methods of detection, the new awareness, the institutions" that lead to earlier and more rigorous detection of cancer. Accordingly, there could be no single logic explaining all cancer trends—cancer had become more, rather than less, complex with time, and each type presented its peculiar social, behavioral, biological puzzle.[84]

An entirely new kind of awareness took hold in the cancer professions: an awareness of differences across cancer types and of many ethnic anomalies, an understanding of diagnostic unevenness making some cancers in some populations more visible than others, a focus on behaviors from sex to smoking, and a powerful leaning toward presumed equalities in cancer. Researchers increasingly presumed that many cancer rates across groups tended toward equality unless modified by social arrangements, behaviors, environment, diet, and customs. Considering the black-white gap in lung cancer, for example, two New York physicians, Milton Rosenblatt and James Lisa, argued that the gap was statistically real but that it disappeared on close examination.

"Bronchogenic carcinoma is most prevalent in the latter decades of life," they noted, "and in general the Negro population does not live so long as the white population." The "race" gap was probably related to this aging gap. "Although some statistical evidence points to a natural immunity of the Negro," they argued, "no conclusions are justified until the life span of the two races is approximately equal."[85] Thus for these specialists, the apparent racial gap was no more than an illusion. Older populations of whites suffered one type of disease, while a younger black population experienced a different disease profile. Looking at lung cancer and the color line in 1956, these experts saw much more than a biological divide. They saw a demographic divide, a gap in life chances, in which "tuberculosis and infectious diseases [were] responsible for higher death rates among Negroes and prevent[ed] them from reaching the cancer age." Rosenblatt and Lisa suggested that "the effect of the difference in age distribution can be eliminated by the use of age specific morbidity or mortality rates," data that was as yet unavailable. If more black people seemed to dodge lung cancer, it was because they had the misfortune of dying earlier and in larger proportions from tuberculosis. In time, the researchers believed, "greater recognition of the disease and consideration of the age survival factor will probably demonstrate in the future a more equal distribution of the disease among all races."[86]

As with cervical cancer, lung cancer theories were also in transition in the 1950s, as some specialists pointed an accusing finger at cigarette smoking behavior among men. Death rates for other cancers had leveled off from 1933 to 1948, but lung specialists voiced alarm at the fourfold increase for bronchial carcinoma, particularly in white men (going from 4.5 per 100,000 in the population to 16.1). It was now second to stomach cancer as the cause of this group's cancer mortality. For white women, the same fifteen-year period saw a twofold increase in death rates, from 2.5 to 5 per 100,000 people—still behind breast, uterus, intestinal, and stomach cancers.[87] A 1948 study characterized lung cancer as "primarily a disease of males, with a predominance over females in the ratio of five or six to one . . . [and additionally noted that] the disease is also primarily one of the white race."[88] Another author in the mid-1950s saw the disease as "twice as frequent in the white as in the Negro race."[89] But race per se was not seen as the driving force. Few could ignore the "high degree of association between cigarette smoking and the occurrence of lung cancer" or the role of exposure to industrial substances and air pollutants.[90] Tobacco was suspect number one in the troubling spike in white men over the age of thirty-five.[91] At the American

Medical Association's 1950 meeting in San Francisco, no topic gained more attention.[92]

The "phenomenal rise . . . [of lung cancer] particularly among males" put another "new" group, the white male and his smoking behavior, into the cancer spotlight. Battle lines formed between those who attacked the cigarette as a causative agent and those who saw a broader range of causes.[93] Clarence Cook Little of the ACS, a staunch believer in the role of heredity, lined up against those who blamed tobacco. But according to Louisiana cancer surgeon Alton Ochsner, "at the turn of the century [lung cancer] almost did not exist and yet at the present time, is the most frequent of all cancers."[94] Ochsner insisted that behavioral change was the key, that this "unprecedented increase . . . is due almost entirely to cigarette smoking," and therefore the link of cancer to habit and custom could not be ignored. Researchers Milton Rosenblatt and James Lisa observed that "one of the arguments put forth in favor of the smoking theory is the prevalence of the disease in males, attributing the sex difference to their heavier smoking habits."[95] But other specialists wondered whether a wider range of environmental factors like "the development of black-top highways and streets" might not instead be responsible. With behavior and environmental exposure now in the foreground, one public health official could even wonder whether "the fact that women, so far, are not exposed to such air pollutants for as many hours per year as are men" accounted for their lower lung cancer rates.[96] According to such views, the indoor safety of domestic life might well be a woman's protection from lung cancer.

As previous examples suggest, cancer types and theories came in increasing varieties, each with its gender or racial entailments. Each cancer type had social patterns of its own, and each type could give rise to racial truisms and claims about etiology and identity. Asked whether viruses might explain lung cancer, New Orleans's Dr. Alton Ochsner wrote to a colleague, "I am convinced that there are certain cancers that are caused by viruses," but he was "not convinced that a virus is responsible for the development of cancer of the lung."[97] Previously unappreciated vectors and mechanisms, from hormones to nicotine to viruses and even smegma, seemed to account for different cancers in different populations.[98] Cervical and lung cancers, two newly prominent malignancies of the 1950, did have distinctive racial distributions, but scholars of the era saw race as a lens onto social difference, rather than as merely a biological problem. Differences in access to diagnosis and treatment across color lines were also seen as defining mortality differences. As well, the rising rates for these two cancers were obviously being driven by improvements in X-ray diagnosis and the Pap smear. Accordingly, many cancer specialists believed that the rise in men's cancer rates overall was illusory, driven by the fact that internal cancers were now being diagnosed more easily than ever before.[99] In these fast-changing times, few generalizations held up under the sustained scrutiny. In some ways, it was far safer to assume that cancer did not discriminate. Thus by the early 1960s, as the biostatistician William Haenszel concluded, "no group ha[d] uniformly high or low rates for all sites considered. Each group presented its pattern of excess and deficits."[100]

Postwar ideals of racial equivalence also filtered into cancer theory. Increasingly, cancer specialists saw the old race questions with skepticism, acknowledging that many factors confounded the gathering and interpretation of data on racial groups and cancerous growths. In this context, few could resist embracing the idea of cancer's fundamental egalitarianism. As Charles Cameron of the American Cancer Society saw it, "there is no reason to believe that people in one part of the world are any less susceptible to cancer in general than anywhere else, or to assume that we today are more prone to cancer than our great-grandparents were. If there is a greater chance to our getting cancer today, the reason is simply that there is a greater chance that we will live into old age."[101] In other words, no generation was truly spared from this threat. Moreover, every cancer, every group, and every specialty told its own story—not only about innate differences but about behavior, custom, and how social differences reshaped what was increasingly coming to be seen as a "democratic disease."

Wisely, most scholars in the 1940s and 1950s refused to endorse an over-arching racial theory of cancer as their predecessors had done; to do so would have been naïve, especially in the face of the disease's expanding diversity. "Biology and environment are so interrelated in determining health status," wrote sociologist and Fisk University president Charles S. Johnson in 1949, "that it is hardly possible or practicable to attempt a separation."[102] Racial awareness and cancer awareness were both in flux, changed by war, urban growth, immigration, specialization, and rising sensitivity toward how the "other half" died.[103] "Viewed from this perspective," Johnson continued, "the health status of the Negro becomes more than a question of medicine, or of hospitals, or of physicians. It is bound up . . . securely with elusive factors of economic levels, cultural status, and the progress of medical science itself."[104] Such scientists insisted that the color line and the cancer challenge were complex issues that transcended biology—calling for social, economic, political, and cultural understanding.[105] Hospitals in Pittsburgh, Los Angeles, Dallas, Atlanta, and other cities were now filled with cancer patients from across the shifting American "racial" spectrum. The war had brought new groups to the American shores—Asians, Pacific Islanders, Jews. And with their arrival, the old logic of race gave way to new confusions in racial classification. But the new age of therapies also provided fresh opportunities for new race theories to develop. As one Delaware physician commented, the black women treated with radiation in his hospital, although initially sicker than white women, survived the therapy better; perhaps, he speculated, "the fortitude and stamina of the Negro patient enable her to survive treatment one would hesitate to use on the white patient."[106] Thus could advances in therapy become the basis for a new round of speculation about race and difference.

The truisms of the first half of the century were melting away, and new unstable, partial truths about cancer and ethnicity, behavior, custom, and social class were emerging. However, cancer scholars in the 1940s and 1950s found themselves at a confusing crossroads in cancer and racial awareness, believing that cancer death rates would even out across the population if all social inequalities disappeared. For Sigismund Peller, the field of statistics needed a clean break from a flawed past when "the arbitrariness of the official mortality data" was rife and experts saw differences where none truly existed.[107] "Premature generalizations" littered the field, creating large "stumbling blocks in the progress of science." He insisted that the state of science was not much improved in 1950: it was afflicted with impoverished data and shallow thinking. As a result, Peller argued that "the study of cancer in nonwhite races is not advanced enough to make it possible to point out differentiating characteristics."[108]

"The more the 'racial' cancers are studied," admitted Paul Steiner, "the greater is the tendency for them as such to vanish."[109] After speaking with Harriet Wilson and many other patients, Rosemary Kent would have agreed. Cancer statistics needed better and more comprehensive data, better means of tracking illnesses and mortality trends, more thorough methods for tracing access to health care and survival differences, and also more thoughtful ways of categorizing groups. For skeptics, the surge in attention to new cancers and to newly studied groups such as Jewish women, southern men, Mexican Americans, and other "nonwhite" groups set the stage for a radical rethinking of how cancer and "race" related to one another. What new racial paradigm would emerge to replace the facile old notion of white female vulnerability and primitive immunity?

Reflecting on the rising political turmoil of the 1960s and the high stakes of health discourse, Ann and Thomas Pettigrew saw that these questions of disease and race classification had sweeping implications. As they wrote in 1963, apparent disease differences were being used to shore up segregation and support the logic of Jim Crow. "Surely, argue many segregationists, the Supreme Court [in its *Brown v. Board of Education* school desegregation ruling] could not have meant that whites must associate with 'diseased Negroes.' The Mississippi legislature even resolved to use health criteria as a possible means of preventing school desegregation," they wrote. The Pettigrews insisted, however, that "segregationists who employ health arguments in their last-ditch defense against racial change are on shaky ground." Cancer trends proved the point, for "when white and Negro females from the same socio-economic backgrounds are studied, the incidence [of cervical cancer] is essentially the same." Health differences were not evidence of innate differences nor to be used as arguments for shoring up segregation, they argued; to the contrary, "the 'racial differences' in health that *do* exist provide further evidence of the societal need for desegregation and improved living conditions for all Americans." Finally, the Pettigrews took issue with the term "race" itself, seeing racial purity as another prosegregation argument. "There are no 'pure' races . . . [but rather] groups socially defined as 'races' in the United States," they argued. "Negro Americans are . . . an example par excellence of a cross-racial group."[110] In decades to come, as the African-American case faded in and out of focus, one could not discuss cancer without acknowledging the era's new race politics or seeing disease differences as linked to the quest for equality.

RACIAL LABELS AND THE RISE
OF A DEMOCRATIC DISEASE

"Cancer strikes persons of all races, creeds, and ideologies," argued one newspaper editorial in 1947. "Neither prince nor pauper, capitalist nor communist, is immune. In the fight against it, all men are on an equal basis." Experts such as radiologist John Moseley insisted, "It is often said that cancer is a great democrat. It does not discriminate because of race, creed, sex or age."

Such observers refused to endorse earlier racial theories of cancer susceptibility and immunity, and they fiercely recast the disease as an egalitarian pathology that knew no color line. For them, it was social inequality (rather than biological difference) that explained observed disparities in incidence and mortality across groups.

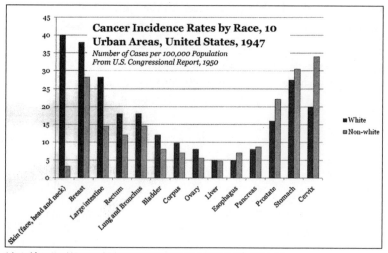

Cancer Incidence Rates by Race, 10 Urban Areas, United States, 1947
Number of Cases per 100,000 Population
From U.S. Congressional Report, 1950

Adapted from Harold Dorn and Sidney Cutler, *Public Health Monograph* 29, 1955, p. 30.

In the annals of epidemiology, the 1940s and 1950s produced new trends and complications in race thinking.

Mortality and incidence charts (such as the one on the facing page from a 1950 Congressional report) told a more complex story of disease and population. Using such incidence data, opinion leaders insisted that each type of cancer told its own story about race and disease. Yet, by using such perverse catch-all terms as "nonwhite," experts of this era promoted a strange new logic of difference. The new population term downplayed the internal diversity of this "other" America, lumping all "nonwhites" (whether Japanese, Chinese, black, Mexican, or Puerto Rican) into one undifferentiated group. A misguided epidemiological race concept from the outset, its utility declined as the composition of nonwhite groups changed and as political pressure grew in the 1960s to count each group's experience separately.

The world war also ushered new groups into American life—Asians and Pacific Islanders, European Jews—and with their arrival, the old logic of race gave way to new confusions in racial classification. The Jewish experience, for example, became a new touchstone in the American race–cancer discussion. Observations about the rareness of cervical carcinoma in Jewish women (alongside low rates among virgins) spurred new theories that showed behavior and sexual custom—rather than race per se—as key determinants of cancer differences in the 1950s. The question of whether these were white or nonwhite trends posed a challenge to older racial nomenclature

5

BETWEEN PROGRESS AND PROTEST

In May 1972, national media such as *Newsweek* magazine, the *Washington Post*, and *ABC News* turned their attention to an American health emergency: scientists at Howard University in Washington, D.C., had discovered an "astounding increase in cancer mortality among the nation's black population in recent years."[1] With the Howard report, public cancer awareness, long focused on the white female population, turned to the black experience. Only a year earlier, President Nixon's "war on cancer" message had failed to comment on any disparities across the color line. The public revelation that mortality rates in black Americans had grown by 32 percent in the eighteen years since 1954, while whites' mortality had increased by only 3 percent, caught cancer experts and the cancer establishment (the NCI, PHS, and ACS) by surprise.[2] "Nobody has really pinned down the causes of the greater increases for blacks," commented a statistician for the American Cancer Society; "we can only speculate."[3] There was something poignant in the fact that it had taken a little-known group of researchers at the historically black university, who published their work in the obscure *Medical Annals of the District of Columbia*, to discover this drift toward increased mortality among black Americans, while scientists in the burgeoning cancer establishment worked unaware. But now, with broad media coverage, the cancer experiences of African Americans took on enhanced meaning.

The Howard report was the culmination of a decades-long transformation that had altered old relationships between medical experts and the public and had politicized cancer awareness. In the 1950s and 1960s, Martin Luther King Jr. had often called segregation "a cancer on the body politic," likening Jim Crow and white supremacy to the insidious malady.[4] King's rhetoric was on the more temperate and restrained side of a public vocabulary of cancer and race that was becoming more angry, accusatory, and politically charged. Through the 1960s, black Americans had engaged in marches and protests and even rioted in the name of equality. Many had died to tear down the color line in voting, education, and civic life. Meanwhile, cancer patients—white, black, and statistically "other"—were marching too, in a drive to seize control of their own destinies. Simultaneously, with the passage of Medicare in 1965, once-invisible elderly citizens of all colors had more fully become part of what Louis Dublin had called the American "insurance experience."[5] Their ailments were now better diagnosed, classified, and documented than they had been at any previous time in history. The politics of health care was changing on many fronts, and tensions brewed between those admitted to the "cured cancer club" and those excluded. By the end of this turbulent decade, relations between these outsiders-looking-in and the so-called cancer establishment had created a tense backdrop for the Howard report.

By the early 1970s, the two signature battles of the 1960s—the fight for racial equality and the struggle for health equality—had merged. Black Americans found themselves facing a less visible but equally deadly enemy.[6] Cancer discourse now turned to the question of racial inequality. But the era was also full of contradictions, with the public at once skeptical about orthodox cancer treatments (radiation, chemotherapy, and so on) while also convinced that unequal access to those treatments was creating survival inequalities. This was a new politics of disease in which, as one journalist reminded readers in *Ebony*, cancer was "not just a white disease" anymore.[7]

The cancer establishment's blindness to the rising tide of death in black America was particularly troubling. Their failure went to the deeper question of political recognition, for authorities seemed unable to even "see" minority groups or understand the minority experience. As Dr. LaSalle D. Leffall Jr. later recalled, "We Howard doctors knew from our experience practicing in a predominantly black hospital that the cure rate for black cancer patients was poorer than for whites, and we sensed the situation was getting worse."[8] If a small band of Howard University researchers could discover such dramatic patterns, what did this say about the cancer establishment nationwide? That it had taken epidemiological experts decades to recognize these disparities pointed to failures of scientific awareness.[9] The study, therefore, fed cynicism about expertise, about progress in the war on cancer, and about racial equality. Moreover, the pathbreaking critique would resonate to such an extent that it catapulted Howard's LaSalle Leffall into the presidency of the American Cancer Society in 1978—the first African American to fill the post. The same year, the black soul singer Minnie Riperton, just recovering from a mastectomy, also ascended to became the ACS's spokesperson for cancer.[10] In the wake of the Howard report, the struggles of black Americans became, for the first time, exemplary of the challenge of cancer awareness.

In this new era, the race question in cancer became not one of primitivism or biology, nor was race a proxy for nonwhite status or social class; rather, it was race as an identity-based political movement that came fully into view. Politicizing cancer in this way around the black experience had far-reaching effects, helping to catalyze and spread a style of identity-based health activism that would have lasting influence and that has become a familiar part of cancer awareness in America. But the roots of that politicization had already been laid in the prior decades.

EXPERTS UNDER SIEGE

The two decades leading up to the Howard report saw intense political skirmishes over cancer—debates defined not by race per se, but by popular frustrations with scientific expertise, by both mainstream and fringe beliefs in emerging cancer cures, and by government activism on behalf of disenfranchised patients. For some cancer patients regarded as beyond hope and incurable, one of the most visible unorthodox treatments of the 1950s and 1960s was Krebiozen—a controversial and ultimately failed drug whose proponents claimed it could cure cancer and whose detractors labeled it a quack remedy.[11] Notably, the drug became a rallying cry over these years for those who felt they had been left behind by medical progress or forgotten by the elitist medical establishment. The long-running Krebiozen saga (animated by angry scientific disputes, libel accusations, competing studies and books, and a nine-month criminal trial) is notable for how it pitted outsiders against organized medicine and defined a new cancer politics.[12]

The Krebiozen story revealed how, alongside the struggles of black Americans for civil rights, other popular passions, hopes, and movements stirred patients to protest and rally against the cancer establishment. The story begins with Andrew Ivy, a highly respected physiology researcher and administrator at the University of Illinois, who announced in March 1951 that a new drug had shown promise in cancer treatment. Hearing Ivy's report, the *Chicago Tribune* optimistically announced that "the age-old search for a chemical bullet that will strike down cancer was believed by scientists to have come a step closer to success here yesterday."[13] The promise of a cure hung in the air as never before, tapping into the frustrations as well as the hopes of many Americans. It was also derided as a "quack cure." But as the story unfolded, it spotlighted new political dimensions of cancer survival, and in so doing opened the way for neglected groups (African Americans among them) to protest against the establishment's self-interested myopia.

At a press conference announcing the drug's potential in 1951, Andrew Ivy sat next to a "semi-bald, modest man" named Stevan Durovic, the mysterious drug's discoverer. According to media reports, Dr. Durovic had "fled from Yugoslavia when the Germans occupied it in 1941," survived the Italian concentration camps, and spent time in Argentina, where he had conducted what he called secret cancer research.[14] His drug needed nothing more than an honest hearing, claimed Ivy. At the press conference, testimonials by women like Mrs. Irene P of Evanston, 40, and Miss Eleanor G, age 36, told of the drug's promise.[15] Within days, hundreds of requests for the drug poured in from doctors and cancer sufferers.[16] Krebiozen tapped into a need, but it also exposed the tension between popular hopes and expert assessment. The American Medical Association soon launched its own review of a hundred patients taking the drug, and within months issued a scathing indictment: of one hundred patients, ninety-eight showed no objective improvement.[17] Accusations and counteraccusations followed. The so-called cancer quacks criticized the American Medical Association for its hasty rejection, and the AMA shot back that Krebiozen offered only the charlatan's false hope.[18] One nurse characterized the fight as the big players versus the "little man": "the federal government, the Food and Drug Administration, the American Medical Association, [and] the entire pharmaceutical industry . . . [are] conspiring against him because 'they' don't want to lose business by allowing the miracle cure to be sold on the open market."[19] These battle lines around cancer care would only harden in the coming years, and the debate would flare and subside though the 1950s and into the 1960s.

Ivy and his followers took up this rhetoric and championed the "little person," the patient who was desperate for a breakthrough but lost in an expanding health-care system with its large bureaucracies and self-serving agendas. To those who believed in Ivy and Krebiozen, the drug's rapid rejection by the medical establishment reflected entrenched "hostility and prejudice" toward mavericks, their unconventional theories, and any outsiders who were snubbed as troublemakers.[20] Initially, Ivy claimed neutrality on the question of Krebiozen's value; all he wanted was a fair hearing. Warning patients against "false hopes," he distributed the drug free of charge to physicians who requested it between 1951 and 1954 so that it might be tested.[21] But the response of organized medicine, particularly to Ivy and Durovic's decision to not release the drug's formula or chemical composition, was sharp and punitive.[22] In November 1951, the Chicago Medical Society suspended Ivy for promoting a "secret remedy," a hallmark of quackery.[23]

As Ivy and Durovic pressed on, extensive media coverage tracked the increasingly angry and politicized debate. "A secret drug cannot be appraised scientifically," insisted one 1952 editorial, echoing the AMA position. "No physician is justified in subjecting a patient to treatment under such conditions."[24] The fight became so heated that the U.S. Congress took up the Krebiozen question. Illinois senator Paul Douglas charged that "the National Cancer Institute and the Food and Drug Administration are 'pawns for organized medicine.'"[25] Other observers accused the AMA of "hasty, capricious, and dishonest" opposition to the drug.[26] Meanwhile, undaunted, the researchers filed for FDA approval.[27] Whom was the public to believe? The heated debate exposed the high stakes linked to cancer care and to Krebiozen. Cancer therapy in the 1950s (with radiation, chemotherapy, radical surgery, and new drugs) hovered on the brink of offering therapeutic relief, but questions of what constituted appropriate treatment went well beyond science. Legislators and common citizens could easily grasp the political implications of the story.[28]

The Krebiozen episode itself had no explicit racial features; but framed as it was as a story of underdogs and marginal patients versus experts, it resonated across class, gender, and racial lines. Since the earliest days of the republic, physicians had portrayed poor and uneducated Americans as susceptible to myths, superstitions, and quackery about illness and cures. Black Americans seemed particularly gullible. "Undoubtedly, mysticism, voodooism, and quackery play an important part in impeding the progress of the Negro in health education," John West, a health officer in Harlem, had written in 1937.[29] But black people were not alone, he continued: "let it not be believed for a moment that such practices are peculiar to the Negro. Superstitions abound in all races." Cancer superstitions were particularly ingrained, but also subject to change.[30] "This belief in magic, superstition, and confidence in quacks is by no means confined to the Negro race," echoed Ray Lyman Wilbur, president of Stanford University and of the American Statistical Association, in 1937. "But we must anticipate that we have several generations before we can expect the average Negro to have an appreciation of medical care equal to that of the highest level of his present white neighbor," he concluded. He looked to radio and literacy to inform and educate the public about health.[31]

To the dismay of leading experts who were intent on labeling Krebiozen a "quack" cure, the Krebiozen movement had a middle-class appeal and thus did not follow the classic script of cancer quackery. Not only was it led by an established scientist but it also attracted an unconventional middle-class following and became a "civil rights" concern for many patients and survivors. Middle-class housewives, U.S. senators, and other elected officials of many stripes counted themselves among the legion of supporters who were frustrated with medical orthodoxy's refusal to endorse the drug.[32] Echoing the tactics of civil rights protesters, by August 1963 some two hundred "Krebiozen marchers" would descend on the White House to begin a "death watch . . . beseeching President Kennedy's aid in their fight" for the drug.[33] In February 1964, a group of roughly a hundred people calling themselves the "Citizen's Committee for Cancer Survivors on Krebiozen" would meet in New York to try to continue the campaign to lift the ban.[34] This mainstream appeal shocked and annoyed the AMA, the NCI, the American Cancer Society, and other authorities. But "without the scientists and the politicians," as one *Los Angeles Times* commenter concluded in 1963, "the Krebiozen boom would never have gotten off the ground nor remained the contentious issue it has [been]."[35] Although the drug fever was led by a scientist, the drug's appeal also exposed a sustained level of public cynicism about scientific orthodoxy, even among the educated classes. This allowed the Krebiozen story to linger as a flashpoint of mainstream concern. As sociologist Andrew Abbott wrote years later, "the public often admires relatively uneducated professionals and heterodox professionals," but "the debates over Laetrile [another unorthodox cancer "cure" in the 1970s] and Krebiozen illustrate the public antipathy to overeducated professional elites."[36]

By its high point, the Krebiozen debate would overlap with other antiestablishment developments; it was playing out, most notably, at the same time that a nascent consumer rights movement was taking shape, prompted in part by Rachel Carson's *Silent Spring* (1962) and Ralph Nader's *Unsafe at Any Speed* (1965), among other works. Popular resentment of orthodox therapies and commercialized promises played a major role in the alliance of patients with

Ivy. In 1966, one letter writer to *Science* concluded that "the Krebiozen case illustrates both the benefits and the hazards of human faith." "When people in distress have a tremendous need to believe in something or somebody, then the forces of society seem powerless to effect an unmasking of the inconsistencies involved in that faith," noted the author. "When a truly effective anticancer agent is developed," he promised, "Krebiozen will be instantly forgotten."[37] As another reporter saw it, "the AMA's initial haste in discrediting Krebiozen had several unfortunate results . . . it certainly prejudiced the atmosphere to a point where nothing short of a miraculous performance could have redeemed Krebiozen in the suspicious eyes of those to whom the AMA journal is a rule-book."[38]

At its inception, however, the Krebiozen story also played into a new therapeutic faith—the widely promoted belief that access to remedies could define, now more than ever before, the line between those who lived and those who died from cancer. In this context, Dr. Ivy's attempt to secure FDA approval for Krebiozen kept the public eye glued to the controversy in the very years when FDA regulatory powers were expanding. The life-and-death implications were fully evident, as were the political and economic stakes. More and more in these post–World War II decades, many Americans looked optimistically to drugmakers for miracle drugs, and also beseechingly to the FDA, the NCI, and government to either confirm or reject the value of such drugs. But quick answers were not forthcoming. In April 1954, the FDA had denied one of the Ivy-Durovic "New Drug Applications" on technical grounds. This did not end the controversy.[39] For another decade, Krebiozen produced "skirmishing around the fringes of the scientific community" as advocates lobbied for a "'fair test' for the product."[40] Popular books took sides, shaping public opinion and pressuring the FDA. One exposé labeled Krebiozen a scam—nothing but a "well-documented story of a worthless 'cancer cure' which enlisted diverse and influential support . . . a story of people—heroes, villains and innocent bystanders."[41] Another book labeled Krebiozen "the drug that split the ranks of organized medicine."[42] As popular pressure continued to mount in the drug's favor, in 1958 the American Cancer Society "expressed an interest in sponsoring a test of the drug."[43] Swayed by similar public pressures, the NCI also engaged in "lengthy negotiations" with the makers over organizing a "fair test" to satisfy the still-angry advocates.[44] The hope of many cancer patients rose again as another application was submitted to the FDA in 1961, accompanied by "an 820-page draft analysis of [Ivy's] results on 4,000 patients."[45]

The debate over Krebiozen's status simmered like a low-grade fever from the 1950s into the early 1960s, as Ivy pushed for other scientists to conduct fair tests, but the political calculus for vetting new drugs was changing fast.[46] In 1961, the government had had enough, and cracked down on the drug amid broader concerns about the drug marketing and side effects. Meanwhile, the FDA's regulatory powers over such investigational drugs had greatly expanded as a result of the thalidomide drug scare in the late 1950s and early 1960s (this sedative, first developed in Germany, had caused birth defects in more than ten thousand children in forty-six countries). In this new regulatory environment, authorities at the Department of Health, Education and Welfare launched a probe in 1963 aimed at forcing Krebiozen's makers "to either provide full details of the drug and its claimed effects or stop distributing it."[47] As Elinor Langer saw it, up until this point "jurisdictional uncertainties [between federal agencies], were mainly responsible for the blank check that FDA has given Krebiozen . . . which its sponsors now claim amount, in effect, to a sanction."[48] In July, the FDA acted firmly, banning the drug from interstate commerce.[49] The director of the NCI, writing to Minnesota surgeon Owen Wangensteen, complained sadly that Ivy had long lost his objectivity on the Krebiozen question: "Ivy has . . . closed his eyes to contrary evidence, and seized upon all sorts of pseudo-scientific gibberish . . . until he finally really came to believe it himself . . . The material [Krebiozen] would long since have been discarded as useless if Ivy had not backed it personally and assisted in the fabrication . . . which has attracted so many gullible patients, their families, and even physicians."[50]

A year later the AMA, at the high point of its power to speak for a unified profession and in the interest of patients, joined again in the assault on the cancer drug, charging that Krebiozen had been sold in violation of the new federal regulations. The U.S. government, allied with scientific authorities, made "its long promised move against the sponsors of the alleged anticancer drugs."[51] Despite the aggressive government action, however, much popular opinion sided with Ivy as a maverick and underdog. Even with Ivy under the cloud of federal indictment, five hundred people (including forty-five cancer patients taking Krebiozen) attended a meeting to honor him and Durovic in the grand ballroom of the Lake Shore Club in Chicago.[52] After months of criminal investigations, federal prosecutors indicted Ivy and Durovic in December 1964 for falsely claiming that Krebiozen was an expensive experimental new drug. It was, the government alleged, "creatinine monohydrate, a common substance which could be purchased at approximately 30 cents per gram."[53] The authorities also charged the two men with submitting false reports to the FDA regarding the recovery of treated patients.[54] The jury trial that followed featured high drama, for although Ivy and Durovic were being charged, expertise itself seemed to be on trial: the AMA stood accused of "intrigue and falsification," FDA inspectors faced charges of deceit, and the NCI was said to do the bidding of these establishment interests.[55]

That the claims and counterclaims surrounding Krebiozen had come to a jury trial in the early 1960s signals much about the new environment of cancer politics and the power of public opinion. The high-profile Krebiozen trial lasted nine excruciating months and echoed the broader crisis of government and political authority that was unfolding in the mid-1960s.[56] The question of this "cancer cure" was placed before twelve average citizens. Government attorneys perhaps overplayed their hand by making what *Science* reporter Elinor Langer called the "plainly extreme" argument that Krebiozen was worthless and that "the men marketing it were not erring scientists but crooks."[57] Ivy's own background and training defied the portrait; he had served on a national advisory cancer council for the PHS and had "represented the Allied governments on the subject of medical ethics at the Nuremberg trials of Nazi physicians accused of war crimes."[58] The defense asked jurors to see Ivy as a scientific insider with unconventional ideas, not as a craven huckster. There was also emotional evidence on both sides. Gary Cathcart, once a "hopeless" twenty-six-year-old cancer victim, testified about how Krebiozen had saved his life. Supported by his physician, jurors heard how Cathcart's "highly malignant tumor had disappeared after Krebiozen injections" fourteen years earlier.[59] But another patient and surgeon, who attributed his own recovery from stomach cancer to the drug, was shown evidence on cross-examination that suggested that he had not in fact had cancer, but rather only a severe stomach ulcer.[60] Krebiozen was therefore useless in this case. Who or what was the jury to believe?

When the trial ended in early 1966 with Ivy and Durovic's acquittal, the government, the AMA, and the NCI were clear losers, receiving a stunning reprimand from a jury of citizens who had been swayed by Ivy's image as a scientist and by the drug's promise. "Krebiozen Backers Win, But Drug Still a Loser," declared the *Chicago Tribune*.[61] Ivy and Durovic had been cleared of charges, but the drug's status was unchanged: lacking FDA approval, it remained banned from the cancer ward. Where the government alleged Ivy's willful dishonesty, jurors, "none of whom had more than a high school education," saw ambiguity and reasonable doubt. "There is no proof that Krebiozen isn't worth anything," one juror insisted; "we did not want to destroy Krebiozen." Another juror argued that Ivy's "reputation is known all over . . . I don't think a man would throw away fifty years of work for humanity and just dump it overboard." "The Krebiozen forces [were] elated but exhausted," wrote Elinor Langer in *Science*. "Krebiozen patients[,] always an effective lobby, are reported to be trying to interest some third party . . . in the possibility of sponsoring a test, and the movement of constituents is also sending ripples through Congress." Even those who dismissed the drug's value were harshly critical of the government. "After 15 years of controversy and a 9-month criminal trial ending in acquittal of all the principals . . . the question of Krebiozen is plainly not yet settled" as a matter of public policy, concluded Langer.[62] The AMA's disappointed president, Morris Fishbein, who had spent much of his career doing battle with the medical quacks, took sharp issue with the jury, questioning "whether a lay jury is competent to judge a medical matter." "It takes at least eight years to train a doctor," he insisted condescendingly. "No layman can expect to understand medicine in a few months."[63] But what Fishbein and others could not see was that Krebiozen was perceived by many observers as part of the political struggles of the era.

The Krebiozen controversy resonated with the antiestablishment sentiments of the time and laid the groundwork for aggrieved groups (women, the poor, ethnic and sexual minorities) to take aim at the hubris and pretense of the cancer establishment. Medical paternalism, deference to scientific expertise, and unquestioning trust in governmental authority that were prevalent in the 1920s and 1930s—all these were being undermined in the sixties. At every turn politics seemed to shape cancer—who got it, which drugs were endorsed, which were not, and who lived and who died.[64] As *Science* reporter Elinor Langer saw it in 1961, many "unresolved controversies collided with new drug laws to produce the Krebiozen panic."[65] The era's disputes were numerous: the reliability of experts versus lay judgment; the economic relationship of the experts with the drug companies; and the power of big enterprises such as the NCI, the ACS, and the FDA to control the options of average patients.[66] For cancer patients—frustrated, marginalized, incurable, and hungry for a cure— Krebiozen became a cause, rallying them to organize in opposition to these forces. For the hopeless, it was better than "the alternative of doing nothing."[67] The case, and its sustained popular skepticism about the "establishment," would reflect a new cancer politics in which the marginal and forgotten might have their say.

BLACK ANGER AND TEARS: REPRESENTING
DISEASE IN THE SIXTIES

As cancer took on increased political significance in the 1960s, cultural representations of the cancer patient shifted. For most of the twentieth century, the iconic figure of the cancer patient in film, magazines, posters, and popular literature had been a vulnerable, white woman. She was the person with the most to fear, with the greatest at stake, and with the richest personal understanding of the disease's implications for herself and her family. In contrast with this fifty-year trend, a few fictional characters stand out. If Ollie Green had offered a rare attempt to imagine cancer in African-American men in the 1920s, two later characters—William Saroyan's Greedy Reed, introduced in his play *Don't Go Away Mad* (1949), and Max Reddick, from John A. Williams's novel *The Man Who Cried I Am* (1969)—show how cancer awareness was, at long last, crossing the color line in the popular imagination. If fictional representations can be said to reflect some of the prevailing cultural beliefs about race and disease, each of these men defied the standard stereotype embodied by characters like the calm, ever-controlled Mary Scott.

When Armenian-American dramatist William Saroyan placed an angry "unlettered young Negro," Greedy Reed, at the center of his play *Don't Go Away Mad*, it highlighted how the idea of cancer, long seen as a disease of women and of whites, was in flux. Artistic choices echoed cultural trends as well as epidemiological thought. Several observers of the time had noted how, as one Atlanta study reported, the "cancer incidence rate among males increased by 21 percent . . . (176 to 212 per 100,000), compared with . . . only 4 percent among females (250 in 1937 to 259 in 1947)."[68] Set in a San Francisco cancer hospital for men, Saroyan's play also reflected the therapeutic pessimism of its time—in fact, it had been originally titled *The Incurables*. At its dramatic core was a African-American man "who, although seemingly indestructible, has been suddenly stricken . . . [a man who earned] his nickname by his insatiable passion for food, drink, and women."[69] Greedy Reed was a kind of brutish, unschooled character, like Bigger Thomas in Richard Wright's *Native Son*, prone to violence and outbursts.

For Saroyan, men—all of varying race and ethnicity—stood at the center of the cancer play, soldiering on like Mary Scott and living out their last days. Epidemiologists could see that men, statistically, were still less likely to die from cancer than women, but they were gaining ground in the grim race. The men in Ward Three in Saroyan's play were a diverse lot: Anglo-Americans,

"Poseyo" the Greek, and Andy Boy, a Chinese man. These post–World War II personifications of cancer were meant to illustrate, as Saroyan wrote, that "despair is never by itself all of the story . . . despair may dominate, it may qualify and color everything else, but everything else is also there." For Saroyan, the story was not about Reed's race—it was about issues that, in his view, transcended race. "In the play," Saroyan explained, "Greedy Reed discovers the dictionary . . . and looks upon a thorough examination of it as the sole means of his (man's) salvation, rejecting the Bible (religious dogma) as well as his fear of and hatred of those whose skin is not colored (mores)." Reed was a "human creature" and the story revolved around "who he thinks he is, what he thinks he is about."[70] For Saroyan, Reed was not a black man, but a man—dying in a cancer ward, forgotten, ignored—along with other doomed men for whom "death is a secondary terror to his major spiritual pain."[71] His postwar drama, like Ruth Southard's 1946 novel *No Sad Songs for Me*, dwelled on resilience and personal triumphs even in death.

Recasting older themes but in intimate terms, pioneering African-American novelist James Baldwin fashioned one character, Florence, the protagonist's aunt, as a cancer victim in his novel *Go Tell It on the Mountain* (1953). The meaning of Florence's cancer echoed earlier beliefs about causation and race. As with so many literary cancer patients, Florence's social aspirations were her undoing. As analyst Charles Scruggs later saw it, "in fleeing the peasant vulgarity of the rural South, Florence soon became trapped by the vulgarity of her own worldly ambitions. Committed to the proposition of upward mobility, she was incapable of compromise."[72] Cancer, in this portrait, followed her transition from South to North, from peasant culture to urban life. In figures like Florence, cancer persisted in popular culture as an index of how black Americans adjusted, or failed to adjust, to a white world.

By contrast with Greedy Reed and Florence, Max Reddick, the character in John A. Williams's late 1960s *The Man Who Cried I Am*, brought a brooding, tortured anger to the American portrait of race and cancer. Reddick was a brave fighter—somewhat like Mary Scott or Greedy Reed—but he was also graphic about what the disease had done to him, where these earlier cancer fighters had spoken in euphemism. Max Reddick was a worldly writer deeply involved in the critical protests and racial transformations of his day. "The story begins [and ends] in Amsterdam," wrote one reviewer, "where Reddick has taken his racial bitterness, his resentment; bitterness intensified by the fact that he is dying from cancer."[73] In Amsterdam, Reddick's flashbacks on his struggles in New York and Washington, his flight to Europe and Africa, gave the work a sweeping boldness, another reviewer noted, akin to Ralph Ellison's *Invisible Man*.[74] The man's situation gave "considerable attention to what happens when an American Negro tries to return to his African past, as well as to the thin sterile existence of the self-exiled Negro writer in Europe," observed another reviewer.[75] But ultimately, Reddick's story (and his cancer) reflected a life in the United States that, though successful, had also been plagued with resentment over segregation, civil rights battles, the rise of African nationalism, and rapidly changing black-white relations. Recalling the events in 1963, Max notes that "so much had happened that day, the day of the March on Washington. Du Bois had died in Ghana the night before . . . But Washington had been the place to be that day. There you could forget that the cancer tests were positive—it was malignant—and that you were going into cobalt treatment soon; you could forget with more than a quarter million people surging around you."[76]

Cancer, used in the novel as a potent, graphic metaphor for the African-American predicament, eats away at Max Reddick. Williams's portrayal of the disease was shocking and explicit—more so than any previous popular representation. Shortly after its publication, one review, titled "When Black Blood Boils," suggested that "even when Reddick is named to head the African bureau of a great news magazine—a white publication—even when he serves briefly on the speed writing staff of a 'young President'—not named but easily identifiable—he is still driven by his own Furies."[77] With his rise, his resentment grows, and a fury (nursed by society itself) spreads. Readers encounter gruesome details in Max's suffering. Toward the end, a "pain had been riding hard between Max's buttocks," rising and subsiding. The pain is unpredictable: "It gripped him at the most inopportune moments and left him breathless, weak, and with his eyes watering." Coping with this recurring pain, Max is caught in an impossible paradox: drowning himself in alcohol relieves his anguish, but the subsequent urination causes intense pain. It is "a vicious cycle. If he didn't drink, he wouldn't have to urinate. To urinate was to suffer the most intense pain. But, if he didn't drink he would have to take either the pills or the morphine . . . The morphine got the pain right by the balls he thought, with a weak chuckle, but it didn't let him operate the way he had to during the day. But then the pain was growing every day."[78]

In Williams's brutally frank portrait, there is also a haunting, noxious odor that accompanies Max's decline. One visitor complains, "There is an awful smell, Max. Do you smell it? Could a small animal from the garden be caught in the eaves and rotting?" The graphic odor of late-stage cancer, so well known to health-care specialists, had rarely if ever been so intertwined with the American experience. "The smell, the cancer smell of rot and death. Sort of sweet, sort of heavy, sort of like being near a corpse on a battlefield and not even seeing it. Max winced in pain and fear. Now he was like anyone else. Mortal. Stinkingly mortal. Until Michelle had spoken he had pretended that the smell was not his." Who or what is responsible for this sad condition? Reddick blames himself, his pretense, his alienation. But he also sees himself in an impossible situation, caught between white racism and black disdain for his accomplishments. "When you're down, scraping through on ham hocks and beans, they don't want to be bothered with you. But when they think you've made it, they're either afraid of you or put you down for being a Tom."[79] His ambition and upward mobility has put Max Reddick into this untenable zone from which cancer has sprung. It is a classic motif—the appearance of cancer in people undergoing mobility and social change— updated for new times. The fictional figure of Max Reddick is a fighter whose ailment has unquestionable political origins; he is a graphic example of a man torn asunder and suffering.

Reddick's cancer reflected the times—an angry, intimate, personalized, and politically charged health identity that made a sharp break with earlier sanitized portraits. Only a few years before *The Man Who Cried I Am* was published, the Rev. Martin Luther King Jr., as noted above, had used cancer imagery much differently: to point to the afflictions of white society. Cancer became a recurring motif in King's speeches.[80] Time and time again through the 1950s and 1960s, King had characterized segregation itself as a "cancer on the body politic," a political disease, a social catastrophe—a white man's malady. "Segregation is on its death bed," he preached in 1956, but it still had formidable "last minute breathing powers." This cancer was kept alive, moreover, by "the guardians of the status-quo [who] are always on hand with their oxygen tents to preserve the dying order." The notion of segregation as a cancer seeped into American political discourse. Whereas in former decades cancer had been understood as a social commentary on white longevity, vulnerable femininity, and the price of privilege, this new conception linked the disease to whiteness in another way. "If democracy is to live, segregation must die," King insisted, and this insidious cancer "must be removed before our democratic health can be realized."[81] But with Max Reddick, the disease metaphor takes on meanings distinct from King's or Saroyan's. Reddick foreshadows the Howard report, pointing to the fact that the "cancer on the American body politic" was now a black man's dilemma as well as a political mystery.

THE HOWARD REPORT AND THE TRANSFORMED
RACIAL ENVIRONMENT

Regarded today by the NCI as a milestone in "efforts to reduce cancer health disparities," the Howard study did indeed mark a turning point in cancer scholarship, a punctuation of earlier trends, and the beginning of a new chapter in epidemiology's awareness of black America.[82] The study, published in 1972, saw cancer as a metaphor about race and the nation. In the immediate aftermath of civil rights protests, the 1968 assassination of Martin Luther King Jr., and urban rioting, this "alarming," "astounding," and "sudden" discovery of cancer in black Americans was greeted with breathless amazement and frustration.[83] What perilous roads had black Americans been traveling that created the "astounding change for such a short period of only 18 years," as the *Chicago Tribune* wondered.[84] "The death toll from cancer . . . has been rising steadily since the beginning of the century, due in part to the control of such major killers as tuberculosis and pneumonia," stated *Newsweek*. But no epidemiologists were prepared for this "striking new feature . . . a sudden, sharp rise in cancer deaths among Negroes."[85] After decades of theorizing about cancer's toll in white America, those trends had taken an unanticipated turn. Why had this alarming increase "escaped attention although it could have easily been spotted . . . as far back as 1960," the Howard researchers asked.[86]

"That article," noted one of the authors, LaSalle D. Leffall Jr., "preliminary as it was, focused attention on the special vulnerability of blacks to cancer. I like to think that it led not only to more and better studies but also to a better understanding of how to deal with a serious national health crisis."[87] But the authors needed to go beyond describing trends to explaining them, and so they speculated and theorized broadly just as experts of earlier eras had done. The wide range of their speculation, coming in the midst of racial protest and anti-establishment skepticism, was dramatic and revealed the myriad interpretive options available at the time. Had African Americans altered their customs— their food habits, living circumstances, and industrial worklife—thereby increasing their environmental exposure to cancer-causing agents? Were particular migration trends, such as the movement of African Americans into cities, shaping these deadly trends? Alternatively, could it be that whites were simply getting access to better diagnosis and more effective treatments, leaving blacks on the margins of a diagnostic and therapeutic revolution in cancer care? Or could the new gap somehow be evidence of a biological vulnerability, thus inverting the theory of black immunity from half a century before? Finally, might the rise be a statistical chimera—an illusion created by the revolutionary shifts in accounting for populations and health in the 1950s and 1960s? Such questions highlight the true complexity, then and now, of tracking cancer across the color line.

The timing of the study and its origins from a small research group in a historically black university in the majority-black District of Columbia, explain its impact. Its authors themselves stood on the margins of the American cancer establishment: an unlikely team of two African-American surgeons along with a German émigré radiologist, a handful of medical students, and a single statistics consultant, none of whom had ever undertaken such an epidemiological project. The first author, German-born Ulrich Henschke, had come to Howard from one of the New York's premier cancer hospitals, Memorial Hospital for the Treatment of Cancer and Allied Diseases, now known as Memorial Sloan-Kettering.[88] Another contributor, Jack White, had followed another path, graduating from Howard's medical school decades earlier, training as a cancer surgeon at Memorial in New York, where he was the first African American accepted to an oncology fellowship, and returning to Howard to found the Freedman's Hospital Tumor Clinic and Cancer Teaching Project.[89] These men needed no NCI study to show them that cancer was a mortal threat in the D.C. community. LaSalle Leffall, the younger of the two surgeons, had followed in Jack White's footsteps, studying under him at Howard, then breaking new ground himself at Memorial before returning to Howard. From White, Leffall learned about radical procedures that were increasingly common in the 1950s—techniques such as radical neck resection for throat cancer that "sometimes involved disfiguring surgery, but . . . offered the possibility of survival." As Leffall later recalled, "American physicians were just beginning to focus on statistics showing that a disproportionate number of African-Americans were dying of cancer."[90] Through the mid- and late 1960s, the two also reported on their cases, published articles about their cure rates, and began noting racial trends in cancer care and mortality.[91] Because none of them—Henschke, White, or Leffall—were trained in the study of epidemiological trends, they turned to a statistical consultant named Claudia Mason.[92]

It would be hard to miss the subdued cynicism toward the cancer establishment expressed by the Howard report when it first appeared in the obscure *Medical Annals of the District of Columbia*—and the unimpressed tone was well founded. For all the sophistication of the NCI's studies, the ACS's epidemiological tracking, the city-by-city reports issued by the PHS, and decades of increasingly savvy cancer health statistics, the team asserted that "to our knowledge, no comprehensive comparison of the cancer mortality in the black and white U.S. population has been made. This is surprising, since the basic data are readily available from the 'Official Vital Statistics of the U.S.A.' [which had maintained statistics specifically on the black, not merely the nonwhite, population]. Even a casual appraisal of the black and white cancer deaths in these volumes shows that black cancer deaths are rising much faster than white cancer deaths. This trend is clearly apparent already from the data up to 1960 but apparently has failed to attract attention."[93] Thus, the report exposed two related mysteries: first, what drove the cancer trends, and second, the deeper problem of why the cancer establishment appeared to be ignorant about these shifts in mortality. How could the nation's best experts have missed this obvious and tragic drift?

Given the racial politics of the time, the popular press presented the findings as the discovery of a true crisis with grave implications. Black men, for example, who decades earlier had been regarded as among the groups least vulnerable to cancer, now appeared most threatened. As one newspaper writer noted, "the principal cancer increase has occurred among black men, mainly in cancer of the prostate and esophagus."[94] Diverging white and black death rates became a metaphor for diverging life chances and the American color line. In one short document, the Howard report echoed many of the cultural debates, the medical cynicism, and the political tensions of the time. "It appears tragic that the Black U.S. population, already burdened with so many handicaps, is experiencing a rise in death rates which is twice as fast as in the White U.S. population," the study's authors wrote.[95] Later, in the journal *Cancer*, they bemoaned that "the rapid increase in black cancer mortality has escaped attention, although it could have been easily spotted from the Official Statistics of the United States as far back as 1960."[96] Imagining a different past, they noted that if the cancer rates had been equal rather than diverging over that period, "black cancer deaths in 1967 [would have been] 7,049 fewer."[97]

Identifying the trend was one thing; explaining it was another. The Howard authors suspected that the gap between standard and substandard care might have grown over these years, since "few Black families have the resources which are required for optimal cancer care."[98] But they also knew that mortality trends were affected by diverse forces. Cancer mortality difference was like a tree bearing many types of fruit; it was rich with multiple possibilities for racial, environmental, social, ecological, cultural, and biological theory. Which theory prevailed reflected much about the surrounding social and political setting.

Surely, the Howard authors suggested, genetic differences between whites and blacks could not explain this tragic eighteen-year-long divergence. Genetic and biological explanation had surely had their day, accounting for higher women's rates as a function of their biology, or explaining lower African-American rates in terms of a racial immunity in much earlier times. But in the post–World War II era, the tables had turned. Not only had the postwar rejection of Nazi racial ideology soured scientists on hasty or simplistic racial theorizing, but it had also moved questions of health difference into the economic, social, and political realm. Landmark legislation like Medicare (passed in 1965 to expand health insurance to the elderly and poor) and major court rulings mandating "nondiscrimination" in hospital care had helped undermine segregated hospitals and drawn many African Americans into the growing American health care and health surveillance system.[99] In such a context, non biological factors seemed the most relevant in explaining disease differences.

Biological theories of health disparities had not disappeared, of course. But the notion that innate group-specific differences in the biological makeup explained the eighteen-year divergence was implausible. "While genetic factors are important," the researchers observed, "it is obvious that the genetic make-up of any population cannot change much in the span of one generation." Biological differences might account for sustained longer-term disparities, such as the higher rates of skin cancer in whites, they maintained. But invoking innate biological difference when so many other possibilities existed seemed merely an excuse for doing nothing. "Genetic factors," they concluded, "cannot explain the rapidly divergent trend . . . from 1950 to 1967."

The era's many health care and social developments offered obvious answers for why some died and others lived. Medicare and Medicaid (both passed into law in 1965) had only just begun to narrow the gap in access to health care, let alone new cancer therapies. Diagnostic innovations such as the Pap smear meant that, unlike earlier in the century, cancer patients were being found earlier in the course of disease—a process that in itself increased "survival after diagnosis." Therapeutic developments in cancer care from radiation to chemotherapy and surgery prompted the Howard team to wonder whether a growing "cure gap" explained the new disparities. "Cure rates directly influence mortality rates," they noted, and so in this era it became possible to argue confidently that differential access to treatments defined the line between survival and death.[100] If all these other factors somehow could be held equal in two groups and differences still persisted, the authors suggested, only then might genetic differences come into play. Attempting to weigh these competing factors, the authors speculated that even though a racial gap in cure rates did exist (a 37 percent cure rate for blacks and 45 percent for whites), this "was not . . . enough to explain the divergent trends" between 1950 and 1967.[101] The death trends could not be explained by a biological difference or by a gap in cure rates, they argued.

Yet another possibility was that, as generations of epidemiologists knew, changes in cancer numbers (incidence, mortality, survival) were unreliable and "trends" might only be statistical illusions. The Howard team acknowledged, for example, that "underreporting of cancers occurs with poor medical care." But for underreporting to play a role, they noted, there would have had to be a sharp eighteen-year reversal in the underreporting of poor people's cancers (so that previously underdiagnosed disease would have to be now over-reported because of now superior medical care than was reported in 1949). Moreover, this trend would have had to be racially biased toward black people. But clearly, they noted, "medical care is not better for blacks than for whites," so these reporting trends could not explain the rise. There were other potential sources of statistical illusion. Some experts suggested, for example, that two problems—the U.S. Census's undercounting of black Americans (by as much as 1.3 percent overall, or by 7 percent in young black males) combined with the rapid increase in African-American access to hospitals and health care—could explain the apparent rise in cancer death rates. Such factors when combined could make it *appear* that more blacks were dying from cancer. But this too was implausible, the authors concluded, because the undercounting would have had to grow incrementally worse each year ("by an improbable 1 percent per year") to produce such an artificial rise in the black mortality rate.[102] Another theory suggested that the relative youth of the black population in America produced lower cancer rates than in the general population, but that the age distribution within the black population had shifted upward during this period—driving up cancer rates *naturally*. The authors entertained all these possibilities, noting that certainly "major changes in the relative age distribution of the black or the white population from 1950 to 1967 could make age adjustment unreliable"; but population statistics did not support the theory. The black population, despite remaining a young population, had grown collectively older ("the percentage of persons over 50 years was 16 percent in 1950 and 17 percent in 1967 for the black population and 22 percent in 1950 and 25 percent in 1967 for the white population"), but such slight differences could not create the eighteen-year divergence. That the Howard team entertained so many diverse theories about disease trends highlights the extent to which the legitimacy of health statistics was in question. It also highlights their awareness of just how many different social factors confounded collection, analysis, and interpretation of the numbers.

Putting aside theories of biology, cure rates, and population estimation, the Howard researchers turned to a newly emerging environmental paradigm: they embraced a dominant view of their era that linked cancer disparities to changes in the environment. To these experts, "environment" was more than air quality—it encompassed a wide range of factors from neighborhood exposures to dangerous workplace chemicals, smoking, alcohol consumption, and diet. As the *Washington Post* reported the findings, "more black men may be cooks, exposed to the fumes of hot cooking oils. More may be outdoor workers in polluted areas."[103] "The magnitude of the change of the black mortality rate," the Howard authors argued, "is . . . entirely compatible with changing environmental factors." Environment was the key, they insisted: "many of the jobs with the greatest exposure to health hazards are now filled by blacks . . . Cigarette smoking seems to have increased much more rapidly in blacks than in whites since 1930 . . . increasing alcohol consumption might be connected to the rapid rise in intra-oral, esophagus, and liver cancer . . . [and] food habits also have changed rapidly in the span of one generation in blacks, while the same changes took much longer in whites."[104] This, of course, was not new: since the 1920s, experts had seen cancer mortality as a cruel paradox of upward mobility—for white people, for African Americans, for immigrants, and for other groups. But the Howard conclusion reflected its own era's intense concern with environmental trauma.[105] Many studies had pointed to the role of asbestos, tainted meat, food coloring, beryllium, and a host of workplace carcinogens on rising cancer rates.[106] To experts and laymen pondering cancer trends, it seemed obvious that "greater exposure to cancer-causing substances" at home and work, especially for the working classes and people "at the bottom of the heap," had driven up their rates.[107]

The Howard group admitted that cancer causation theories were a dime a dozen, and that "the relative importance of these factors [dietary, socioeconomic, errors in Census enumeration, lower cure rates, genetic differences in susceptibility] is different for each individual cancer." In the end, these experts admitted that their own explanation was a hedge: "one can only speculate at this time about the causes of the more rapid rise in cancer deaths in the black U.S. population."[108] They ended on an ominous warning for fellow researchers in the cancer establishment: if evidence went uncollected and if attention to cancer across the color line did not grow, more African Americans would perish. "The increase in black cancer mortality does not show any indication of flattening out. In fact, in some cancers, the trend seems to be accelerating," they cautioned. The report called for reform within those elite institutions that had followed cancer closely yet failed to detect these trends: "plans should be formulated to cope with the expected further rapid increase in black cancer patients."[109] If funds were not allocated to cancer care across the color line, the mortality gap would widen. "Cancer management is so difficult and time consuming, that the already overloaded and understaffed facilities for medical care of black patients will be put under a severe strain by an increase of black cancer patients of about 5 percent per year."[110]

Long on speculation, the report was most effective at naming the problem and criticizing the cancer establishment for its failure to gather intelligence, particularly with regard to "racial" health patterns. Coming a year after the U.S. Census had introduced never-before-used population categories such as "Hispanic," along with self-identification rather than third-party identification, the report's most scathing indictment focused on the simple fact that the NCI used the outmoded racial classification "non white" to track cancer—causing its own failure of detection: "[I]t lumps all minority groups together under 'non-white,' and . . . it assigns to the state of Maryland the data of the District of Columbia, although the District of Columbia has a larger population than 11 states."[111] The NCI's best overview of cancer trends since 1950 (Report 33) did not even "give figures for black, but only for a group called 'non-whites,'" noted the D.C. researchers.[112] Indeed, Report 33 had stressed not race but gender as the new cancer challenge of that era. "The racial differences are mentioned only casually in the last sentence . . . and no comment is offered," the Howard authors noted dryly.[113]

The message behind their critique was that racial classifications carried great weight in shaping the awareness of experts themselves. Classification mattered for patients as well—for being classified translated into recognition, created powerful and lasting perceptions, and shaped policy and the distribution of resources. But classifications could also manufacture illusions. If epidemiologists persisted in grouping nonwhite peoples as *nonwhite*, what could be learned about the particular situations of Puerto Rican-, Mexican-, Chinese-, Japanese-, and Latin-American people? Complicating matters, this nonwhite population had been transformed during the era (from the 1940s, when "nonwhite" came into epidemiological vogue, to the 1970s, which gave rise to new Census-based racial categories). In 1970, the U.S. Census, after decades of classifying Mexican Americans, Puerto Ricans, and Latin Americans as "white," shifted its practice—introducing a new category ("persons of Spanish origin").[114] The 1970 Census disclosed that there were just over 9 million such people among the 203 million in the U.S. population; 93 percent of them were "white" and 5 percent "Negro."[115] In short, at the very moment the Howard report was published, racial categories were in flux, and it was clear that terms like "nonwhite" only obscured experts' ability to see vital differences in the population. The Howard authors guessed that "the great majority of the non-whites are blacks (91.3 percent) in 1967." But surely, better terminology than "nonwhite" was needed. "It is well known . . . that cancer of the nasopharynx is more frequent in American Chinese and cancer of the gallbladder is more frequent in American Indians than in other racial groups," observed White, Leffall, Henschke, and the others. "Therefore, it would be most desirable to have cancer mortality rates for each of the subgroups, which make up the 'non-white' groups."[116]

The Howard report highlighted a new truth: that the gathering of population health statistics and the categorization by group was inseparable from the politics of recognition and representation, and that categorization itself produced disparities. Political limitations, not medical or biological ones, shaped experts' ability to recognize the racial gap. The criticism was aimed squarely at the collectors of cancer data. The whole surveillance enterprise needed an overhaul.[117] The NCI, a federal institute sensitive to political criticism, responded with a new program and promised to gather more accurate cancer data and to address the perplexing problem of group representation. The NCI had been tracking cancer trends for decades, relying on a patchwork of state registries and participating university hospitals since the 1950s.[118] But the numbers were always questionable; as NCI historian Michael Shimkin wrote, the "cancer population that was included of course was not a random sample, and undoubtedly under-represented poorer areas and hospitals that served such areas." Representation had always bedeviled such enterprises, and, as two experts later admitted, "proof of representativeness is difficult under the best of circumstances . . ."[119]

Created soon after the Howard report, the NCI's new cancer surveillance program, called SEER (Surveillance, Epidemiology, and End-Results), saw representation as a political and also a scientific necessity. The program's architects chose seven sites "because of their diverse ethnic subgroups and because of ongoing registration activities": five states (Connecticut, Iowa, New Mexico, Utah, and Hawaii) and two metropolitan areas (Detroit and San

Francisco–Oakland).[120] In 1974, New Orleans and Seattle–Puget Sound were added to further diversify the data; in 1975, Atlanta was added "under the rationale that this data would increase coverage of the African-American population."[121] Yet the new SEER program continued to categorize Cuban Americans, Mexican Americans, Latin Americans, and Spanish Americans as one single group, "Caucasians of Spanish surname or Spanish origin"—some of those very practices of lumping that the Howard report had criticized.[122] Indeed, every few years, in an unending quest to truly represent the American situation, the SEER data would expand, change, and recategorize.[123] All the while, immigration (for example from Vietnam and Southeast Asia), demographic change, and classification quandaries would complicate the quest for representative sampling that was catalyzed by the Howard report.[124]

Cancer in the 1970s was far more than a deadly disease; from the Krebiozen episode through the Howard study, it had become a symbol of a new antiauthoritarian politics driven by marginal groups and calls to racial awareness. Attention had turned to groups living and dying on the margins of American society (the elderly, children, African Americans) and to the inability of the so-called cancer establishment to notice, let alone analyze and remedy, their condition. Although President Nixon had declared a national war on cancer with no mention of race, within a year the African-American cancer condition had become a crucial part of that war. The NCI and other organizations became interested in the unequal burden of cancer in black America. Nearly thirty years after the Howard study, other reports continued to document the "unequal burden of cancer" for blacks and ethnic minorities and their "unequal treatment" in the health-care system.[125] Ideas on the fringes of mainstream practice had migrated to the center, pushed by the political protests and racial awareness of the sixties. Events of the time left their mark not only on society and politics but also in epidemiology and the study of cancer. In this era as before, experts speculated feverishly about cancer as a lens onto society; but after the Howard study a central question was why the disease selected more of its victims among black Americans. A vast web of social transformations in neighborhoods, work environments, health care, and consumer practices (rather than biological ones) seemed to be driving these trends.

Among its many effects, the report transformed the career of LaSalle Leffall. Within a few years of coauthoring the report, the Howard-based surgeon would climb from marginal critic to being president of the American Cancer

Society, the first African American named to the coveted post at the center of the American cancer establishment.[126] By the end of the decade, the cancer experiences of well-known black Americans—not only Minnie Riperton but also Fannie Lou Hamer, Duke Ellington, and Audre Lorde, among others—would be read as evidence of a new reality. While experts bemoaned that "the cure rates for black cancer patients are considerably lower than for white cancer patients," Minnie Riperton made her tragic, brief ascent into popular cancer awareness.[127] As American Cancer Society national spokesperson after her mastectomy, Riperton carried a grim message: cancer, she proclaimed, had crossed another color line. Of course the stories of the Howard report, Leffall, and Hamer obscure a more complex, decades-long transformation. The roots of this new awareness of a democratic cancer in the 1970s—in epidemiology, in cultural representation, and in awareness—had been laid by the social changes of the 1960s and by economic and cultural shifts many decades earlier. But even with the new public face of cancer, old questions remained unanswered, such as whether these disease trends were new, whether they were really old trends being perceived for the first time with new eyes, or whether they were merely beliefs generated by the particular political moment.

Experts had long called attention to the racial gaps in survival after diagnosis, and in the post-1970s era, this data would become a crucial touchstone for theorizing about racial, gender, and social differences. Data on differential survival were not entirely new, of course. One 1947 Atlanta study had found, for example, that 76 percent of whites were still alive six months after the discovery of a malignancy and treatment, and 71 percent lived to see the one-year anniversary of their treatment. For residents of color, on the other hand, only 53 percent survived the first six months after treatment, and 47 percent lived an entire year. "Colored males," researcher Sidney Cutler had noted, "had an especially low survival rate—only 38 percent survived twelve months." Why the difference? Cutler found that black patients were more likely to be diagnosed with advanced disease.[128] Survivor politics emerged in new and contentious forms. As one writer noted, "across the United States there are people who are genuinely convinced that they have gained added months and years of life, in their struggle against cancer, by their use of krebiozen."[129] In truth, however, many other forces—early screening, chemotherapy, radical surgery, and a host of new therapies—were swelling the ranks of cancer survivors and activists decade by decade. More people knew their status as cancer patients at earlier and earlier stages of disease.[130] In the 1960s and 1970s, survival gaps attracted the growing interest of scholars in a society attuned to social and racial disparities. White cancer patients did better in cancer treatment than nonwhites, one report suggested—with whites living "an average 40 percent longer than blacks who get cancer." White women enjoyed "the best chance for survival, followed, in order, by black women, white men and black men."[131] The politics of survivors only expanded, with the NCI's SEER statistics documenting 3 million cancer survivors in 1971, growing to over 10 million strong by 2002.[132] Susan Sontag's *Illness as Metaphor* (1978) and Audre Lorde's *Cancer Journals* (1980; the memoir of a black lesbian cancer survivor) contributed new voices to this emerging genre of cancer politics.[133]

To an extent seldom seen in other eras, cancer scholars in the 1970s and 1980s appreciated that health differences were socially constructed and politically malleable, but they also accepted that these disparities could be illusory because of the vagaries of data collection and racial categorization. Samuel Epstein's *Politics of Cancer* (1978) insisted that increasing cancer rates were driven by "avoidable exposures to environmental and occupational carcinogens" and that "the reckless culpability of the cancer establishment—the National Cancer Institute (NCI) and the American Cancer Society (ACS)" was to blame for the peril facing all Americans.[134] Between the 1950s and the 1980s, argued the British epidemiologist Richard Peto, there was no progress in cancer care, and little had really changed in the accuracy of recording cancer deaths; but there *was* "significant improvement in registering nonfatal cancer cases." The gap in reporting, he insisted, created the mirage of progress. It was an "apparent gain . . . a result of the fact that many of the survivors were not recorded 30 years ago." A skeptic in skeptical times, Peto acknowledged that "there has been some improvement . . . but it's less extreme than the crude relative survival rates would suggest."[135]

Antiestablishment skepticism even politicized the sacred question of progress in the war on cancer. Had there been statistically provable progress in cancer treatment, or were "the highly touted gains in 'survival rates' . . . a statistical mirage, caused more by changes in the way cancer is detected and defined than by any real gains?" asked a reporter in 1984. Skepticism was evident in such headlines as "Cancer Progress: Are the Statistics Telling the Truth?" Critics alleged that self-serving financial interest generated the myth of progress: "The more cures the press releases claim, the more money cancer organizations raise," argued Hayden Bush, director of a regional cancer center in Ontario, Canada. But the establishment fought back. With his institute under attack, the NCI's director, Vincent T. DeVita Jr., dismissed such talk as "a bunch of nonsense." Survival gains were real, DeVita insisted; in the 1950s, "only about 33 percent of all cancer patients were surviving five years. Now it is 50 percent." And after the election of Ronald Reagan in 1980, a report by his secretary of Health and Human Services politicized cancer anew, insisting that the link between environment and occupational hazards to cancer had been overblown: "only seven percent of all cancers were caused by environmental and occupational exposures or chemical food additives."[136] "The shift," commented a *New York Times* reporter, "may partly reflect the differing approaches of the Carter Administration, with its emphasis on Federal actions to safeguard the environment, and the Reagan Administration, with its emphasis on self-help solutions rather than regulation."[137]

Cutting across race, gender, politics, and epidemiology, the American cancer debate had taken a politically tumultuous and scientifically contentious turn. The social agitation of the 1970s generated a disease politics specific to the era, one that was overtly focused on cancer and black identity, on the social mediation of cancer knowledge, and on cancer as an index of social inequality. Objective "facts" could not be taken for granted. Were survivors of cancer more numerous than ever because patients were receiving better therapies or, as some skeptics warned, because "early detection was starting the survival clock" so much earlier that, by definition, the survival time from diagnosis to death was being artificially inflated?[138] Had cancer truly crossed a color line? In the atmosphere of the 1970s and 1980s, this was no longer a biological question or a question of civilization and primitivism. It was a political question, touching on issues of inequality and political recognition. And who could be trusted to remedy this wrong? The intense interest in cancer among black Americans exposed (albeit through the particular stories of Minnie Riperton and the fictional character Max Reddick) just how little was known about individual struggles across the color line, how impoverished official awareness was, and how deeply connected political interests and disease had become.

CHALLENGING THE CANCER ESTABLISHMENT

In the early 1970s, a little-known research group at Howard University discovered a new trend: cancer mortality in black Americans had increased dramatically over the preceding eighteen years. One of its authors, LaSalle Leffall Jr., later commented, "Preliminary as it was, [the study] focused attention on the special vulnerability of blacks to cancer. I like to think that it led not only to more and better studies but also to a better understanding of how to deal with a serious national health crisis." But why had it taken two decades for these facts to come to public light?

By 1970, the rise of such institutions as the National Cancer Institute, the U.S. Public Health Service, and the American Cancer Society had set the stage for a national "war on cancer." Yet the establishment's blindness to cancer trends in black America became a metaphor, highlighting problems of political and epidemiological recognition of the minority experience among the experts themselves.

In this context, the story of the twenty-nine-year-old singer and cancer victim Minnie Riperton (right) became a stark symbol of what *Ebony* magazine described as "the disease's growing and tragic destruction of black people." The disease was "not a white disease anymore," it proclaimed. Portrayed as a new kind of survivor, Riperton appeared on the *Tonight Show* to "reassure millions of women that losing a breast need not mean the end of the world." She lectured nationally to black women and to a broader public and even became honorary chairman of the American Cancer Society's education crusade.

Thus did the decade of the 1970s see old truisms die and new ones emerge—about expertise and popular knowledge, about race and cancer vulnerability, and about disease and group identity. In this new context, experts and lay commentators returned to questions they had been pondering for the entire century—what perilous roads had black Americans been traveling that created these modern health disparities?

6

THE NEW POLITICS OF OLD DIFFERENCES

The 1990s generated multiple cancer mysteries across America—troubling spikes in mortality, puzzling dips in incidence, and intense political activism around sometimes real and sometimes illusory epidemics. There was, for example, the discovery of nation's highest breast cancer incidence in wealthy, white Marin County, California. Women in the county just north of San Francisco blamed the water or air, but some researchers insisted that "women in the Bay Area are making decisions—such as delaying childbirth or not breast-feeding"—that made them more likely to develop the disease.[1] There was also, according to an NCI study, the puzzle of why black men were "still the Americans most likely to get and die of cancer," with prostate cancer a particular worry.[2] It was a stunning turnaround from earlier decades when such men were seen as largely immune from the disease's ravages. Many researchers looked to socioeconomic factors to explain the mortality gap, but others wondered whether elements of racial biology, for example, "a protein known as prostate specific antigen [PSA] in the blood of black men," might be responsible.[3] Asian women posed another national paradox. A 1996 NCI study hailed as the first to go beyond "black and white, adding eleven new [ethnic] categories," found that new immigrant Asian groups had large gaps of knowledge that put them at risk and produced disturbing variations. In Vietnamese-American women, cervical cancer was shockingly high, while in Japanese-American women it was well below the national average.[4] In Chinese Americans, lung cancer rates were low despite high rates of cigarette consumption, a finding that prompted one researcher to wonder whether some kind of "ethnic metabolism" protected them from carcinogens that caused disease in other groups.[5] Finally, epidemiologists also puzzled over a so-called Hispanic epidemiological paradox: "despite a high incidence of poverty and, too often, meager access to medical care," Hispanic infant mortality remained low and the mortality rate "from cancer and heart disease—the two leading killers in the country—was 22 and 35 percent lower, respectively, than the national average."[6]

As these spikes, dips, and variations in health indicators appeared across the American ethnic spectrum, observers seized on them to recycle classic themes from the history of cancer—from the critique of conspicuous consumption to women's failures at breast-feeding, from the advantages of the Western lifestyle to the perils of migration, from the danger of smoking and exposure to cancer environments to the enduring question of ethnic metabolism and racial biology—dressing up these old theories in new garb to address the population anxieties of a new era. By the 1980s, these cancer spikes had become a dominant feature of the evening news. And just as in the 1920s, disease trends not only commanded attention but also resonated with the prevailing identity politics of the time. Disease statistics were more than mere numbers; statistics attracted increased news coverage of the particular group at issue, and public attention translated into legislative interest, research dollars, and health-care resources for doctors and researchers as well. Columnist Roger Hernandez commented, for example, that both liberals and conservatives could praise the so-called Latino health paradox. To those who wanted immigrants to assimilate to American norms, the statistics could be said to show that "immigrants who put aside Hispanic culture to assimilate into the American middle class lose something of value," becoming less healthy. On the other hand, the numbers suggested that "the cultural values that individuals hold, rather than government programs, is what really matters," and that ethnic minority groups could solve their own health problems without government help. This idea, Hernandez believed, challenged "the conventional wisdom of liberals."[7] As had been true for decades before, the rising or falling rates had to be interpreted, and the higher- or lower-than-average indices could be used for different cultural ends and political purposes.

The 1980s and 1990s cancer discourse caricatured the era's identity politics, making illness a stage on which gender debates, racial politics, and ethnic tensions were acted out. In 1984, for example, the U.S. Congress established "National Breast Cancer Awareness Month." In 1987, Congress designated a "National Minority Cancer Awareness Week."[8] In 1990, the prostate cancer awareness group Us TOO was created and used prostate cancer as a tool for awakening men's health activism. And in 1996, no sooner had President Clinton signed a law authorizing a breast cancer postal stamp to raise money and awareness than legislators insisted on "a special stamp to raise funds for prostate cancer."[9] As Juanne Clarke found in her own analysis, in the 1990s "competition with breast cancer continues to be a theme in the articles on prostate cancer," with its advocates hoping that those with the disease would "finally get some respect."[10] A widening array of groups used cancer trends, statistics, and theories to do political work—not only to frame their identity differences but also to shape biomedical knowledge, to position themselves for resources, and to engage in the era's culture wars. The pink ribbons had become omnipresent, prompting Barbara Ehrenreich (herself a breast cancer survivor) to lament that breast cancer "is the biggest disease on the cultural map, bigger than AIDS, cystic fibrosis, and spinal injury, bigger even than those more prolific killers of women—heart disease, lung cancer, and stroke."[11]

A St. Louis woman, Kathie B., afflicted with what she called "the dirty cancer" [liver cancer], echoed Ehrenreich's complaint that breast cancer's immense popularity deflected public and medical attention from her own battle.[12] Frustration came in many colors. As one prostate cancer specialist complained in 2006, "[T]here are still more people doing research on breast cancer than on prostate cancer . . . [and] more industry support for research on breast cancer drugs."[13] The numbers were used to rationalize resentment and to launch discussions over who or what was responsible for inequalities in mortality and in public awareness. From Marin County, California, to Houston, Texas, to St. Louis, Missouri, 1990s-era cancer discourse was characterized by crosscutting resentments—reflecting the diversity of disease types, and of the populations at issue, as well as the multiple medical, scientific, corporate, and public health agendas that had become invested in cancer awareness.

In this context, cancer proved to be a potent vehicle for theorizing about "race," ethnicity, culture, and the new world of group differences, just as it had been since the birth of cancer awareness a hundred years earlier. But some aspects of the debate were new. As *New York Times* science columnist Gina Kolata noted, an aggressive diagnostics industry was generating novel tests that were "moving rapidly into the marketplace before there [was] a medical consensus on their value or how to use them."[14] New tests for genes associated with breast cancer (such as the BRCA-1 and BRCA-2 genes, which were said to have a higher-than-average frequency in Ashkenazi Jewish women), for example, opened new business possibilities in disease detection; and the marketing of these tests inevitably made use of the era's identity politics. Suddenly, patients and doctors confronted the possibility of detecting "cancer" decades before any actual disease appeared; such tests also opened the way to controversial treatments like the "preventive mastectomy." Similarly, the PSA test (a test not for cancer per se, but linked to prostate cancer *risk*) raised challenging problems in disease detection, and for men's views on their health, aging, and sexuality. Many wondered if these tests truly saved lives or if they were only producing anxiety, ushering in unnecessary treatments, and constructing new "at risk" social groups. Marketed aggressively, these innovations in cancer detection (alongside older ones like mammography and BSE) and new therapies like hormone replacement therapy played critical roles in the era's identity politics.

Every spike in cancer trends, each new genetic test or novel diagnostic tool provoked cancer specialists to think anew about disease and difference, but their theories continued to reflect stunning inconsistencies in how race was conceptualized. Epidemiological awareness had long been afflicted with a perverse racial awareness, with black people and many nonwhites often imagined as biological groups, other groups such as Asians seen as harboring a mix of biological and malleable "ethnic" features, and whites usually written about as individuals with inner lives and anxieties. In this awareness as throughout the past century, whiteness was hopelessly undertheorized as a racial concept. "Race," in short, meant different things and carried different connotations when applied to each group. Epidemiological and popular awareness often echoed the same confusion. In the 1990s these classic tendencies resurfaced with the era's interest in white affluence and women's lifestyles, "black blood" and racial biology, and the resurgence of theories of "ethnic metabolism."

THE RETURN OF RACIAL BIOLOGY: PSA AND THE PROSTATE CANCER EPIDEMIC

Between 1971 and 1990, the incidence of prostate cancer among American males increased by 65 percent, although the rise in death rate was only 16 percent.[15] The largest mortality increases came in 1990 (20 percent) and 1991

(19 percent).[16] Because African Americans had the highest prostate cancer rates, this troubling story intersected with questions of black male identity and the ongoing search for equality in health care. For much of the twentieth century, prostate cancer had been a minor presence in America's ever-shifting cancer consciousness. And where black men had once been seen as almost "immune" from such malignancies, the tide apparently had turned. Physicians and epidemiologists detected an apparent men's health crisis, with strong racial overtones. In prostate cancer as in many other cancer types, patients, doctors, and health advocates seized on the statistics in their consciousness raising, political battles, and cultural appeals for equal access to resources. With prostate cancer leading the way, the 1990s saw a resurgence of interest not only in men's health but also in racial theories purporting to illuminate what made black men different from their white counterparts.

Many advocates, from men's health groups to urologists to surgeons and oncologists, cheered the advent of a new prostate-specific antigen (PSA) test, for at first it seemed to do work on several fronts. First, the PSA did diagnostic work, promising to identify men's cancer at earlier stages and possibly improving outcomes because of early intervention. Second, it did public health work, opening new possibilities in screening the population and spreading awareness. Third, it did epidemiological work, promising that aggressive diagnosis might reduce the black-white mortality gap.[17] And finally the PSA test promised to do cultural work in moving prostate cancer into the limelight. For many activists and scientists, breast cancer was viewed as the "privileged" cancer and as a premier woman's issue, attracting a relative wealth of public attention, foundation support, government research dollars, and health-care resources. Prostate cancer advocates bemoaned that "their" disease received lesser drug and chemotherapy research funding than breast cancer.[18] Testing and early detection promised, however, to redress this imbalance, increasing the profile of the disease by spotlighting the large numbers of sufferers.

From the outset, prostate cancer advocates pushed a flawed "early detection" analogy with breast cancer, portraying the PSA incorrectly as akin with breast and cervical cancer screening tools.[19] On one level, the comparison of prostate cancer and breast cancer was politically obvious: one was the male cancer, the other was the female cancer. But after that, the parallels ended. All prostate tumors were not alike; most progressed very slowly—much more slowly than breast tumors—and many failed to develop in an orderly fashion through typical stages.[20] Prostate cancer was often a slow-moving cancer; it was often said that elderly men were more likely to die *with* prostate cancer than *from* it. Breast cancers, by contrast, were more menacing. Moreover, for the women's cancers it had taken generations for current diagnostic and screening practices—from Pap smears and breast self-examination (BSE) in the 1950s to mammograms in the 1960s—to be integrated into women's cancer consciousness. These interventions had long histories of promising patients hope and giving physicians the sense that they could track cancer's warning signs and save lives.[21] Culturally speaking, the prostate had nothing of the wide symbolic significance of the breast. The idea of prostate health was relatively new and carried little cultural cachet. Most American men knew very little about the prostate gland—its location or its role in semen production, in sexuality, or in urology. The arrival of PSA, first discovered in 1979 and still untested in the 1990s, had altered this calculus; but its arrival had been relatively sudden, with no historical antecedents for men.[22] Moreover, as elevated PSA scores did not necessarily indicate the presence of cancer, nor low scores suggest the definite absence of cancer, the precision of PSA as a screening tool remained an open question. The status of PSA stood in sharp contrast to the mammogram, the Pap smear, and the breast self-exam, which had longer histories and firmer, if still debated, places in disease screening.

Much of the new disease politics was driven by the business of testing. "To test or not to test," worried the specialists in the 1990s. The PSA test, like other aggressively marketed tools, produced multiple clinical, scientific, commercial, and intellectual confusions. Its advocates contended that, whatever the flaws, the test was a reliable "tumor marker." A high score along with any enlargement detected by a digital rectal exam indicated the need for a biopsy. For many urologists and primary care physicians, *not* ordering a PSA test became a liability concern.[23] Some advocates also demurred that "if you don't offer the testing, the patients will get it anyway. They will go anywhere, to another country if they have to."[24] When in 1998, for example, the FDA approved an improved PSA test developed by the company Beckman Coulter, the new test had an immediate appeal despite its uncertainties. One author declared that "men don't want to be biopsied unless it is absolutely necessary, due to the expense, the pain, anxiety and possible complications . . . The Hybritech Free PSA will spare many men that ordeal," he promised, speaking in support of the burgeoning PSA testing industry.[25]

Some observers rightly feared that the rapid expansion of disease testing could have many unintended consequences, contributing, for example, to the rising costs of unnecessary treatments and an epidemic of needless overdiagnosis. Troubling questions swirled around the whole cancer testing enterprise in the 1990s, around newly minted genetic tests, and even around well-established practices like mammography—a linchpin in early breast cancer detection.[26] The discovery of the BRCA-1 and BRCA-2 genes for breast cancer in 1994 had produced new tests and raised hopes, but it also fomented ethical and practical questions. What, after all, did a positive test actually mean for a woman's risk? Did it mean one would definitely develop the cancer years down the road, or just that one was at higher risk—and how much higher than average? Many women who tested positive, some of whom had tragic family histories with the disease, were opting for "preventive mastectomies," raising other concerns. In the case of PSA, critics worried that the tool was creating a false increase in cases. As researchers like Arnold Potosky observed, the sweeping "changes in this intensive medical surveillance" were themselves producing an "epidemic" as a direct by-product of the tests. The "exponential increase in PSA testing in the general population from 1988 to 1991" had produced several perverse new trends, driving up the rate of needle biopsies. They concluded: "The recent dramatic epidemic of prostate cancer is likely the result of the increasing detection of tumors resulting from increased PSA screening."[27]

Despite these uncertainties, PSA nevertheless emerged as basis for racial speculation. Some experts praised PSA's promise not only in battling prostate cancer but also in addressing racial disparities and in theorizing about race and health difference in black men. As the test came into wider use, the new data from patients generated apparently strong biological evidence of racial differences. Why, experts wondered, were PSA levels more elevated in black men than in white men? A single antigen produced by the prostate to help liquefy semen, PSA became the basis for shaping many of the decade's discussions of prostate disease and theories of race difference. To bolster the argument for aggressive PSA testing, its proponents waved the red flag of racial disparities—insisting that the test might help reduce those disparities in a tragedy where "American blacks have the highest incidence and mortality rates from prostate cancer in the world."[28] The claim was a mix of clinical hope and marketing bravado. In 1996, urologist Judd Moul and colleagues took the argument a step further. They argued that because of the high "level of a protein known as prostate specific antigen in the blood of blacks," PSA testing in black men "needs to be modified to improve detection among blacks."[29] Moul and his colleague argued that when a doctor considered how to advise an African-American man about his prostate test results, he should use a different scale than for a white man because "when 'average' ranges were used as a reference, many cases of cancer would not be detected in blacks."[30] Under their proposed change, the evaluation of a "normal" range would depend not only on the patient's age but also on race: white men in the 50-to-59 age range, for example, could be assigned an age-specific "normal" reference range of 0.0–3.5 with a biopsy recommended above 3.5; but in the same age group black men's reference range would be 0.0–4.0. These ideas for tailoring the test to address the existing racial disparity proved compelling. Urologists like Joseph Oesterling, who had found that PSA levels were lower in Japanese men, were optimistic about the prospects: "We're going to find more early curable cancers in black men," he predicted.[31] In its heyday, then, PSA was touted as a test that could be tailored to race differences and as a remedy for disparities. As one research group insisted in 1997, "PSA detects more cancers than rectal examination in both races, although this advantage is pronounced in black men." They acknowledged, however, that "PSA had more false-positive results than rectal examination in black men"—a flaw that would foreshadow some of the complexities to come.[32]

Many researchers knew, however, that PSA was not a reliable biological reference point, and regarded any racial theories founded upon such new and unstable evidence as flawed or even dangerous. Skepticism was especially warranted in light of the disease's and PSA's variability not only by ethnicity but also by the patient's social situation. Moreover, the more PSA variations (by region, by class, across groups, and in a single individual from time to time) were studied, the more problems emerged. Researchers learned, for example, that PSA scores correlated with behavior as well as with race and class. Men were urged to "refrain [from having sex] for 48 hours ahead of a PSA exam," since "ejaculation can skew a prostate cancer test"; and in one study race differences "showed up only among poorer black men with no health insurance besides Medicare . . . [while] among patients who had private health insurance . . . no significant racial difference in PSA" was found.[33] The correlation between high PSA scores and cancer, sexual activity, race, and class raised obvious questions about the test's accuracy in detecting true cancers. As Potosky and his colleagues noted, "[T]he rapid diffusion of screening interventions that have the ability to detect latent asymptomatic disease [and] geographical variability in the adoption of PSA testing underscores uncertainty and disagreement about its value."[34] Variations by region were also increasingly obvious, suggesting that PSA was a less than ideal screening tool.

The assumed correlations between race biology and cancer remained flimsy and vigorously disputed, with true believers in tests like the PSA squaring off against those who saw PSA as an unreliable marker of cancer, let alone of race. "One potential explanation for the racial differences in the incidence of prostate cancer is difference in hormone levels," insisted one group of biologically inclined scholars, linking supposedly high testosterone levels in black men to aggressive tumor growth and thus to higher mortality. But another group questioned the theory, noting that their own study of 453 men (264 white and 189 African-American) showed that "there was no statistical difference in the mean serum testosterone levels with respect to race in those patients with positive biopsies." Was race biology a factor in prostate cancer? Should race be taken into account when judging the risk of untreated cancer, or the pace of treatment? "Our data do not support the need to consider race when estimating the probability that a man has prostate cancer," this second group insisted.[35] Another study of serum PSA levels in African Americans, whites, and Hispanics concluded that "differences do exist," but "whether these differences are due to biologic or sociologic reasons, or a combination of both, is not known at this time and needs further study."[36]

One vexing problem with PSA was that its levels in an individual or in a population could change for multiple reasons. One study, for example, saw "a substantial decline in the mean PSA level for African-American patients, particularly in the years 1991 to 1995," and noted that "by 1994 to 1995, PSA levels among African-Americans declined to values comparable to those of whites." How was it, some experts wondered, that PSA trends could change so rapidly over time? How could biological evidence linked to cancer undergo such a rapid shift over four years? Could it be that the PSA reflected not black biology, but the changing social situation of patients? Perhaps, this group speculated, "because of the disparity in medical care between whites and African-Americans, the PSA levels among the better-cared-for whites may have been lower than those for African-Americans even before the current increase in PSA screening."[37] Some urologists focused on diet, rejecting the notion of fundamental biological differences.[38] "The change in the racial differences in PSA levels from a wider difference in the earlier years to a narrower difference in the later years of the study between whites and African-Americans, supports the hypothesis that sociological factors account for racial differences in prostate cancer in the United States," they concluded.[39] PSA differences, they argued, reflected many factors: social difference, the movement of black men into and out of clinics relative to white men, and so on. By the late 1990s, most authorities acknowledged that the test's links to cancer were tenuous at best. "Various benign conditions . . . can affect PSA levels," acknowledged one group; "serum PSA is a tumor marker which is organ-specific, but not cancer-specific."[40] Yet, the PSA—flaws and all—had become a touchstone of the debate on race biology and cancer, generating new race theories and reviving old ones.

In its recent heyday, then, the PSA test highlighted how an "epidemic" could be constructed, created by a new commercial diagnostic test, by rapid shifts in monitoring and surveillance, and by increasing attention to a targeted population. This was an old, epistemological problem in the history of cancer awareness, now returned in a new light. As we saw in chapter 1, ever since the early twentieth century, health statisticians had known that a "rise" in cancer deaths could reflect a true increase in cases or simply improvements in monitoring and diagnosing cases that had always been there. For all the sophistication of the PSA test, the puzzle had not changed. If anything, it became worse in the age of highly sensitive, aggressively marketed testing that pushed the boundaries of detection. By the late 1990s it was clear that, as the surgeon Peter Albertsen bluntly put it, "the epidemiology of prostate cancer remains an enigma . . . The last two decades have witnessed a dramatic increase in the incidence of this disease, yet despite extensive use of aggressive treatment regimes the mortality rate from prostate cancer remains unchanged."[41] The PSA had confused the epidemiological picture, but so too had other factors, such as gender and racial identity politics, and the slowness of prostate tumor growth. These illusions were also evident in mammography. "Breast cancer incidence increased most rapidly among white women between 1980 and 1988," commented one American Cancer Society epidemiologist in 2006, "during the period when mammography was widely disseminated." Separating the "real" rise from the effects produced by the introduction of new technologies like mammography proved to be challenging.[42]

As epidemiologists had long understood, new tests could create powerful false impressions. When tests like the PSA appeared they caused physicians to rethink their older assessments of when the disease started and its stages of severity. A more sensitive test detected cases that previously had fallen under the radar. One by-product was an illusion of progress, because earlier diagnosis necessarily meant a longer survival from time of diagnosis. Another illusion produced by earlier detection and the re categorization of disease stages was what some scholars called the "Will Rogers Phenomenon" or "the Okie effect." The American humorist Will Rogers, himself a native of Oklahoma, had once apparently quipped that "when the Okies left Oklahoma during the Dustbowl and went to California, they raised the average intelligence of both states."[43] This bit of Depression-era humor (although perhaps apocryphal) pointed to a paradox of progress associated with the simple movement of people from one location to another. The Okies were the least intelligent in Oklahoma, but they were highly intelligent compared to the average Californian, or so the joke went. The simple fact of their migration had perverse effects on each state without changing any underlying reality. The dismissive quip was picked up as a metaphor in the mid-1980s by epidemiologists trying to explain how a new cancer test could create similar illusions about rising cancer survival rates. As the authors pointed out in the *New England Journal of Medicine*, the effect was evident when a new diagnostic imaging technique for lung cancer emerged in the 1970s. Under the older diagnostic regime, patients had been separated into, say, two categories—one consisting of patients with less severe disease who could expect longer survival times, and the second with greater severity and shorter survival times. When new, more sensitive diagnostic techniques came into wider use in the 1970s, imaging tests found that some patients who once appeared to have minor disease were, in fact, more severely ill than believed. The "Okie effect" moved the sickest patients from the less severe group into the group with more severe symptoms. Of course, these migrating patients had less severe disease relative to their new group and were likely to survive longer. Merely by transferring this subgroup from one category to another (a process called "stage migration" in the literature) the survival rates in both groups had increased.[44] It was a profound epistemological illusion, they wrote, produced by increased sensitivity in lung cancer diagnosis.

Despite PSA's many flaws, the true believers continued to rely on PSA evidence (and the sense that incidence was rising fast) to compete for attention with breast cancer advocates; but skepticism was growing. Philadelphia physician Leonard Gomella insisted that PSA was finding *real* cancers—"that the widespread use of PSA has begun to clear the 'backlog' of undiagnosed cases of prostate cancer . . . [and] we now may be reaching the true incidence of the disease in the population." For Gomella, PSA encouraged parity with breast cancer. "When compared with breast cancer screening," he argued, "the costs per case discovered are substantially less for prostate cancer . . . [T]he tide . . . may be beginning to turn, and PSA-based screening may ultimately prove to be the decisive weapon in the battle against prostate cancer."[45] But reviewing the statistics, the effects produced by PSA were clearly not entirely believable to the experts themselves. In their own hospital, University of Chicago researchers surveyed PSA data from 1988 to 1995. They found remarkable changes over this short period, discovering that "in 1988 PSA levels were twice as high in African-Americans as in whites, but by 1995 they had declined to a value similar to that in whites." These kinds of rapid shifts suggested that something was wrong with the test itself, for how could such a dramatic seven-year shift reflect anything other than a statistical effect? Perhaps this was the ghostly product of stage migration? In both blacks and whites, the Chicago researchers found, the increasing use of PSA meant that "a higher percentage of men will be diagnosed with more favorable prostate cancers."[46]

By 2000, professional enthusiasm for the PSA test was weakening and so too were its links to cancer and to race biology. Even its advocates admitted soberly that PSA tests produced too much overdiagnosis. The rapid rise and fall of PSA through the 1990s reveals less about a prostate cancer *epidemic*, and more about the commercial diagnostics and scientists' flights of diagnostic and racial imagination.[47] Increasingly, studies confirmed that the faith in PSA was misplaced. It "misses most tumors," physicians admitted; its value as a screening tool was called into question.[48] Authorities coalesced around the view that there was "no lifesaving boost" from the test, a skepticism that would also arise with breast self-examination a few years later.[49] "As has happened in the past with genetics," one molecular biologist had commented early on in 1995, "the technology far precedes the response to what we're going to do with the technology."[50] In PSA's heyday, its advocates were slow to acknowledge this truth. By 2000, however, many physicians saw prostate cancer diagnosis as a tortured zone of uncertainty. They looked askance at many aspects of the test, and they rejected the racial adjustments that Moul and his colleagues had proposed. The argument for PSA as a biological index of race difference had evaporated.

The misplaced faith that aggressive PSA testing in black men could remedy the racial divide in prostate cancer generated perverse effects: PSA and increased biopsy led patients more quickly into surgery, and produced "a sharp increase in radical prostatectomy [surgical removal of the prostate gland] rates."[51] But who benefited from these trends? Not patients, apparently. Ironically, noted one study in 2000, "black men who undergo radical prosta-tectomies . . . for clinically localized prostate cancer have worse outcomes."[52] For many men, PSA was a ticket to unnecessary surgery. African-American urologist Isaac Powell argued that changing the cutoff for black men would merely pull more of them into a system of treatment that did not serve them well, producing only more biopsies and ever-increasing numbers of radical prostatectomies, but little real benefit for the patients. As another study in

2004 noted, "given that overdiagnosis is already a considerable problem when the standard threshold of 4.0 ng/mL is used, further lowering of the threshold would result in even more clinically insignificant cancers being detected." The question was not whether the PSA detected "cancer," noted the authors. Their study documented that "many men with PSA less than 4.0 ng/mL may have prostate cancer, but whether these cancers are clinically meaningful is an entirely different matter."[53] Such researchers looked beyond the PSA to other factors to explain the higher rates and lower survival in black men: they looked to "differences in access to care, the quality of the care received, and the impact of co-morbid conditions."[54]

In 2004, urological surgeon Thomas Stamey, an early advocate of PSA, declared his loss of faith, boldly insisting that "the prostate specific antigen era in the United States is over for prostate cancer." "[W]hat happened in the last 20 years?" he asked, looking back over the two decades.[55] PSA had distorted cancer awareness in men, Stamey asserted: "Men need to realize that prostate cancer [usually a slow developing malady] is something we all get if we live long enough . . . [P]rostate cancer is ubiquitous . . . we all get it, and it goes with increasing age—but at the end of the road [it is associated with] a pretty small death rate [because] when men get to be 60, the competing causes of death are huge—strokes, accidents, and other causes."[56] But how could the predictive value of a test change so much over time? Stamey was asked. "That's a very good question," he responded. "One possible answer is that we have so overscreened men in the United States with PSA that . . . we have removed all the big cancers and we are left only with the small microscopic ones . . . About 20 years ago . . . we reported that if you plotted the size of the largest cancer in the prostate that had been removed with the level of blood PSA before it was removed, that there was a reasonable relationship" between the two; but it "wasn't . . . perfect" because the PSA had only a 43 percent predictive relationship to finding cancer. Over time, however, the relationship diminished. "In the last five years it's now only 2 percent," stated Stamey, "so that's negligible. That allows me to say that PSA today in the United States no longer has any relationship to the cancer except for 2 percent of men." In this account, the test had done its work by overidentifying cancer cases, creating cancer cases where no clinically important cancer existed, and now there was no more work for it to do.

By 2006, more than a decade after PSA's first emergence as a popular diagnostic test, one patient commented on the many uncertainties it had generated: "Before my PSA test, the doctor told me that a score of less than four is considered 'safe.' My PSA was less than one, but the doctor ordered a biopsy based on a digital rectal exam . . . The biopsy showed that cancer was present and I had my prostate surgically removed. Doesn't that mean that the PSA test is useless?"[57] Urologists were also critical. "I think we need to recognize today that PSA is related today to the benign enlargement of the prostate and not to the cancer," Stamey commented. "That says we must find a new cancer marker."[58] Indeed, PSA had failed on multiple levels: as a marker for cancer, as a reliable conduit for men's health awareness, as a remedy for health disparities, and most obviously as a proxy in the long-running effort to link cancer to racial biology.

ETHNIC TRANSFORMATIONS: THE ASIAN PARADOX AND CERVICAL CANCER

While the emergence of an "epidemic" of prostate cancer in black men resuscitated familiar stories about race biology, the discovery of distinct patterns of cervical cancer in Vietnamese women opened a new discussion of Asian ethnic diversity, culture, and biology. The starkly higher incidence rates of cervical cancer in this community forced epidemiologists to recognize that "Vietnamese" was not synonymous with "Asian." Race, in this context, seemed to be an obviously unhelpful concept, and discussions about the disparity looked back to the Vietnamese experience broadly defined, taking a historical and sociological view of disease causation.

In studying Asian cancer trends, public health experts acknowledged that they confronted not one but multiple mysteries, hinging not on "race" but on complex notions of Asian ethnicities—Korean, Japanese, Chinese, Vietnamese, Filipino, and so on. As one California newspaper writer noted in 2004, "the overall cancer picture of Asian Americans is a relatively healthy one," but "variations among the very diverse Asian populations in California told a more complicated story." Cancer incidence for all Asians had dropped 5.9 percent from 1988 to 2001; deaths from cancer had declined 16.3 percent. But "Koreans saw only a 0.2 percent drop in incidence, and Filipinos experienced a 2.5 percent increase in their cancer death rate."[59] Moreover, awareness of cancer resources also varied by group. As one researcher explained, "Regarding awareness of cancer clinical trials and interest in participating, Chinese, Vietnamese, and Cambodians were more knowledgeable but less willing to take part while Koreans were less likely to [be] aware of the meaning of trials but showed more keenness in involvement."[60] These questions regarding Asian diversity shaped a new kind of identity politics. As one Portland-based health educator put it, "[B]ecause Asian Americans are often lumped together in health data, disparities among them can be overlooked."[61]

Asian cancer rates were an emerging public health challenge, but data and resources to address the challenge appeared to be sparse, especially by comparison with other minority groups. "We searched the literature using the keywords 'Asian' and 'health' and came up with something like 48 citations," stated one Ohio State University researcher in 2000. "That compares with more than 300 citations for blacks . . . There's just no data, especially cancer data . . ." For such researchers, the comparison with black Americans highlighted the need for reform and resources. Asian cancer trends reflected a unique crisis. One news account from 2000 reported that "in comparing racial ethnic groups, Asian-American women are the only group in which cancer is the leading cause of death. Among the others, heart disease is the leading cause." Such a statement, while compelling and accurate, was also misleading. Asian-American women as a group experienced lower heart disease mortality than did other Americans—a fact that, by definition, pushed cancer into the *most deadly* category. By 2000, calls for reform were being heard. A new $7.6 million National Cancer Institute initiative to reduce cancer disparities among the country's 10 million Asian Americans promised action to remedy the complex challenges facing this diverse population.[62]

Perhaps because of the obvious nationality-based differences across Asian groups, most researchers saw *race* as a useless concept in understanding the complexity of the Asian cancer experience. But the problem of race terminology when applied to Asians only highlighted a deeper problem with the race concept in general. An authoritative 1999 Institute of Medicine report, *The Unequal Burden of Cancer*, insisted that the "use of the term 'race' is scientifically inaccurate because it implies fundamental biological differences among groups that do not exist." Asians were merely one case in point. Asians "included Vietnamese . . . other south Asians, Koreans, Japanese, Chinese, Indians and others who are ethnically and culturally very different," noted the report.[63] Each group also experienced different cancer rates.[64] The IOM study went further, noting the limits of other race categories. "Having people in cancer studies in traditional racial categories—white, black, Asian or Pacific Islander, or Native American—makes it hard to pinpoint factors affecting incidence of the disease and its treatment within subgroups."[65] As one author noted, building on the IOM report, tracking health trends in Asians was especially difficult since they were "the fastest growing minority . . . and one of the most diverse and poorly understood minority groups" in the country.[66]

The Vietnamese experience pointed beyond biological *race* (indeed, the term "race" was rarely employed), thus illustrating profound inconsistencies in group classification. Commentators instead situated this cancer epidemic in a troubling and complex story of Southeast Asian refugee history. Any focus on race or genetic group differences tended, as one critic noted, to "mask the influence of ethnic background and life style difference that could be big factors in cancer."[67] In Vietnamese American women, for example, cervical cancer was "five times higher than that of white women and seven times higher than for Japanese American women, who have the lowest incidence in America," reported an Oregon newspaper in 2001.[68] In states like Oregon, where the Vietnamese population had grown, sensitivity to the issue had increased alongside popular interest in the Vietnamese-American experience. After 1975 and the American military withdrawal from Vietnam, the arrival of "boat people" from the countryside and fishing villages created a small Vietnamese refugee population in the United States. This first wave was followed by a second wave of freed political detainees and survivors of prison camps. And then in the mid-1990s, after the normalization of U.S.-Vietnamese relations, there came a third significant immigration wave.[69] Between 1990 and 2000, the American Vietnamese population doubled to over 1 million (going from 0.2 percent of the U.S. population in 1990 to 0.4 percent in 2000).[70] In Houston, for example, the numbers of Vietnamese leaped from 2 percent of the city's population to 3.2 percent; and by the end of the 1990s, the city's M. D. Anderson Cancer Center had created a Center for Research on Minority Health to address emerging needs.[71] Commenting on that city's fast-growing immigrant communities, one Houston-based advocate noted that "Southeast Asians have a variety of needs that other Asians don't have . . . When we are consolidated, the nuances are lost. We have probably missed out on a good amount of funding because of the inability to assess our needs."[72] In understanding health and cancer trends in such communities, health experts insisted that race biology was less important than "cultural and behavioral actions, beliefs, lifestyle patterns, diet, environmental living conditions and other factors."[73] Another problem was the real possibility of ethnic misclassification and that "approximately 20 percent of cancer cases classified as Vietnamese are probably not Vietnamese." This possibility suggested that "the higher incidence rates for Vietnamese in the United States than in Vietnam partly may reflect such classification error," and that such errors were symptomatic of common American cultural misunderstandings regarding Asian peoples.[74]

Like beliefs about prostate cancer and black men, portraits of cancer in Vietnamese people proved to be malleable—evolving remarkably in the 1970s, '80s, and '90s—in this case not with diagnostic technology but with each immigration wave. During the first phase, researchers often connected higher cancer rates in Vietnamese populations (as well as in American Vietnam veterans) to exposure to dioxin during the war.[75] In an era sensitive to environmental cancer causation and the effects of war, scientists associated an "endless . . . parade of chemicals" with the cancer trends they saw—from DDT to the synthetic hormone DES to asbestos, benzene, and a growing range of industrial and food products.[76] The war itself had produced chemical carnage, unleashing carcinogens on the Vietnamese people—the most notorious being the herbicide Agent Orange, a chemical cocktail containing dioxin. Thousands of tons had been used to defoliate the jungles of Vietnam. In the 1970s and early 1980s, therefore, experts saw disparities in cancer rates as a direct consequence of environmental exposure. The Vietnam story was merely another case of this general, and obvious, linkage.

According to another emerging theory, it was not life in Asia but the adoption of American ways of life that produced puzzling spikes in Asian-American cancer rates, increasing cancer risks for such groups. Here, other Asian groups and cancers became the reference point. Breast cancer (a disease with low prevalence in Asia) offered updated proof of the civilization theory that had been around for almost a century. "For Asian-Americans who lived in this country for 10 years or longer," one 1997 news account noted, breast cancer rates slowly increased with each year in the new country. And, sadly, for women of Far East Asian descent born in America, whatever breast cancer advantage their mothers had had in the old country was lost to the younger generation: "American-born women of Asian descent have a risk similar to that for white women."[77] In this telling, migration increased risk. "Within the migrating generation of Asian-Americans," explained another study, "breast cancer risk appeared to increase relatively rapidly, doubling after a decade of residence in the West and then leveling off."[78] The increased risk also depended on where immigrants had formerly lived. Migrants from rural communities saw "risk . . . triple over two decades." For these groups (Japanese, Chinese, and Filipino), the migration from East to West framed a dangerous transition: "exposure to the West" brought higher cancer rates and death rates that outpaced the women in their homelands.[79]

Just as their counterparts early in the twentieth century had worried that black migration northward increased cancer rates, researchers in the 1990s observed that "westernization" explained the Asian-American cancer transition and spun data into theories of modernization. "Asians in U.S. Adopt Unhealthy Habits," one newspaper headline insisted, implicating newfound prosperity and adoption of Western lifestyles. One researcher quoted in 1992 observed that "73 percent [of Vietnamese immigrants in the U.S.] ate more beef than they did in Vietnam, 57 percent ate more pork and 48 percent ate more eggs." By assimilating Western diets and smoking practices, such Asian groups were said to be "cultivating a lung cancer and heart disease crisis."[80] The popular press echoed such views. As one Canadian reporter noted about Canada's Chinese immigrants, "cancers of the breast, colon, prostate and others that have ravaged Western societies, but traditionally caused far less damage in the Far East, are now on the rise here. A leading theory suggests that . . . economic growth puts more money in people's pockets and they develop a taste for Western-style foods."[81]

Reprising classic notions of cancer as a disease of civilization, commentators speculated that perhaps cancer was the price Asians paid for "falling prey to smoking and a high-fat diet—two major risk factors that may play key roles in an emerging health crisis."[82] These new ways, combined with traditional stigmas, silences, and shame associated with cancer, proved to be a deadly combination, epidemiologists worried. It was said that Asians brought with them a traditionally Confucian approach to diseases such as breast cancer and a "typical modesty" that resulted in women's deep reluctance to practice breast self-examination. For many observers writing about the Asian-American cancer experience in the 1990s, the dominant storyline hinged not on biology but on a classic paradox of migration and assimilation—an encounter between modernity and tradition that adapted to new times ideas of civilization and primitivism from one hundred years ago.[83]

Alongside the theories of westernization also came half-baked ideas about Asian "ethnic metabolism," suggesting that epidemiologists were not wholly averse to race biology arguments where Asians were concerned. For example, one 2002 San Francisco study of lung cancer took up the mystery of why Chinese Americans had lower lung cancer rates than Latinos or whites, even though smoking rates were just as high. The researchers speculated that "Chinese-Americans metabolize nicotine more slowly than Latinos and whites, and that they take in less nicotine from each cigarette smoked than Latinos or whites."[84] This imagined difference in ethnic metabolism could, the authors suggested, explain their "lower risk of lung cancer from cigarette smoking than white Americans."[85] Yet, for other scholars, smoking was a prime culprit. In Asia, noted one California researcher, Hao Tang, "men smoke at a higher rate than men in California, while women smoke at a lower rate. But those [women's] rates creep closer to the American norm the more Asian immigrants become incorporated into U.S. society." "Smoking becomes a symbol of freedom, especially with ethnic women," he surmised; hence its rise explained the cancer trend.[86] Thus, cancer in Asian populations could be framed any number of ways: as a migration drama, as a story of westernization, freedom, and dangerous adoption of new habits such as high-fat diets instead of old soy diets, as a narrative about the persistence of modesty as impediments of self-examination, or as the effects of "ethnic biology."[87]

In Vietnamese women, cervical cancer was interpreted against this broader backdrop, as a lens onto the group's social transformation. What made this case unique was how some researchers also linked this case to social turmoil in Southeast Asia and to women's difficult migrations amidst war.[88] As early as the 1980s some authorities had pointed to a hidden "male factor" in the "transmission" of high cervical cancer rates in these women.[89] The discovery of the link between human papillomavirus (HPV) and cervical cancer in the late 1970s reinvigorated an age-old linkage between sex, cervical cancer risk, and men as vectors. As in the 1950s, men and sex appeared onstage as crucial factors. If cancer was caused by HPV, then the Vietnam War had stimulated a deadly viral traffic. Women became more sexually vulnerable in wartime, especially in an environment where "normative social customs hold women to strict codes of sexual monogamy but allow most men to have multiple pre- and postnuptial partners, including commercial sex workers, who may serve as important reservoirs of high risk subtypes of HPV." One theory held that the health effects of exposure were not immediate, but delayed, manifesting themselves for immigrants only after arrival in America. Thus "because the average time interval between initial infection with HPV and the diagnosis of invasive cervical cancer may exceed 20 years, contemporary cervical cancer rates" reflected "carcinogenic pathways initiated during" the war, from 1959 through the mid-1970s.[90] In such accounts, the burden of cancer was tied to the military struggles of America in Vietnam, to decades of social destabilization, and to the sexual vulnerability of women in wartime. As some experts saw it, this new American health problem had virological and social roots in the American campaign abroad.[91]

MYSTERY IN MARIN: CANCER AS
A BURDEN OF AFFLUENCE

Where the prostate cancer "epidemic" created illusions of *race difference*, and the cervical cancer puzzle pointed to diverse Asian *ethnic transformations*, the puzzle of breast cancer's spike in Marin County reflected (in the minds of some experts) neither race nor ethnicity but a white culture where privilege and affluence was believed to breed vulnerability.[92] Although the whites of Marin had diverse ethnic backgrounds themselves, few commentators sought to read ethnicity into the local mystery or to put a racial biological label on this cancer spike. Perhaps it was the absence of historical knowledge about these women who resided in wealthy Marin that led to these deracialized accounts. This asymmetry in the interpretation of cancer rates among Vietnamese and in Marin County women draws our attention to long-standing patterns within cancer discourse of personalizing white women's risk.

"Women in these scenic valleys north of San Francisco are being diagnosed with invasive breast cancer at a higher rate than experts have found anywhere in the United States," noted one news story.[93] The mysterious leap in cancer among Marin's "white non-Hispanic women" revisited a long-standing theme with roots in the early twentieth century: the link between women, affluence, and cancer. "Breast Cancer mid Affluence," read a headline from 2003; "Unseen Killer Stalks Marin," reported another.[94] A sense of disbelief filled these news accounts: "there is no logical reason Marin County— where women hike pristine trails, eat organic and see their doctors regularly— has more breast cancer than almost any place on Earth. There is no reason that the numbers continue to climb." Rates of breast cancer had increased by 60 percent from 1991 to 1999, and "in a single year, from 1998 to 1999, the rate jumped 20 percent," noted the *San Francisco Chronicle*, a statistic that "has sent a new wave of panic through the community."[95] Wealthy Marin County, "long-famed as a mecca for wealthy hot-tubbers, has recently acquired a darker distinction," intoned one writer in the *Washington Post*.[96]

From the outset, the findings were personalized and politicized. The challenge of breast cancer in Marin became inextricably bound up with questions of identity, how these women lived, the air they breathed, what foods they ate, how many children they had, their socioeconomic status, how nearby and distant industries influenced their lives, and many other factors. Marin County women suspected their environment was to blame, calling for studies of the local water, soil, air, and food.[97] U.S. Senator Dianne Feinstein of California broadened the debate, asking federal officials and scientists for answers: "[I]s it diet? environment? genetic? what is it?" And women in other such "cancer clusters," from Toms River, New Jersey, to Louisiana's "cancer alley" along the Mississippi River, asked similar questions.[98]

But where the women of Marin looked to environmental causation to explain the high rates of cancer in their community, epidemiologists saw the region as an unremarkable cancer cluster, suggesting that these "higher-than-expected concentrations of similar cancers in one discrete area" were not necessarily cause for alarm.[99] The underlying reason for each cluster was often difficult to pin down.[100] As early as 1988, experts knew, for example, not only that "New Jersey had a problem" and a long "reputation as a cancer alley," but also that the state had vast problems with underground cancer-causing radiation in the form of radon.[101] Interest in these clusters grew in the 1990s, driven by residents who were "leery of landfills, worried about waste products and edgy about electromagnetic radiation."[102] Marin County, however, had none of these environmental problems—no radon, landfills, or electromagnetic wires. Indeed its status as a privileged enclave gave residents a strong sense of health security. What people in Marin possessed was notably higher-than-normal wealth, high social status, abundant health awareness, and a distinctly white complexion. Women there diligently sought out screening for cancer, engaged in systematic breast self-examination, and were aggressive health care consumers. Ironically, some experts believed that these very factors (and not the environment) explained the county's cancer spike.

Most public health authorities placed Marin County women at the center of a perfect storm of cultural awareness and social factors that combined to drive cancer rates up. Even those sympathetic with the situation in Marin County saw little cause for environmental scrutiny. Instead, these experts pointed to education and household income in Marin. As epidemiologist Elizabeth Clarke confirmed, "[E]ducated, professional women . . . generally have better access to medical care, including screening for cancer; that leads to more diagnoses."[103] Indeed, their access to health care may even have put them at greater risk, since "better medical care may have included more combined hormone replacement therapy."[104] Already in 2002, hormone replacement therapy (HRT) was linked to higher rates of cancer. Conflicting data about the risks and benefits swirled around new HRT drug products such as Wyeth Pharmaceutical's drugs Premarin and Prempro; HRT drugs were among the most frequently prescribed for women older than fifty.[105] Some studies suggested that "a type of breast cancer associated with the use of combination hormone replacement therapy appears to be on the rise and may account for some or all of the increasing incidence of the disease nationwide."[106] Another author speculated that "educated, affluent women may be checked for breast cancer more regularly and have better detection rates. Their diet may be different. Or they may have children later in life."[107] (Having children later in life had long been understood to be a factor in increasing breast cancer risk.)

But some commentators, like Ruth Rosen, deeply resented these arguments as blaming women for the lives they chose to lead. Rosen insisted that "the women of Marin were [being] maligned. They were too white, too rich, too educated, too selfish to bear children at a 'proper' young age. These were called 'risk factors'" And she concluded sarcastically, "Then, it turned out that the rate . . . was not, in fact, off the charts—just slightly higher than the rest of the Bay Area."[108] But in time, scientific consensus settled on HRT and Marin women's affluent consumption as the chief culprits. HRT had become increasingly popular in the 1980s and 1990s as a treatment to relieve hot flashes and menopausal symptoms, and its link to increasing cancer risk pushed some authorities to see Marin's case as a tale of conspicuous consumption by women hoping to improve their postmenopausal lives.[109] Instead, this theory suggested, these women courted cancer. Affluence, in other words, more than "race" or ethnicity, was believed to explain these trends.

But adding to the Marin mystery was another possibility: that the spike, like the epidemic of prostate cancer, was merely an illusion. To be sure, women in Marin suffered from breast cancer and died from the disease. But were these numbers any greater than in other counties? As one *Washington Post* story noted, epidemiologists like Christina Clarke believed that the county's "attributes as one of the nation's smallest urban counties" could explain the "epidemic." The spike in incidence was a statistical chimera akin with the so-called Will Rogers effect discussed above. "Its 250,000 residents are predominantly white and well-off financially, characteristics long associated with higher rates of breast cancer. Cancer rates are reported for counties, but not for cities and towns. If they were," Clarke noted, "places such as Beverly Hills, Calif., or Chevy Chase might exhibit similarly high breast cancer rates."[110] The epidemic, in this view, was the product of Marin's skewed wealth profile and its small size compared to other counties, factors that combined to produce curious statistical effects on the cancer rates. The rates could not be taken at face value. The cancer profile in Marin could be explained away as part of the expected norm for such populations in America.

While much of the coverage of Marin's mystery suggested that breast cancer was more a disease of affluence than of race, epidemiologists increasingly saw the disease as a more complex metaphor for life and cancer death across the modern economic divide. As epidemiologist Nancy Krieger wrote in 2002, "[T]he conventional view that breast cancer is a 'disease of affluence' is increasingly at odds with the empirical evidence and lived experiences of poorer women." The new reality was double-edged, such scientists now concluded; as Krieger noted, "white women are more likely to be diagnosed with breast cancer, but Black women are more likely to die of the disease."[111] The new truth could be seen in towns like Moraga and Richmond, just east of Marin in Contra Costa County, with the "second-highest breast cancer" rate, just behind Marin. As one news story described the situation, Mrs. Hogan, from Moraga in Contra Costa County, was fastidious, "white and well off," living in a town that was "85 percent white, with a median household income of nearly $70,000." Regarding her risk of breast cancer, Mrs. Hogan noted earnestly: "I was very aware . . . I was a fanatic about breast self-examination and mammograms, the whole bit." When her diagnosis came, it was an utter surprise; yet she still remained in control. "At each step in her treatment, Hogan called the shots, and her insurance company picked up the tab," noted a *San Francisco Chronicle* writer. In the nearby town of Richmond, Mrs. Terrell lived in poorer circumstances. Richmond was "70 percent minority, with a median income of less than half of Moraga." Access to cancer care was more difficult for Mrs. Terrell. While women like Mrs. Hogan were more likely to develop breast cancer, it was black women like Mrs. Terrell who faced the higher mortality rates.[112] So it was that cancer in Marin County and the Bay Area was fore grounded as a class and economic story of whiteness.

Woven through the Marin coverage was the belief, arcing back across the century, that women were in peril and self-examination promised survival. If faith in PSA cancer detection was linked to men's identity politics in the 1990s, many women's faith in breast self-examination was fiercely tied to their ideas about self-control and identity. White women were the most proficient at it; married women performed the technique particularly well; and epidemiologists worried that other groups (Asians, Hispanics, black women) lagged in their proficiency.[113] "For Latinas and Asians," one study wondered, did "cultural taboos against talking about or touching one's body . . . result in the avoidance of self-exams and screenings" and thus higher death rates?[114] Over fifty years, the breast self-examination had become an article of faith for

How Cancer Crossed the Color Line

mainstream middle-class women, a form of cultural outreach, and a tool of women's empowerment. Women had thoroughly incorporated the practice into their routines. It seemed obvious to many that breast self-examination could explain the white woman's mortality advantage over black women.

To read the news reports of this era was to see many other troubling yet often illusory "epidemics" popping up across the social spectrum—in black men, Asian groups, and whites—each giving rise to its peculiar style of race talk. In the instance of black men and prostate cancer, experts attempted to grapple with what they saw as "racial differences" in cancer; in the case of Vietnamese women and cervical cancer, they spoke of "ethnicity" and culture; and in the instance of culturally "white" women in well-to-do Marin County, their explanations often hinged on questions of economic and class difference. The asymmetries not only highlight the differences in how groups with their varying social features and social psychology are described in America, but they also expose the ways in which health experts in the 1990s and today imagine race and difference in disparate ways.

In truth, the troubling cancer spikes in prostate cancer, breast cancer, and cervical cancer are complex and illusive phenomena shaped by many social and biological factors. But each type became reduced, in the minds of authorities, to particular identity-linked factors: affluence, poverty, "black blood," "ethnic metabolism," and so on. The aggressive marketing of genetic and non-genetic tests tended to reinforce biological arguments. They also added further complexity to the cancer debate because they found "cancers" long before they were truly life-threatening—making cancer into an entirely different type of disease than it had been when diagnosis typically came at a later stage. New testing possibilities created intense pressures for screening, which could effortlessly merge with American identity politics, linking cancer detection to the needs and experiences of diverse groups.[115] Thus, at the heart of the era's scientific, political, and racial controversies sat a range of diagnostic innovations such as the newfangled prostate-specific antigen, the breast self-examination, the mammogram, and innovative genetic testing, the value of which was much debated.[116]

The role of these tools in shaping personal identity and health awareness became particularly evident when breast cancer experts, reassessing the value of BSE, encountered a potent backlash from women. In 2001, a remarkable finding based on a ten-year study of women in Shanghai, China, suggested that BSE was useless in improving their survival. "Routinely Teaching Breast Self-Examination Is Dead," pronounced an editorial in the *Journal of the*

National Cancer Institute. But public reaction showed how the study threat-ened deeply held notions of self-surveillance and self-protection that had been established decades earlier. One writer named Elaine Fogel responded skeptically, adding that she had "received calls from irate breast-cancer survi-vors who found their lumps on their own and argued the key to beating cancer is early detection." As a *Toronto Sun* article stated, "Fogel says she believes with-out BSEs, tumours potentially have a year to grow before the next clinical test."[117] The reaction to the establishment's rejection of BSE was combative. Two years later, when the *Journal of the National Cancer Institute* published the results of the now-complete China study, one newspaper reported that even "the American Cancer Society [took] exception to the research, noting that the conclusions do not necessarily apply in the United States, where there is a higher incidence of breast cancer. The Cancer Society still recommends monthly self-exams as a way to find a tumor in its early stages." Even the author of the Shanghai study acknowledged that the findings ran strongly contrary to long-cultivated belief and practice: "That is not what women want to hear. I wish we didn't have to be the bearer of that news, but it is what we found."[118] Those who had diligently learned the technique (white women and married women were said to be most proficient) were most fierce in rejecting the study.[119]

In fact, ardent BSE advocates were concerned not with jettisoning the practice, but with bringing this form of awareness to new immigrants and women of color—those who had not yet adopted these standard practices of modern health awareness, and whose cultural beliefs impeded the practice because of their so-called Asian modesty, or cultural/sexual stigma in Latina cultures about touching the body. It was therefore believed that self-examina-tions were a valuable tool in cultural uplift across the color line. In the words of "8-year breast cancer survivor, Lourdes Hernandez," profiled in the *Hous-ton Chronicle* in October 2003, "I really want to encourage women—particu-larly in the Hispanic and African-American communities—to do self exams and to get their mammograms."[120] Commenting on the BSE controversy, one editorial concluded that "despite the latest verdict against self-examination, virtually all experts agree that it is important for women to be aware of the normal texture and appearance of their breasts and alert to any changes."[121] Its advocates spoke more bluntly: "To come out blankly and say not to do [BSEs] anymore," commented one observer resentfully, "is wrong."[122]

Facing a backlash, authorities quickly scrambled to show that they remained attentive to these personal, internalized beliefs in women's ability to safeguard their own lives. Despite finding that BSE was "more expensive than it first appears," that it was "difficult to learn to do well," and most important, that "it does not reduce the risk of dying of breast cancer," specialists acknowledged that women schooled in the practice were finding smaller and smaller tumors. But this "reduction in the size of lumps discovered by women themselves" was not necessarily life-saving.[123] Yet editorialists at the *Journal of the National Cancer Institute* ultimately bowed to women's insistence in the value of BSE. The Shanghai trial did not mean "that we can forget about women's awareness of the importance of seeking clinical evaluation for incidentally discovered breast lumps," they wrote. Whatever science said, the practice would endure. Such women had internalized their own risk perceptions, and "although this awareness may have negative effects (. . . anxiety and heightened risk perceptions)," their belief in the practice had a tiny clinical value, the authorities acknowledged. More important, they concluded, women "may also feel empowered and more in control with this knowledge. . . . Routinely teaching BSE may be dead, but giving women information . . . should live on."[124]

THE NEW POLITICS OF OLD DIFFERENCES

To read the news and medical reports of the 1990s was to see troubling epidemics across the social spectrum: rising cancer mortality in wealthy Marin County, California; high cervical cancer rates among Vietnamese women; heavy prostate cancer mortality among African-American men. Cancer awareness reflected the identity politics of these years, as a widening array of groups used disease trends, statistics, and other evidence to position themselves in the fight for resources, to frame their resentments and differences, or to engage in the era's so-called gender and culture wars.

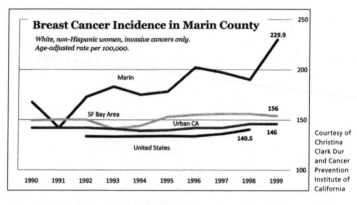

Breast Cancer Incidence in Marin County
White, non-Hispanic women, invasive cancers only.
Age-adjusted rate per 100,000.

Marin — 229.9

SF Bay Area — 156

Urban CA — 146

United States — 140.5

1990 1991 1992 1993 1994 1995 1996 1997 1998 1999

250 200 150 100

Courtesy of Christina Clark Dur and Cancer Prevention Institute of California

One epidemiological mystery was why cancer rates in affluent, white, Marin County had spiked upward (above). Was it the conspicuous consumption of hormone replacement therapy or the fact that (as one expert put it) "its 250,000 residents are predominantly white and well-off financially, characteristics long associated with higher rates of breast cancer"? The age-old links between cancer, whiteness, and affluence revisited theories about privilege, cancer, and women's identity that had deep roots in American cancer awareness.

A second puzzle was how to explain high rates of cervical cancer among Vietnamese-American women alongside very low rates among Japanese-American women. Such disparities within the "Asian" population underlined the limits of American racial categories. As one commentator noted, Asians were the "fastest growing minority . . . and one of the most diverse and poorly understood minority groups" in the country; however, Koreans, Indians, Southeast Asians, Japanese, and other distinct groups were "often lumped together in health data," with disparities among them overlooked.

Photo by Leigh Vogel/ Getty Images

A third mystery surrounded the rising incidence of prostate cancer and its particularly high mortality rate among African-American men. In March 2010, actor Louis Gossett Jr. (above), in Congressional testimony, linked awareness to the complexities of black men's sexual identity: "The examination of prostate cancer especially in places like Louisiana, Detroit . . . places of the macho African-American . . . turns him off . . . because you know what you have to do to examine the prostate. . . . [Digital rectal examination] really literally makes him put it aside, put it in the back of his head and forget about it. As a result more deaths happen because he doesn't want to go through the experience. This is what I get from emails and letters and faxes. . . . He doesn't want to hear about not being able to make love, wearing diapers, and incontinence. So he takes it, puts it in his back pocket and forgets about it . . . [and because of this] we lose an African-American or two every day to prostate cancer."

Scientists, physicians, and an aggressive diagnostics industry were tuned in to these cultural and gender developments, playing on the identity politics of the era and pushing new cancer tests like the PSA test "into the marketplace before there is a medical consensus on their value or how to use them," according to the *New York Times*.

CONCLUSION: THE COLOR OF CANCER

It took more than half a century from the birth of American cancer awareness in the 1920s to the 1970s for rhythm and blues singer Minnie Riperton to become a national spokeswoman for early diagnosis, prevention, and the courageous fight for survival. Riperton was emblematic of an awakening in health and racial consciousness, but her story had been foreshadowed by events as early as the 1920s, when African Americans began to move into urban spaces where cancer was more likely to be diagnosed. And even after Riperton's death, the politics of cancer and the color line continued to evolve. It would be still several more decades before an elderly African American named Sam Frost took the stage. Testifying about his own struggles and inner conflicts with the disease before the President's Cancer Panel in November 2000, Mr. Frost stood out against the long lineage of mostly white middle-class women who had embodied cancer awareness. His was a new cancer portrait for a new era—a prostate cancer survivor from a small town in South Carolina, who spoke of how a prostate-specific antigen (PSA) test (a new invention of the 1990s) became his initial vehicle to disease awareness. "In 1995," said Frost, "I had an elevated PSA of 4.0 and I was told to check every year . . . But I didn't. In '97, I had a PSA of 8.7, which is bad . . . I went to the doctor and [learned that] we've got to go through a biopsy . . . The doctor said, call me so you can get your results."[1]

After decades on the periphery of public discussion, men like Mr. Frost were ushered by the promises of the PSA test into this troubling zone of cancer awareness where conflicts were plentiful, knowledge was constantly changing, and fears and hopes mingled uneasily with unstable scientific claims. The reliability of the test that had shaped his cancer awareness was itself the topic of contentious debate. Treatments also were uncertain; sometimes, in fact, they were worse than the disease. "It was the after effects that will kill you," he told the audience about his prostate surgery. "You have to go to the bathroom [but] you can't urinate." "You go from being a healthy male with a virile sex drive to nothing." "Everything is fine but the sex . . . See, they don't tell you that. I was told everything would be working in six to eight weeks. And dummy me, I believed them." In an age of concern about black-white disparities in cancer mortality, Frost's profile speaks powerfully to the realities of racial vulnerability and pervasive skepticism about society's ability to fix those disparities.[2]

Cancer awareness, from its inception, had always mixed hope, faith, and belief in self-control with fear, inner torment, and profound uncertainty. In 2000, it was Sam Frost's turn to embody long-standing conflicts and contradictions within cancer awareness. "To be honest with you," he acknowledged to the sympathetic audience, "if [a man] knew beforehand that going to the doctor he would get a digital rectal exam, he's not going. But if you tell him, well, come in and I'll do a PSA; well, 'What's that?' 'Blood test.' He'll come."[3] He had faced many other challenges and gone through many shifts in his own thinking to get to the stage where he felt comfortable speaking to others: "See the average man does not know what the prostate is," he complained. "Let's be honest . . . you've got people dying out here every day from this disease that don't know." Initially, not even the PSA test could allay his anxiety. "Why are you going to call the doctor to tell you that you got cancer? I didn't call him. He had to find me." For many men, he said, the route to cancer awareness required traveling through many anxieties about their bodies. Echoing this characterization in his March 2010 testimony before Congress, actor Louis Gossett Jr. (who has just announced his own prostate cancer diagnosis) noted that the "macho African-American . . . doesn't want to hear about not being able to make love, wearing diapers, and incontinence," let alone digital rectal exams. "So he takes it [his anxiety], puts it in his back pocket and forgets about it."[4] In Sam Frost's own view, this was what made the PSA test an effective outreach tool. The yet unproven blood test became a vehicle to new personal awareness.[5] Once regarded as a hush-hush, even shameful death sentence targeting vulnerable "civilized" women, cancer had been transformed over the decades by new tests, by activist patients and survivors, by ever-expanding disease surveillance, and by changing political and personal awareness.

As the preceding chapters have shown, the discourse of public health carries powerful "hidden arguments" and cancer awareness, from its very origins early in the twentieth century, was a cultural battleground over how right thinking and right living could safeguard one's health, with race as a powerful subtext.[6] Early in the twentieth century, the principal concern of experts was why well-off, sophisticated white women were afflicted more often than others, and the experts tailored cancer awareness to speak to these women's inner anxieties. As historian Leslie Reagan eloquently stated, "public health educational materials do more than simply provide information. They are cultural products that participate in and produce cultural meanings as they name, describe, and depict disease."[7] Cancer invited a steady flow of conjecture about why women were more vulnerable than men, why white women were specially vulnerable, and other such curiosities. But population shifts, disease trends, and evolving political realities slowly moved men, African Americans, Asians, and other groups into contexts where cancer diagnosis and surveillance were more common. Although in the 1930s experts belabored the claim that "cancer of the breast is the penalty women pay for failing to bear and particularly to nurse children," by midcentury these stark claims were coming undone.[8] Internal cancers were more diagnosable, contributing to an increase in the detection of men's cancers and prompting wholesale revisions in theories of the gender and biological aspects of susceptibility. Theories of African-American immunity also faded. By the 1950s and 1960s, the face of cancer had become more diverse, cancer survivors were more vocal, and cancer awareness had become closely linked to political struggles of citizens against the establishment and of people on the margins seeking honesty, fairness, equal recognition—and medical attention. In her 1980 book *Illness as Metaphor*, for example, Susan Sontag insisted that experts themselves generated much noxious cancer ideology: "cancer patients are lied to, not just because the disease is (or is thought to be) a death sentence, but because it is felt to be obscene—in the original meaning of that word: ill-omened, abominable, repugnant to the senses."[9] In truth, the PSA test and Sam Frost were both latecomers to a drama that had been unfolding slowly over decades, reshaping popular and epidemiological consciousness about disease and difference.

It had taken many decades for the inner psychological struggles and conflicts of men like Sam Frost and Louis Gossett to matter in American cancer discourse. In the 1920s, when cancer awareness emerged as a new cultural ideal, the outreach efforts targeted a narrow demographic group. Cancer awareness followed two different trajectories, two distinct paths defined by the American color line. One pathway focused on communicating with vulnerable white women, using novels, magazines, film, mass media, and doctor-patient encounters to stress feminine vulnerabilities, the need to move beyond modesty, fear, disgust, and stigma, and the development of habits of self-surveillance. The other trajectory focused on black people and nonwhites not as individuals with complex human qualities but as undifferentiated social categories. These people were said to be increasingly susceptible to cancer because of their complicated encounters with "civilization." In writing about this other cancer challenge, authorities rarely if ever viewed these people as having emotional depth, intimate fears, or psychological dimensions. Over the many decades when cancer awareness took shape, the overwhelming tendency was to speak to the individual psychological attributes of "modern" white women while also expressing concern about the colored multitudes. This historical fact established a powerful legacy in epidemiological awareness and in American cancer communication. How cancer crossed the color line is, then, the story of how these portraits evolved. It was a line of color and psyche that Minnie Riperton had breached in the 1970s and that Mr. Frost and Mr. Gossett stood astride three decades later.

Why does it matter how cancer and race are personified on the public stage? Why is it important how cancer vulnerability has been portrayed? Sitting near Mr. Frost at the President's Cancer Panel was Harlem surgeon Harold Freeman, who had organized the forum and who saw the struggle for awareness as a political battle for health-care resources and equal access to care. For Freeman, Mr. Frost's testimony was another skirmish in this war. Freeman lamented that "we have a political system that responds to the public as I see it . . . the AIDS money was the highest per case, $34,000 per death, and it [funding] went down the line from breast to prostate to colon and lung [where there] was very little." The competition made "awareness" into a political enterprise. Besides, commented Wayne Tuckson, a colorectal surgeon from Louisville, Kentucky, patients had many other reasons to be skeptical: "If the patients *did* come to a screening program there was no guarantee these patients were going to get treated, and if they were, what was going to be the quality of the treatment?" The rhetoric of cancer awareness was filled with such contradictions—not only for Mr. Frost struggling with his postsurgical challenges, but also for doctors like Tuckson. "The point seems to be that our political system and the funding of healthcare and research seems to be driven by who can make the loudest protest, or the squeaky wheel," Harold Freeman concluded. "We don't have a great amount of advocacy for colon cancer, for example, or pancreatic cancer. So the question is, what is the political answer for this, if there is one." As it always had been, awareness was unevenly distributed, reflecting the divisions and disparities of society itself.[10]

Sharing the stage with Mr. Frost and Dr. Freeman was Dr. Gilbert Friedell, a cancer specialist from Lexington, Kentucky, who insisted that race was a distraction in the struggle for cancer awareness and equal opportunity in health care. For Friedell, the compelling factor in cancer disparities was not race or ethnicity per se, but rather the wealth-poverty divide. Among the rural, white Appalachian women he served, Friedell noted, "you'll notice that these are similar incidence figures [compared with black women nationwide] and they're different from the white population in general . . . The Appalachian population is rural, it's poor . . . and its problems with cancer, in many ways, are exactly the same as those of the minorities that we've been talking about." Friedell insisted that "if we're really going to make progress in this you have to compare different population, incidence, mortality and so forth with the lower 10 to 15 percent of the white population in terms of the economy." As he saw it, many of the Appalachian people he served faced the same challenges as people living in Harold Freeman's Harlem—commonalities obscured by a focus on race. Moreover, both men agreed that advocacy made a difference in awareness, funding, and survival. "The reason money isn't someplace is because there's no squeaky wheel."[11] For all the progress in battling this enigmatic disease, the story of who lived and who died continued to be shaped by economic disparities, differences in access to diagnosis and therapy, and skewed public imagery of disease.

If race obscures the health challenge today, as Dr. Friedell argued, the preceding pages reveal that race has *always* been a confounding element in the study of American health disparities.[12] Race could make alternately a political characterization or a biological claim; it was often a legal and social reality for citizens determining where one could live or travel, or it could be a convenient administrative concept for government having little to do with biological difference. In the early and mid-twentieth century, physicians and scientists thought of "race" not as biology alone, but as culture, heritage, biology, and custom (collapsed into the rubrics of civilization and primitivism). At midcentury and later, other authorities regarded "race" as biologically suspect, and as more of a proxy for class and socioeconomic differences. Moreover, epidemiological constructions like "nonwhite" introduced administrative conveniences of race, lumping many groups into one. Racial categories in the U.S. Census shifted over time, with early terminology defined by the categorizers and more recent categories reflecting the political identities of those being categorized. As the story of cancer and the color line clearly shows, it is impossible to reconcile the Census's meanings of race with the biologist's, the geneticist's, and the political activist's. "Race . . . may be only a cloak for our ignorance," wrote Maurice Fishberg presciently in his 1911 study, *The Jews: A Study of Race and Environment.*[13] Indeed, looking at the next hundred years one is struck by the constantly changing meanings, connotations, and categories of "race" within cancer epidemiology—shifts that echoed the disjointed complexity and large sweep of American racial discourse.

The story of cancer and the color line therefore becomes the story of cancer's transformation *and* of racialization—by which I mean, the processes by which scientists used the disease to create narratives of difference. Many of the differences imagined in one era would not stand the test of time. Yet in each era, these views were regarded as authoritative and influential. Scientific, medical, biological, and epidemiological theories of disease and identity shaped public views, informed public policy, and determined how health care resources were distributed. Early on, for example, racialized images of white womanhood and vulnerability, tales of black primitives advancing toward civilization, and concerns about racial competition shaped the epidemiological imagination. These detailed and seemingly well-informed theories of disease and difference proved to be notoriously unstable. They would be refined in later eras as new evidence came in, or rejected when new diagnostic practices brought to light fresh data on cancer trends. They would also be altered, as we have seen, by the restive demographic and political currents. Sometimes, however, old anxieties about race and cancer would return in a later era; for example, the early twentieth-century notion of cancer as a disease of civilization was recycled in recent years to speak to the observations about, for example, immigration, modernization, and rising breast cancer rates among Asian-American women. Some racial infatuations—for example the notion of the special vulnerability of white women—could stand the test of time. Other obsessions about black racial biology could be completely inverted, so that early twentieth-century notions of black "immunity" were replaced by equally flawed early twenty-first-century theories of prostate specific antigen, black biological vulnerability, and prostate cancer. These race beliefs can only be fully understood when we see them as by-products of each era's broader politics of difference.

Today's experts who research and write and speak about health and difference (particularly those championing genetic and biological theories of health difference) would do well to place themselves along this complicated continuum of epidemiological thought. They need not go far back in time to learn the lessons of the complexities of race—these complexities are all around us. They could learn from Venus Gines, for example, another presenter at the President's Cancer Panel in 2000, who spoke after Sam Frost. A project coordinator of Latin Cancer Awareness in Georgia, she took subtle aim at prevailing racial beliefs, explaining that "a lot of the Latino activists feel that when you say Hispanic you're talking about a statistical category."[14] While it is obvious that American Hispanics and "Latinos" are clearly not one singular group (hailing from such diverse locales as Spain, South America, Central America, or Cuba) and that whites, too, have never been a homogeneous population group, they are both commonly classified as such in health studies. As we have seen, this logic of race and cancer has little to do with biology and much to do with the social and political meanings of race, as well as with epidemiological conveniences and popular beliefs. Recall, for example, how the earnest pathologist Paul Steiner, in his expansive 1954 study of cancer, race, and geography, could defer his definition of race to the fact that "the newsboy on the corner has no difficulty in most instances in distinguishing between the three main racial stocks here studied." In the end, because of the many uncertainties surrounding racial awareness, precisely how cancer crossed the color line cannot be pinpointed. There is no particular date and event marking the transformation but only a series of lurching shifts in disease, demographics, and the politics of diagnosis, surveillance, racial categorization, and perception.

The prominence of particular individuals in cancer consciousness helps us to mark these shifts—from Jane Addams to Mary Scott and Babe Zaharias, from Ollie Weaver to Greedy Reed to Max Reddick, and from Minnie Riperton to Sam Frost and onward to others yet to be named. However, their place in cancer's racial transformation cannot be fully understood without also appreciating the long history of expert attention to whites and the prominence of whiteness as a political and epidemiological focus. White cancer trends have been a source of enduring fascination against which nonwhite and minority experiences have been contrasted and assessed. Yet in line with Dr. Friedell's observations, there has been little attention to the complexity of this diverse demographic group or to the ways that white health is analyzed. "White" is regarded as one homogeneous and unchanging point of reference rather than as a category in constant flux. The twentieth century began with interest in a *white* population that was heavily Anglo-American, with other groups such as Irish, Jews, or Mexicans on the margins of whiteness. In time, the marginal ethnicities were slowly brought into the fold; and in recent decades, there has been a bifurcated reclassification of Latino Americans (with some labeled "white" and others not), even as Latinos have grown as a separate yet internally diverse population. Although the category *nonwhite* fell out of epidemiological vogue several decades ago, *white* has persisted, sometimes drawing "other" groups into the fold and variously serving as a specious biological category in health studies, a strong marker of social difference, an administrative concept, and a potent political force. Understanding and applying these complexities of "color" and "race" remains a critical challenge in health scholarship, public policy, and society.

No one concerned with group differences and social inequality can do without social categories of identity; they offer outlines (albeit impersonal ones) of the nation's divisions. The point here is not to do away with categories of difference, but rather to distinguish more carefully among the many meanings of race. Thus, a so-called race-blind approach to studying health differences would be a failure, since it would only replicate the myopia, blinders, and the unequal representation that has long plagued cancer awareness. In other words, the collecting of data using racial or ethnic categories remains essential for identifying health inequalities. At the same time, though, we need to recognize that while racial analysis can tell us that differences exist across so-called racial groups, they don't explain *why* those differences exist; nor can those social differences be attributed to biological notions of race. As the previous pages show, such population categories are not timeless, and must be used with greater care—particularly by health experts who do the job of interpreting disease in relationship to race. Those who have claimed that racial categories are proxies for biological or genetic differences are proven to have erred many times in history. There is no need to repeat these mistakes of the past, for racial categories are best understood as historically evolving surrogates standing in for, and conflating, social differences, cultural practices, biological variations, and political categorizations.

The last one hundred years can be read as a guide to the ever-changing complexity of race—a biological, epidemiological, political, social, and ideological concept. The last hundred years can also be read as a historical warning, teaching us to avoid the easy allure of oversimplified narratives of biological difference and to expand the American racial vocabulary. Surely, the times call for subtlety in categorization. Neither race nor cancer will sit still as Americans grapple with health challenges in years to come.

In the administrative flux of race, the 2000 U.S. Census let respondents check more than one identity category, and the bureau warned that "data on race from Census 2000 are not directly comparable with those from the 1990 census and previous censuses due, in large part, to giving respondents the option."[15] In 2010, the census added a historical twist—returning the outmoded term "Negro" to the form alongside "Black and African-American" in an effort to accommodate older African Americans who still identified with a racial term others saw as a legacy of Jim Crow.[16] In the biology of race, the front shifted as genetics experts boldly argued that genomic similarities (rather than phenotypic appearance per se) could be used to confirm ideas of race biology difference, or to refine or refute them. Genetic analysis, such experts argued, could even lead to new population classifications and to drugs tailored for effectiveness in those groups and genetic "races."[17] These claims are (to a large degree) repackaged ideas from the past, which, as social scientists Barbara Koenig, Sandra Soo-Jin Lee, and Sarah Richardson have noted, are also driven by gene-based businesses that have a "tremendous financial incentive to package 'race' as a genetically underwritten commodity."[18] As to the demographics of race, here too changes are afoot. The rising prevalence of biracial and multiracial families (most prominently embodied by Barack Obama, whose mother was a white Kansan and father a native Kenyan) also threatens to undo old racial formulations.[19] Looking ahead at birth trends in 2009, the Census Bureau predicted the loss of an American white majority: "white children would become a minority in 2023 and the overall white population would follow in 2042."[20] Not surprisingly, the ethnic complexity of this "white" population remains unspecified. In decades to come, we must think carefully about the promise, limitations, and extraordinary power of these categories to both locate and obscure the realities of health and difference in America. This task is made easier, one hopes, by taking the long view of how cancer crossed the color line.

NOTES

Introduction

1. John Rockwell, "Minnie Riperton, 31; Soul Singer Lectured Nationally on Cancer," *New York Times* (July 13, 1979), A14; Jack Slater, "The Terrible Rise of Cancer Among Blacks," *Ebony* (November 1979), 132.

2. Dennis Hunt, "Riperton: 'I'm Happy to Be Alive,'" *Los Angeles Times* (April 4, 1977).

3. Ulrich Henschke, LaSalle Leffall Jr., Claudia Mason, Andreas Reinhold, Roy Schneider, and Jack White, "Alarming Increase of the Cancer Mortality in the U.S. Black Population (1950–1967)," *Cancer* 31 (April 1973): 763–68, 767. "Singer Honored," *Los Angeles Sentinel* (April 21, 1977), A4.

4. John Rockwell, "Minnie Riperton, 31 . . . ," A14; "Minnie Riperton, 31; Sang, Wrote 'Loving You,'" *Washington Post* (July 13, 1979), D7.

5. See American Cancer Society television commercial featuring Riperton: www.youtube.com/watch?v=p8GSd957Zpw. Last accessed November 2008.

6. Jennings Parrott, "Newsmakers—Rickover Can't See Admirals for Stars," *Los Angeles Times* (April 5, 1977), 2; "Carter Gives Cancer's Courage Award to Black Entertainer Riperton," *Atlanta Daily World* (April 12, 1977), 1.

7. Jack Slater, "The Terrible Rise . . ." 131.

8. Dennis Hunt, "Minnie Riperton: A Heroic Saga," *Los Angeles Times* (July 22, 1979), L74.

9. "Minnie Riperton, 31; Sang, Wrote 'Loving You,'" D7; "Singer Minnie Riperton Dies," *Chicago Tribune* (July 13, 1979), B7; Michael Seiler, "Minnie Riperton Loses Struggle Against Cancer," *Los Angeles Times* (July 13, 1979), SD–A16.

10. "A Month-Long Tribute to Singer Minnie Riperton," *Los Angeles Times* (July 16, 1980), G3; "A Run for Life: 2nd Annual Minnie Riperton Cancer Action Run Scheduled Next Weekend," *Los Angeles Times* (November 4, 1984), SE6.

11. "Two Courageous Women," *Chicago Tribune* (October 21, 1974), A2.

12. W. E. B. Du Bois, *The Souls of Black Folk* (Chicago: A. C. McClurg and Co., 1903)

13. Elida Evans, *A Psychological Study of Cancer* (New York: Dodd, Mead, 1926), 70.

14. Nikolas Rose, *The Politics of Life Itself: Biomedicine, Power and Subjectivity in the Twenty-First Century* (Princeton, NJ: Princeton University Press, 2007), 26.

15. The book, then, is an excursion into the "archeology of medical [and epidemiological] perception," to modify Foucault's language, a study of the history and cultural politics of statistics. Michel Foucault, *The Birth of the Clinic: An Archeology of Medical Perception* (New York: Vintage Books, 1994), 24.

16. The literature on the history of breast cancer has dominated cancer scholarship, reflecting the growth of women's studies, women's history, and women's health as fields of scientific and social investigation and as topics of contemporary political importance. Barron Lerner, *The Breast Cancer Wars: Hope, Fear, and the Pursuit of a Cure in Twentieth-Century America* (New York: Oxford University Press, 2001); Robert Aronowitz, *Unnatural History: Breast Cancer and American Society* (New York: Cambridge University Press, 2007); Barbara Clow, *Negotiating Disease: Power and Cancer, 1900–1950* (Montreal: McGill-Queen's University Press, 2001); Kristen Gardner, *Early Detection: Women, Cancer, and Awareness Campaigns in the Twentieth-Century United States* (Chapel Hill: University of North Carolina Press, 2006); James Patterson, *The Dread Disease: Cancer and Modern American Culture* (Cambridge, MA: Harvard University Press, 1987); Ellen Leopold, *A Darker Ribbon: Breast Cancer, Women, and Their Doctors in the Twentieth Century* (Boston: Beacon Press, 1999). One exploration of the role of race in the history of cancer, set in Nazi-era Germany, is Robert Proctor, *The Nazi War on Cancer* (Princeton, NJ: Princeton University Press, 1999). See also the recent collection edited by David Cantor, "Special Issue: Cancer in the Twentieth Century," *Bulletin of the History of Medicine* 81 (Spring 2007).

17. Some readers, taking note of this book's focus on race, ethnicity, and gender, may see the book as a study of "intersectionality," a common term these days that refers to how race intersects with class and gender in a variety of social contexts and problems. Kimberlé W. Crenshaw, "Mapping the Margins: Intersectionality, Identity Politics, and Violence Against Women of Color," *Stanford University Law Review* 43, no. 6 (1991): 1241–99. Yet the goal here is not to promote a particular theory or approach to the study of the disease, health, or the past. Rather, it is to highlight the historical roots of current beliefs, and to examine the social and political processes that guide our beliefs about difference in health and in American society.

18. Preston Valien, "General Demographic Characteristics of the Negro Population in the United States," *Journal of Negro Education* 32 (Autumn 1963): 329–36, 329.

19. www.censusscope.org/aboutCensus2000.html.

20. On the uncertainties surrounding epidemiology, see Gerald Grob, *The Deadly Truth: A History of Disease in America* (Cambridge, MA: Harvard University Press, 2003).

21. J. Howard Beard, "The Avoidable Loss of Life," *Scientific Monthly* 2 (February 1916): 105–17, quote on 113.

22. Joseph William Schereschewsky, "The Increase in Cancer Mortality," *American Journal of Public Health* 16 (May 1926): 475–77, 476.

23. Herbert L. Dunn, "The Evaluation of the Effect Upon Mortality Statistics of the Selection of the Primary Cause of Death," *Journal of the American Statistical Association* 31 (March 1936): 113–23, quote on 114; Walter F. Willcox, "On the Alleged Increase of Cancer: [Part 1]," *Publications of the American Statistical Association* 15 (September 1917): 701–49, quote on 737. On the growth of cancer registries, see Amy Fairchild, Ronald Bayer, and James Colgrove, *Searching Eyes: Privacy, the State, and Disease Surveillance in America* (Berkeley: University of California Press, 2007), 113.

24. There is "little doubt that cancer is more easily diagnosed, because more accessible, in females," one physician wrote in 1915. William Seaman Bainbridge, author of *The Cancer Problem* (1914), quoted in "Is the Increase in Cancer Real or Only Apparent?" *Current Opinion*, August 1915, 110. Some forty years later, another author would ask in *Reader's Digest*, "Does the fact of being a woman increase the chances of developing cancer?" Yes came the answer, "more cancer is reported in women than among men . . . but because the disease strikes women in external or accessible organs, it can be detected earlier than in men." "Cancer and the Woman's Sex," *Reader's Digest* (September 1955).

25. John H. Schaefer, M.D., Assistant Medical Director, State of California, Department of Employment, to Alton Ochsner, M.D., May 5, 1955, Box 21, Folder 5, Alton Ochsner Papers, Williams Research Center, Historic New Orleans Collection.

26. William M. Rich, "Some Cancer Statistics," OBGY.NET, www.obgyn.net/women/women.asp?page=/women/articles/rich/stats.

27. Barney G. Glaser and Anselm L. Strauss, "Awareness Contexts and Social Interaction," *American Sociological Review* 29 (October 1964): 670.

28. On racial formations, see Michael Omi and Howard Winant, *Racial Formation in the United States: From the 1960s to the 1980s* (New York: Routledge, 1986).

29. As ethicist James Childress writes, "efforts to rescue identified individuals have symbolic value. They are gestures not merely tasks." The classic distinction comes from the work of economist Thomas Schelling. See James Childress, *Practical Reasoning in Bioethics* (Bloomington: Indiana University Press, 1997), 23.

30. Willy Meyer, *Cancer: Its Origins, Its Development, and Its Self-Perpetuation* (New York: Paul Hoeber, 1931).

31. J. Ellis Barker, "Cancer and the Black Man," *Fortnightly Review* 117 (January/June, 1925): 381–93.

32. And "the menace of a common enemy and the inspiration of fighting it together may have a sorely needed and deeply significant religious and moral force." "Cancer Army," *Time* (March 27, 1937), 49–56.

33. "The Battle Against Cancer," *American Mercury* (1945).

34. Emerson Day, "Cancer and a Woman's Sex," *Reader's Digest* 67 (September 1955), 88–89.

35. It was impossible "to determine how large a part of the increase in cancer of the inaccessible organs is due to the improvement in diagnostic methods which has taken place in the last 20 years," wrote Mary Gover in 1937. Mary Gover, "Trend of Mortality among Southern Negroes since 1920," *Journal of Negro Education* 6 (July 1937): 276–288, quote on 285.

36. Sigismund Peller, *Cancer in Man* (New York: International Universities Press, 1952), 226–27.

37. Charles Cameron, *The Truth About Cancer* (Englewood Cliffs, NJ: Prentice Hall, 1956), 29.

38. "New Appointment," *New York Amsterdam News* (January 21, 1956), 8.

39. "Cancer in Negroes," *Newsweek* (May 29, 1972), 47.

40. See for example, Lisa Cartwright, "Community and the Public Body in Breast Cancer Media Activism," *Cultural Studies* 12 (2) 1998: 117–38.

Chapter 1

1. Louis Dublin, "The Chance of Death from Cancer," in *Cancer Control: Report of an International Symposium Held under the Auspices of the American Society for the Control of Cancer* (New York: Surgical Publishing Co., 1927), 280.

2. "Jane Addams Ill in Tokio," *New York Times* (June 27, 1923), 19; "Jane Addams to Be Operated on Today," *Washington Post* (June 27, 1923), 1.

3. "Letter, June 26, 1923, to Addams's nephew Stanley Linn." University of Illinois at Chicago, Jane Addams Memorial Collection, Stanley Linn Family Papers (Accessed at Alexander Library, Rutgers University). Reel 15, Ind: 1066.

4. "My Dear Esther, letter, June 26, 1923," Jane Addams Collection, Stanley Linn Family Papers, Reel 15, Ind: 1050.

5. For example, the tragic story of Princess Anastasia (the so-called Dollar Princess, an American heiress widowed after the death of the magnificently wealthy William Leeds, the "Tin-Plate King") received brief coverage in the newspapers of the day. She "spent a considerable part of her immense fortune on renowned physicians of a dozen nationalities, seeking a cure," but "the strain of a busy social season in Paris and London was too much for her . . . the disease reasserted itself." "Princess Anastasia Is Dead of Cancer," *New York Times*, August 30, 1923, 1.

6. F. C. Wood, "Must Women Die of Cancer?" *The Woman Citizen* (1927).

7. American Society for the Control of Cancer, *Essential Facts about Cancer: A Handbook for the Medical Professional* (New York: American Society for the Control of Cancer, 1924), 11.

8. "Cancer Less Common Among Women with Large Families," *Science News Letter* (January 14, 1939), 23.

9. "Since my operation I have been very well," wrote one woman to Cabot in 1913. "I seem to be in a healthful state [but] my womb falls down. . . . Do you think I am unwise in not doing something for these troubles? If so what shall I do?" Letter to Richard Cabot, September 26, 1913, "Case #144, Cancer of the Breast, Mrs. Packard, 50 years old," Richard C. Cabot Papers, Harvard University Archives, Pusey Library, Cambridge, MA, Box 5 of 8, vol. 25 (April 20, 1913 to September 29, 1913).

10. Louis I. Dublin, "A Statistical Analysis of Mortality from Cancer," in Henry Baldwin Ward, ed., *Some Fundamental Aspects of the Cancer Problem* (New York: Science Press, 1937), 237–41, quote on 239.

11. Another expert noted, "no organ is free from attack . . . though the organs most commonly affected are the breasts in women who have not borne children and the organs of reproduction in those who have borne children." P. Brooke Bland, "Cancer in Women," *Hygeia* (May 1930), 460.

12. J. H. J. Upham, "The Woman of Middle Age and Some of Her Health Problems," *Hygeia* 5 (4) (April 1927), 187–89; J. B. Carnett, "Cancer of the Breast," *Hygeia* (March 1930).

13. "You Can Tell the Doctor," *Hygeia* (September 1942).

14. Leila Charlton Knox, "Cancer: A Woman's Problem," *Hygeia* 5 (June 1927), 293–95, 294.

15. "Cancer Contest Winner," *Hygeia* (January 1941). As David Riesman warned in *Hygeia*, "many persons who bleed from the rectum attribute this to bleeding hemorrhoids or piles, and in nineteen out of twenty cases that is the correct interpretation; but it may be a sign of an early growth in the rectum." Only a physician could tell the difference. David Riesman, "What You Should Know about Cancer," *Hygeia* (1935).

16. A recent study of mass print media from 1996 to 2001, for example, found that themes of maternity, femininity, and family roles figured prominently in the North American breast cancer literature. See Juanne Nancarrow Clarke, "A Comparison of Breast, Testicular, and Prostate Cancer in Mass Print Media (1996–2001)," *Social Science and Medicine* 59 (2004): 541–51.

17. C. C. Little, "The Social Significance of Cancer," in Henry Baldwin Ward, *Some Fundamental Aspects of the Cancer Problem* (New York: Science Press, 1937), 244.

18. Leila Charlton Knox, "Cancer: A Woman's Problem," 293–95. This message is discussed extensively in "'Do Not Delay': The War Against Time," Chapter 6 in Robert Aronowitz, *Unnatural History: Breast Cancer and American Society* (New York: Cambridge University Press, 2007).

19. Little, "Social Significance," 244.

20. Virginia Gardner, "Vanity, Modesty, and Cancer," *Hygeia* (April 1933), 300–302.

21. L. Dublin, Edwin Kopf, and George Van Buren, *Cancer Mortality: Among Insured Wage Earners and Their Families: The Experience of the Metropolitan Life Insurance Company Industrial Department, 1911–1922* (New York: Metropolitan Life Insurance Company, 1925), 3.

22. Herbert Snow, "The Great Cancer Problem," *The Nineteenth Century* (September 1920): 508–12, quote on 509.

23. On moral management, see, for example, Keith Wailoo, "Chlorosis Remembered: Disease and the Moral Management of American Women," in *Drawing Blood: Technology and Disease Identity in Twentieth-Century America* (Baltimore: Johns Hopkins University Press, 1997).

24. "The Control of Cancer," *American Journal of Public Health* (April 1925): 297–98.

25. Walter F. Willcox, "On the Alleged Increase of Cancer: [Part 1]," *Publications of the American Statistical Association* 15 (September 1917): 701–749, quote on 709. See chart on 713.

26. Many of the ideas and themes relating to women and cancer vulnerability built upon notions that had also been prominent in the nineteenth century regarding upper-class women's special delicacy and vulnerability to disease. See Sheila Rothman, *Living in the Shadow of Death: Tuberculosis and the Social Experience of Illness in American Society* (New York: Basic Books, 1994); Regina Markell Morantz-Sanchez, *Sympathy and Science: Women Physicians in American Medicine* (New York: Oxford University Press, 1985); Judith Walzer Leavitt, *Brought to Bed: Childbearing in America, 1750–1950* (New York: Oxford University Press, 1986); and Charles Rosenberg and Carroll Smith-Rosenberg, "The Female Animal: Medical and Biological Views of Women and Her Role in Nineteenth-Century America," *Journal of American History* 60 (September 1973): 332–56. A particularly important study of the intersections of disease and gender discourse is Nancy Tomes, *The Gospel of Germs: Men, Women, and the Microbe in American Life* (Cambridge, MA: Harvard University Press, 1998).

27. Irving Fisher, "Some Impending National Problems," *Journal of Political Economy* 24 (July 1916): 694–712, quote on 703.

28. William Woglom, "Cancer the Scourge of God," *Atlantic Monthly* 141 (June 1928), 807–12.

29. American Society for the Control of Cancer, *Essential Facts About Cancer: A Handbook for the Medical Professional* (New York: American Society for the Control of Cancer, 1924), 11.

30. "Science News: Breast Cancer in Relation to Childbearing and Nursing," *Science* 80 (September 1934): 8–9.

31. Upham, "The Woman of Middle Age," 187–89.

32. Hearing the word "benign," Addams's companion called it "The best news! The tumor was benign and while they insisted on the radical operation and there are hard days ahead—hard weeks ahead, I fear—nothing matters for it is not cancer." Letter, June 27, 1923, to Stanley Linn, Jane Addams Collection, Stanley Linn Family Papers, Reel 15. Ind: 1067.

33. Leila Charlton Knox, "Cancer: A Woman's Problem," *Hygeia* 5 (June 1927) 293–95, 294.

34. J. C. Barnett, "Cancer of the Breast," *Hygeia* (March 1930), 261. More often, the deadlier problem was undetected disease, for "cancer, particularly when it affects

the internal organs, is sometimes extraordinarily difficult to diagnose," lamented William Woglom in *Hygeia*. "Errors are still being made, though the number of wrong diagnoses is much smaller than it was," he wrote. William Woglom, "Does Meat Cause Cancer?" *Hygeia* 1 (1): 23–24.

35. Barnett, "Cancer of the Breast," 261.

36. Anne A. Ferris, "The Nursing Care of Cancer Patients," *American Journal of Nursing* 30 (July 1930): 814–20, quote on 18.

37. I. S. Falk, "Fundamental Facts on the Costs of Medical Care," *Milbank Memorial Fund Quarterly Bulletin* 11 (April 1933): 130–53, quote on 139. When he wrote these words, Falk had only recently served as associate director in charge of research for the Committee on the Coast of Medical Care, a groundbreaking study. See *Medical Care for the American People: The Final Report of the Committee on the Costs of Medical Care* (Chicago: University of Chicago Press, 1932). See also I. S. Falk, C. Rufus Rorem, and Martha D. Ring, *The Cost of Medical Care: A Summary of Investigations on the Economic Aspects of the Prevention and Care of Illness* (Chicago: University of Chicago Press, 1933). See also Grace Abbott, "The Social Security Act and Relief," *University of Chicago Law Review* 4 (December 1936): 45–68, quote on 67, and Ray Lyman Wilbur, "The Costs of Medical Care," *Scientific Monthly* 39 (September 1934): 235–39, quote on 236.

38. Mabel C. Willard to Richard Cabot, January 14, 1912, Box 4 of 8, vol. 20 (June 27, 1911 to November 17, 1911), Cabot Papers.

39. Richard C. Cabot to Dr. H. L. Conner, April 15, 1912. "Case #56, Gastric Cancer?" Mrs. Charles H. Davis, 58 yrs. Box 4 or 8, volume 22 (March 2, 1912, to June 14, 1912), Cabot Papers.

40. On the ambiguities of cancer diagnosis in breast cancer, for example, see Robert Aronowitz, *Unnatural History: Breast Cancer and American Society* (New York: Cambridge University Press, 2007).

41. "She was taken ill in the night on Tuesday . . . the pain was way down in the groin on the left side . . . they got Dr. Curtis [and] he came downstairs to see me afterwards, and said that there was a mass there of some kind which would have to be taken away at once," wrote Addams's companion. Letter to Stanley Linn, May 25, 1935, Jane Addams Collection, Stanley Linn Family Papers, Death File, Reel 45. Ind: 1267–68.

42. "Jane Addams Dies in Her 75th Year," *New York Times* (May 22, 1935), 1.

43. Mr. A. M. Burt to Richard Cabot, May 24, 1913, "Case #43, Gastric Cancer, Mr. A. M. Burt, 70 yrs., May 24, 1913," Box 5 of 8, vol. 25 (April 20, 1913, to September 29, 1913), Cabot Papers.

44. Elida Evans, *A Psychological Study of Cancer* (New York: Dodd, Mead, 1926), 60.

45. On the relationship of right living and Anglo-American cultural ideals, see Charles E. Rosenberg, ed., *Right Living: An Anglo-American Tradition of Self-Help Medicine and Hygiene* (Baltimore: Johns Hopkins University Press, 2003).

46. Evans, *A Psychological Study of Cancer*, 11. "We know that the libido, or energy, of women is chiefly in the reproductive organs, for the maternal instinct of women is very strong and seldom satisfied," Evans wrote.

47. "Social Problems Have Proven Basis of Heredity," *New York Times* (January 12, 1913), SM 10.

48. Wendy Kline, *Building a Better Race: Gender, Sexuality, and Eugenics from the Turn of the Century to the Baby Boom* (Berkeley: University of California Press, 2005), 16–17.

49. "Says Tallest Humans Are Cancer's Victims—Swiss Specialist Tells British Conference That Nordic Race Leads Disease Sufferers," *New York Times* (July 21, 1928), 7.

50. Cited in Helen Kirchoff and R. H. Rigdon, "Frequency of Cancer in the White and Negro: A Study Based Upon Necropsies," *Southern Medical Journal* 49 (August 1955): 834. Other studies echoed these findings. See, for example, the table on p. 521 of William H. Guilfoy, "The Death-Rate of the City of New York as Affected by the Cosmopolitan Character of Its Population," *Publications of the American Statistical Association* 10 (December 1907): 515–22.

51. Louis I. Dublin, "The Mortality of Foreign Race Stocks," *Scientific Monthly* 14 (January 1922): 94–104. The statistics, in his view, told the story of race "stocks" and their cancer tendencies. For men, the Italian rate was 56.6 per 100,000 (over age 10), followed by native-born Americans (78.1), English (107.8), German (126.1), Irish (136.4), and Russian (mostly Jewish) at 141.1. The rates were all higher in women than men, with the stark exception of Russian Jews. For women, the Italian rate was 80.8, followed by Russian (Jewish) (123.7), native-born American (131.1), English (158.9), German (159.9), and Irish (171.7).

52. C. Jeff Miller, "The Prophylaxis of Cancer, with Special Reference to the Cervix Uteri," *New Orleans Medical and Surgical Journal* 81 (1928): 253–60, quote on 254–55.

53. Francis Carter Wood, "Must Women Die of Cancer?" *The Woman Citizen* (1927).

54. Riesman, "What You Should Know About Cancer."

55. Louis Wright, "Cancer as It Affects the Negro," *Opportunity* 6 (June 1928): 169–70, 187.

56. LeRoy Broun, "The Saving of Life in Cancer." *American Journal of Nursing* 25 (March 1925): 194–98, quote on 197.

57. "I'm Not Afraid of Cancer," *Hygeia* (February 1933).

58. Shields Warren, "Cancer—An Unsolved Problem," *Hygeia* 5 (November 1927), 571–74.

59. Gottfried Benn, "Husband and Wife Going Through a Cancer Ward," in *Gottfried Benn: Selected Poems*, edited by Friedrich Wilhelm Wodtke (Oxford: Oxford University Press, 1970), 51–52. "Undoubtedly," wrote one Benn scholar, "Benn works with hyperbole in these poems, and he does so intentionally. He is bitter." Edgar Lohner, "The Development of Gottfried Benn's Idea of Expression as Value," *German Quarterly* 26 (January 1953): 39–54, quote on 42.

60. LeRoy Broun, "Saving Life in Cancer Cases," *American Journal of Nursing* 25 (March 1925): 194–98, quote on 197.

61. William Preble to Richard Cabot, April 5, 1919, Cabot Papers, "Case #9, Bladder Cancer," Box 7 of 8, vol. 9 (February 12, 1919, to September 18, 1919). These concerns about the "offensive odors and unpleasant sights due to the sloughing of tissues and secondary infections," so frequent in the disease, continued to be a source of concern. Quote appears in Lala L. Handorf and Thyra E. Pedersen, "Nursing Care in Terminal Cancer," *American Journal of Nursing* 50 (October 1950): 643–46, quote on 644.

62. One example, however, was the death of former president Ulysses S. Grant, described by James Patterson in his book *The Dread Disease: Cancer and Modern American Culture* (Cambridge, MA: Harvard University Press, 1987).

63. Benn, "Husband and Wife," 51–52.

64. Woglom, "Cancer the Scourge of God." Quoting a Michigan physician in 1934, two authors in the *ASCC Bulletin* noted that "cancer entails a social stigma; thus physicians are prevailed upon to falsify death returns." Walter Willcox, "Statistics of Causes of Death," *ASCC Bulletin* (April 1934), 8–9; cited in James Patterson, *The Dread Disease: Cancer and Modern American Culture* (Cambridge, MA: Harvard University Press, 1987), 111. As J. H. J. Upham noted about breast cancer in 1927, "if there is such a taint in the family, these organs should be guarded as much as possible." Upham, "The Woman of Middle Age," 187–89.

65. Writing in the late 1930s, Louis Dublin noted "that the importance of cancer as a cause of death has been, and still is, understated cannot be denied." Dublin and Lotka, *Twenty-Five Years of Health Progress* (New York: Metropolitan Life Insurance Company, 1937), 115.

66. "Whatever We Do," *New York Times* (December 4, 1927), BR6.

67. "Expatriates: The Gilded Caravan," *New York Times* (October 16, 1927), BR9; Henry Longan Stuart, "White Man's Burden in a First Novel: Black Valley," *New York Times* (January 10, 1926), BR9.

68. Mary Hastings Bradley, *Pattern of Three* (New York: D. Appleton-Century, 1937), 8. Subsequent quotes in this paragraph on 11, 258–59.

69. Bradley, *Pattern of Three*, 261, 272.

70. Case #33, Cancer of the Breast, Mrs. James Graham, 42 years old, March 23, 1912, Box 4 of 8, vol. 22 (March 2, 1912, to June 14, 1912), Cabot Papers.

71. "The Truth About Cancer," *American Journal of Public Health* 15 (1925): 338–39, quote on 338.

72. James Linn to Stanley Linn, 1935 (date unspecified), Jane Addams Collection, Stanley Linn Family Papers, VII, Death File: A. Family correspondence (Reel 45, Indicator: 1252).

73. Evans, *A Psychological Study of Cancer*, 70.

74. Edith Wharton, "Diagnosis," in R.W. B. Lewis, ed., *The Collected Short Stories of Edith Wharton* (New York: Charles Scribner's Sons, 1968), vol. 2, 726.

75. Evans, *A Psychological Study of Cancer*, 40, 14.

76. "Maryland: Causes of Death," *Journal of the American Medical Association* 87 (October 23, 1926): 1399.

77. C. C. Little, "The Social Significance of Cancer," in Henry Baldwin Ward, *Some Fundamental Aspects of the Cancer Problem* (New York: Science Press, 1937), 244. H. J. Deehman, "The Mortality from Cancer among People of Different Races," in *Cancer Control* (Chicago: Surgical Publishing Co. of Chicago, 1927), 250.

78. "Cancer in Women," *Newsweek* 16 (July 15, 1940), 40.

79. U.S. Census Bureau, 1930 statistics. The Hispanic data was crudely measured in 1940. www.census.gov/population/documentation/twps0056/tab01.pdf. By 1930, the percentage of African Americans living in the South had dropped from 85 percent in 1920 to 79 percent, and the northward rural-to-urban movement of blacks continued for decades, reshaping Americans' awareness of the social and health condition of black people. In 1940, the southern percentage was 77 percent; in 1950, it was 68 percent; and in 1960, the percentage had dropped to 60 percent. By the early 1970s, the percentage had settled near 50 percent.

80. Kristen Gardner, *Early Detection: Women, Cancer, and Awareness Campaigns in the Twentieth-Century United States* (Chapel Hill: University of North Carolina Press, 2006), 14.

81. Elizabeth Etheridge, *The Butterfly Caste: A Social History of Pellagra in the South* (Westport, CT: Greenwood, 1972); John Ettling, *The Germ of Laziness: Rockefeller Philanthropy and Public Health in the New South* (Cambridge, MA: Harvard University Press, 1981); Edward Beardsley, *History of Neglect: Health Care for Blacks and Mill Workers in the Twentieth-Century South* (Knoxville: University of Tennessee Press, 1987).

82. Louis Dublin, *Mortality Statistics of Insured Wage-Earners and Their Families* (New York: Metropolitan Life Insurance Company, 1919), 149. There were even those few, like England's E. F. Bashford, who insisted that "cancer is not limited to white men" and that "carcinoma is [indeed] found in savage races." But Bashford's views were in the distinct minority, although his division of the world into civilized and savages was quite commonplace. E. F. Bashford cited in "What Research in Cancer Shows," *New York Times* (November 7, 1909), C7.

83. Walter R. Chivers, "Northward Migration and the Health of Negroes," *Journal of Negro Education* 8 (January 1939): 34–43, quote on 43.

84. Some cancers, said Samuel Hopkins Adams writing in the *Ladies' Home Journal* in 1913, were unavoidable, but in most of them, stupidity, ignorance, and fear in women was responsible. Samuel Hopkins Adams, "What Can We Do About Cancer?" *Ladies' Home Journal* (May 1913), 22.

85. Gardner, "Vanity, Modesty, and Cancer."

86. Commenting on these trends in 1931, a female journalist could note that "only in the last generation or two has there been any intelligent cooperation between women and the medical profession in the effort to reduce the annual sacrifice to the disease." Gardner, "Vanity, Modesty, and Cancer."

87. C. Jeff Miller, "Special Problems of the Colored Woman," *Southern Medical Journal* 25 (1932): 734.

88. C. Jeff Miller, "The Prophylaxis of Cancer, with Special Reference to the Cervix Uteri," *New Orleans Medical and Surgical Journal* 81 (1928): 253–60, quote on 253.

89. Writing in 1928, one observer noted that some 16 million people lived outside the registration states (with 101 million covered by the registration data). The non-registration states were Colorado, Georgia, Louisiana, Nevada, New Mexico, Oklahoma, South Carolina, South Dakota, and Texas. "About one-third of our Negro population (35.2 percent) is found in these states," he noted. "This Negro population . . . is a rural population and has a fairly large rate of increase." Warren S. Thompson, "Population," *American Journal of Sociology* 34 (July 1928): 3–15, quote on 7–8. See also Herbert S. Klein, *A Population History of the United States* (New York: Cambridge University Press, 2004), 153–54.

Chapter 2

1. John Harvey Kellogg, *The Monster Malady: Cancer and the Coming Plague of the Race* (Battle Creek, MI: Good Health Publishing Co., 1913), 64.

2. J. Ellis Barker, "Cancer and the Black Man," *Fortnightly Review* 117 (Jan.–June, 1925), 392.

3. Willy Meyer, *Cancer: Its Origins, Its Development, and Its Self-Perpetuation* (New York: Paul Hoeber, 1931), 236.

4. Elida Evans, *A Psychological Study of Cancer* (New York: Dodd, Mead, 1926), 70.

5. "Can't Blame Cancer on Civilization," *Science News Letter* 32 (November 13, 1927): 313.

6. Ira De A. Reid, "Mirrors of Harlem-Investigations and Problems of America's Largest Colored Community," *Social Forces* 5 (June 1927): 628–34, quote on 632.

7. H. L. Mencken, "The Johns Hopkins Hospital. XX. Conclusion," *Baltimore Sun* (July 1937), clipping in Alan Mason Chesney Papers, Folder: Johns Hopkins Hospital, Mencken, H. L., Articles on JHH, 1935–1937.

8. J. W. Schereschewksy, "The Increase in Cancer Mortality," *American Journal of Public Health* 16 (May 1926): 475–77.

9. By the late 1930s, Carl Weller of the University of Michigan would insist that "if cancer is a disease of civilized life, it is . . . because civilized life enabled the average man to live much longer than a primitive way of life does . . . Not many Haitians or other primitive peoples live to the age at which cancer appears. When they do, they evidently are just as apt to have cancer as civilized peoples." Carl Weller quoted in "Can't Blame Cancer on Civilization," 313.

10. Jacques W. Redway, "Spread of Cancer from Geographer's Standpoint," *Washington Post* (June 29, 1924), SM2.

11. "Civilized Man's Diet as the Cause of His Ills," *New York Times* (January 29, 1929), 135.

12. The 1937 statistics showed a similarly large gap, with the white female mortality rate at 89.9 per 100,000, the white male rate at 85.8, the colored female rate at 94.9, and the black male rate at 58.3. Louis Dublin and Alfred Lotka, *Twenty-Five Years of Health Progress* (New York: Metropolitan Life Insurance Company, 1937), 169.

13. Redway, "Spread of Cancer," SM2.

14. Kellogg, *Monster Malady*, 66.

15. Louis Dublin, *Mortality Statistics of Insured Wage-Earners and Their Families* (New York: Metropolitan Life Insurance Company, 1919), 150.

16. Kellogg, *Monster Malady*, 66.

17. Louis Wright, "Cancer As It Affects the Negro," *Opportunity* 6 (June 1928); 169–170, 187.

18. James M. Reinhardt, "The Negro: Is He a Biological Inferior?" *American Journal of Sociology* 33 (September 1927): 248–61, quote on 255.

19. Louis Dublin, "The Health of the Negro," *Annals of the American Academy of Political and Social Science* 140 (November, 1928): 77–85. Later revised and updated in Louis Dublin, "The Problem of Negro Health as Revealed by Vital Statistics," *Journal of Negro Education* 6 (July 1937): 268–75.

20. Walter F. Willcox, "On the Alleged Increase of Cancer: [Part 1]," *Publications of the American Statistical Association* 15 (September 1917): 744–46.

21. Willcox, "On the Alleged Increase," 744–46.

22. Dublin, "The Health of the Negro," 1.

23. James Marquis, *The Metropolitan Life: A Study of Business Growth* (New York: Viking, 1947), 338.

24. Frederick Hoffman, "Race Traits and Tendencies of the American Negro," *Publications of the American Economics Association* 11 (August 1896), 1–329.

25. Marquis vigorously defended the practice: "There is no more discrimination against colored people than against workers in hazardous employments. Time and time again, it has been demonstrated that the mortality of colored lives is sizably greater than that of whites." Marquis, *Metropolitan Life*, 338.

26. One 1920 report in Georgia found that "forty-three percent of all the deaths from cancer last year were white females. There were 23.4 percent negro females and only 5.1 percent negro males." "Death Analysis Shows Dangers of Cancer," *Atlanta Constitution* (May 13, 1920), 5.

27. The story of Ollie and Lettie Weaver, first published in a collection called *Wide Fields* in 1926, reappeared in a later collection entitled *Salvation on a String*. Paul Green, "The Humble Ones," *Salvation on a String and Other Tales of the South* (New York: Harper, 1946), 61.

28. Ibid., 66–67. Men like Ollie rarely complained, Green commented in 1930 article; they had "developed . . . a dignity, a stoicism to evil and pain unknown to his white neighbor." Paul Green, "Some Notes on North Carolina," *English Journal* 19 (May 1930): 351–56, quote on 356.

29. Green, "Humble Ones," 71, 76.

30. Ivan Taylor, "Salvation on a String," *Journal of Negro Education* 16 (Spring 1947): 203–4, quote on 204.

31. "'Wide Fields,'" *New York Times*, 63. Hoffman et al., "Folklore in Literature," *Journal of American Folklore* (1957): 6.

32. See discussion of in chapter 4.

33. T. Lynn Smith, "The Redistribution of the Negro Population of the United States, 1910–1960," *Journal of Negro History* 51 (July 1966): 155–73, quote on 159.

34. U.S. Census Bureau, *The Social and Economic Status of the Black Population in the United States: An Historical Overview* (U.S. Department of Commerce, Bureau of the Census: U.S. Government Printing Office, 1979).

35. Grace Abbott, "The Social Security Act and Relief," *University of Chicago Law Review* 4 (December 1936): 45–68, quote on 67.

36. Dorn believed in "eschewing irresponsible speculation" in favor of real data. "Harold F. Dorn, 1906–1963," *Population Index* 29 (July 1963): 237–42, quote on 238. See also Harold Dorn, "The Effect of Rural-Urban Migration upon Death Rates," *Population* 1 (November 1934): 95–114; Harold Dorn, "Migration and the Growth of Cities," *Social Forces* 16 (March 1938): 328–37; Harold Dorn, "The Relative Amount of Ill-Health in Rural and Urban Communities," *Public Health Reports* 53 (July 15, 1938): 1181–95; Harold Dorn, "The Incidence of Cancer in Cook County, Illinois, 1937," *Public Health Reports* 55 (April 12, 1940): 628–50.

37. Edgar Sydenstricker, "Health in the New Deal," *Annals of the American Academy of Political and Social Science* 176 (November 1934): 131–37.

38. Abbott, "The Social Security Act," 67. See also Clark Tibbitts, "The Socio-Economic Background of Negro Health Status," *Journal of Negro Education* 6 (July 1937): 413–28.

39. George St. J. Perrott and Dorothy F. Holland, "Health as an Element in Social Security," *Annals of the American Academy of Political and Social Science* 202 (March 1939): 116–36 quote on 127.

40. Thomas Parran, "A General Introductory Statement of the Problems of the Health Status and Health Education of Negroes," *Journal of Negro Education* 6 (July 1937): 263–66, quote on 266. Perrott and Holland, "The Need for Adequate Data," 362.

41. Harold Dorn, "The Effect of Allocation of Non-Resident Deaths upon Official Mortality Statistics," *Journal of the American Statistical Association* 27 (December 1932); 401–12, quote on 401.

42. Samuel Jackson Holmes, *The Negro's Struggle for Survival: A Study of Human Ecology* (Berkeley: University of California Press, 1937), 205.

43. J. W. Schereschewsky, "Survey of the Facilities for Treatment of Cancer in Western, Southern and Eastern Georgia," Georgia Department of Archives and History, Atlanta, RG-SG-Series: 26–2–3, Box 5, Folder: Cancer Control, p. 1. Department of Public Health, Director's Subject Files. (hereafter, DPH-Georgia).

44. J. W. Schereschewsky, "Survey . . . Georgia," Box 5, p. 3, DPH-Georgia.

45. J. W. Schereschewsky, "Survey . . . Georgia," Box 5, p. 1, DPH-Georgia.

46. J. W. Schereschewsky, "Survey . . . Georgia," Box 5, p. 11, DPH-Georgia.

47. J. W. Schereschewsky, "Survey . . . Georgia," Box 5, p. 5, DPH-Georgia.

48. J. W. Schereschewsky, "Survey . . . Georgia," Box 5, p. 12, DPH-Georgia.

49. R. Mosteller, M.D., Director, Division of Cancer Control, to U.S. Congressman Carl Vinson, January 14, 1939, Box 12, Folder: Cancer Control, p. 1, DPH-Georgia.

50. "Georgia Club Women Join in Fight Against Cancer," *Atlanta Daily World* (March 25, 1938), 2.

51. "Report of the Division of Cancer Control, Georgia State Department of Health for the Year 1939," Box 11, Folder: Cancer Control, p. 1, DPH-Georgia.

52. "Harold F. Dorn, 1906–1963," *Population Index* 29 (July 1963): 237–42, quote on 238.

53. Amy Fairchild, Ronald Bayer, and James Colgrove, *Searching Eyes: Privacy, the State, and Disease Surveillance in America* (Berkeley: University of California Press, 2007), 123.

54. Sigismund Peller, *Cancer Research Since 1900* (New York: Philosophical Library, 1979), 108–9.

55. See, for example, Keith Wailoo, *Dying in the City of the Blues: Sickle Cell Anemia and the Politics of Race and Health* (Chapel Hill: University of North Carolina Press, 2001); Edward Beardsley, *A History of Neglect: Health Care for Blacks and Mill Workers in the Twentieth-Century South* (Knoxville: University of Tennessee Press, 1987).

56. Isidore Cohn, "Statistics," *Southern Surgeon* 10 (September 1941): 686–88, quote on 686.

57. Maurice Sorsby, *Cancer and Race: A Study of the Incidence of Cancer among Jews* (London: John Bale, Sons and Danielsson, 1931), v.

58. Ibid., 77.

59. Louis I. Dublin, "The Mortality of Foreign Race Stocks," *Scientific Monthly* 14 (January 1922): 94–104, quote on 104.

60. Sorsby, *Cancer and Race*, 1.

61. Ibid., 4.

62. Quotes in this paragraph are found in Sorsby, *Cancer and Race*, 40, 78, 66–67.

63. Mary Gover, *Cancer Mortality in the United States, III, Geographic Variation in Recorded Cancer Mortality for Detailed Sites, for an Average of the Years 1930–1932* (Washington, DC: U.S. Government Printing Office, 1940), 66.

64. Quotes in this paragraph are found in Sorsby, *Cancer and Race*, 66, 86–90.

65. Ibid., 86–90.

66. See, for instance, the comments of Rabbi Leo Franklin on the medical basis of Mosaic code. Rabbi Leo Franklin, "Orthodox Jewish Customs in Their Relation to the Nursing Profession," *American Journal of Nursing* 14 (October 1913): 11–18, quote on 13.

67. Sorsby, *Cancer and Race*, 89.

68. P. Weir and C. C. Little, "The Incidence of Uterine Cancer in Jews and Gentiles," *Journal of Heredity* 25 (1934): 277–80, quote on 280.

69. "Maurice Sorsby" [obituary], *British Medical Journal* 1 (April 23, 1949): 730.

70. S. J. Holmes, "The Increasing Growth-Rate of the Negro Population," *American Journal of Sociology* 42 (September 1936): 202–14, quote on 204. See also Samuel Jackson Holmes, *The Negro's Struggle for Survival: A Study in Human Ecology* (Berkeley: University of California Press, 1937), 105.

71. Holmes, *Negro's Struggle for Survival*, 105.

72. Ibid., 2.

73. Holmes, "Increasing Growth-Rate," 207.

74. S. J. Holmes, "The Differential Mortality from Cancer in the White and Colored Population," *American Journal of Cancer* 25 (October 1935): 358–76; S. J. Holmes, "The Principal Causes of Death Among Negroes: A General Comparative Statement," *Journal of Negro Education* 6 (July 1937): 289–302. Holmes's other works include *Studies in Evolution and Eugenics* (New York: Harcourt Brace, 1923); *The Eugenic Predicament* (New York: Harcourt Brace, 1933); and *Human Genetics and Its Social Impact* (New York: McGraw-Hill, 1936)

75. Holmes, "Principal Causes of Death . . . ," 298.

76. Holmes, "Differential Mortality from Cancer . . . ," 368–69. See also Holmes, *Negro's Struggle for Survival*, 105.

77. Holmes, "Differential Mortality from Cancer . . . ," 360, 368–69, 374.

78. Ibid., 361.

79. Despite the fact that "there was probably an undercount of Negroes . . . and there has been some controversy over its extent," Samual Jackson Holmes believed that the meaningful conclusions could still be drawn. Ibid., 358.

80. Holmes, "Increasing Growth-Rate," 203.

81. Holmes, "Principal Causes of Death . . . ," 298–99, 300.

82. Ibid., 300.

83. Holmes, *Negro's Struggle for Survival*, 105–6.

84. He wrote that "the marked prevalence of uterine cancer in colored females . . . would naturally affect the birth rate of the colored population more than of the whites. Hence the cancer mortality that is really effective in the long run in its influence on the survival rates of the two races is probably exercising its most destructive effect on the colored, and hence the Negro population of the United States." Holmes, "Principal Causes of Death . . . ," 301.

85. Holmes, "Increasing Growth-Rate," 205.

86. Holmes, *Negro's Struggle for Survival*, 107.

87. Holmes, "Principal Causes of Death . . . ," 302.

88. Holmes, *Negro's Struggle for Survival*, 131.

89. Tuberculosis quote is from New York physician George G. Ornstein, "The Leading Causes of Death Among Negroes: Tuberculosis," *Journal of Negro Education* 6 (July 1937): 303–9, quote on 307–8. The second quote, "racial differences," is from George St. J. Perrott and Dorothy Holland, "The Need for Adequate Data on Current Illness among Negroes," *Journal of Negro Education* 6 (July 1937): 350–63, quote on 362.

90. Holmes, "Principal Causes of Death . . . ," 302.

91. M. O. Bousfield, "Race Health an Important Factor in Community Health, Says Doctor," *Chicago Defender* (May 4, 1935), 24. "The advocates of this insinuation have been pushed further and further in the background so that today one seldom hears of Frederick L. Hoffman and Lotrop Stoddard," Bousefield wrote.

92. Holmes, *Negro's Struggle for Survival*, 212–13.

93. Holmes, "Increasing Growth-Rate," 209, 208.

94. Harold Dorn, "Comment," *American Journal of Sociology* 42 (September 1936): 211–12, quote on 212.

95. Holmes, "Differential Mortality from Cancer . . . ," 363. Louis Dublin argued that black women also suffered from higher rates of breast cancer Dublin, "The Health of the Negro," 8.

96. Holmes, *Negro's Struggle for Survival*, 107–8.

97. Ibid.

98. Wright, "Cancer as It Affects the Negro," 169–70; Holmes, *Negro's Struggle for Survival*, 107–8.

99. Holmes, *Negro's Struggle for Survival*, 107–8.

100. Dublin, "The Problem of Negro Health . . . ," 273. See also Louis Dublin and Alfred Lotka, *Twenty-Five Years of Health Progress* (New York: Metropolitan Life Insurance Company, 1937), 178.

101. Louis Dublin, "The Problem of Negro Health . . . ," 273. Dublin and Lotka, *Twenty-Five Years of Health Progress*, 178.

102. Isidore Cohn, "Statistics," *Southern Surgeon* 10 (September 1941): 686–88, quote on 687.

103. Isidore Cohen, "Carcinoma of the Breast in the Negro," *Annals of Surgery* 107 (1938): 716.

104. "Cancer Teaches a Lesson in Democracy," *Science News Letter* 35 (March 11, 1939): 152.

105. "Why Should Cancer Interest Us?" *Yale Review* (December 1943).

106. Wm. S. Quinland and J. R. Cuff, "Primary Carcinoma in the Negro," *Archives of Pathology* 30 (1940): 393–402, quote on 402.

107. Lewis K. McMillan, "Light Which Two World Wars Throw Upon the Plight of the American Negro," *Journal of Negro Education* 12 (Summer 1943): 429–37. As McMillan wrote, "Whereas the many mixtures of millions of white strangers who have flocked to our shores . . . have been eagerly taken into the very bosom of the nation, blessed with its boundless opportunity and fattened and enriched with its fabulous wealth, the thoroughly Americanized Negro has been forced to live apart to himself," 430.

108. Helene Margaret, "The Negro Fad," *Forum and Century* 87 (January 1932): 40, 41.

109. Dublin, "The Problem of Negro Health . . . ," 274.

110. Margaret, "The Negro Fad," 41–42.

111. Milton Rosenau, *Preventive Medicine and Hygiene* (New York: D. Appleton, 1935), 416.

112. Cohn, "Carcinoma of the Breast in the Negro," 716.

113. D. Lewis and W. R. Reinhoff, "A Study of the Results of Operations for the Cure of Cancer of the Breast Performed at the Johns Hopkins Hospital from 1899 to 1931," *Annals of Surgery* 95 (1932): 336–400, quote on 342–45.

Chapter 3

1. "It's Right to Lie in Some Cases, Doctors Told," *Chicago Daily Tribune* (March 29, 1955), 23C.

2. Kristen Gardner, *Early Detection: Women, Cancer, and Awareness Campaigns in the Twentieth-Century United States* (Chapel Hill: University of North Carolina Press, 2006), 127.

3. Francis Ashley Faught, "Foretell Cancer!" *Hygeia* 17 (December 1939): 1067.

4. Florence Hunt, "An Open Letter to Club Women of Georgia," *Atlanta Daily World* (April 20, 1938), 6.

5. "Movie May Help Save Lives of Cancer Victims," *Science News Letter* 53 (March 4, 1950): 132; "Cancer Signs Put on Film: Free Movie Shows Women How to Make Own Examination," *New York Times* (October 16, 1950), 45; A. H. Weiler, "By Way of Report," *New York Times* (November 27, 1949), X5. The film, *Cancer: The Problem of Early Detection*, won first prize in the medicine and science films division.

6. As early as the 1920s, Thomas C. Edwards of the National Health Council had noted that "the special value of the motion picture in health education is that it can make a powerful emotional appeal." Thomas C. Edwards, "Health Pictures and Their Value," *Annals of the American Academy of Political and Social Science* 128 (November 1926): 133–38. See also Darrell A. Dance, "Health Films," *Hollywood Quarterly* 1 (April 1946): 328–30.

7. Bosley Crowther, "The Screen in Review: Margaret Sullavan Returns in 'No Sad Songs for Me,' New Feature at Music Hall," *New York Times* (April 28, 1950), 26. See also Andrea Parke, "The Sickle's Shadow," *New York Times* (January 9, 1944), BR5.

8. Mae Tinee, "Cancer Movie Daring But Has Its Weaknesses," *Chicago Daily Tribune* (May 11, 1950), C10.

9. Philip K. Scheuer, "Grim Realism and Soul-Searching Stamp Hollywood Films in 1950: Moviemakers Get Tough in Tearing Apart Own Institute and Some of Society's Ills," *Los Angeles Times* (December 24, 1950), C1.

10. Daniel Bernardi, "Introduction: Race and the Hollywood Style," in Daniel Bernardi, ed., *Classic Hollywood, Classic Whiteness* (Minneapolis: University of Minnesota Press, 2001), xv–xvii.

11. Elaine Tyler May, *Homeward Bound: American Families in the Cold War Era* (New York: Basic Books, 1988).

12. "Screen News Here and in Hollywood," *New York Times* (January 11, 1944), 23.

13. Frank Daugherty, "Buddy Adler, Exhibitor-Producer," *New York Times* (April 16, 1950), X5.

14. Ibid., X5. "Unmentionable Aspects," *New York Times* (December 11, 1949), X6. See also "Canada Lee Signs for Role in Film," *New York Times* (December 25, 1946), 33; "New Leading Role for Irene Dunne," *New York Times* (August 21, 1946), 34; "Hedda Hopper: Looking at Hollywood," *Los Angeles Times* (December 23, 1946), A7.

15. "300 Notables at Rites for Sam Wood," *Los Angeles Times* (September 25, 1949), A3; Frank Daugherty, "Buddy Adler," X5; Hedda Hopper, "Miss Sullavan Signs . . . ," A6.

16. "The character," Sullavan said, "is a dramatic study of fortitude, not a medical case history." "Unmentionable Aspects," X6.

17. William T. Fitts Jr. and I. S. Ravdin, "What Philadelphia Physicians Tell Patients with Cancer," *Journal of the American Medical Association* 153 (November 7, 1953): 901–4.

18. See, for example, John Brody, "I Lost My Battle with Cancer," *Saturday Evening Post* 221 (February 5, 1949), 23, 85–86; Simonne Fabien (adapted from the French by Peggy Lamson), "You Shall Become a Man: A Mother Who Would Not Let Her Son Die," *Ladies' Home Journal* 72 (July 1955), 84–88, 90, 93, 96–98, 100; Herbert King, "I Lost My Voice to Cancer," *Saturday Evening Post* 229 (September 1, 1956), 20–21, 71–73; Gretta Palmer, "I Had Cancer: Face Your Danger in Time," *Ladies' Home Journal* (July 1947), 143–45, 147–48, 150–53; Laura Benson, "I Live with Inoperable Cancer," *Today's Health* 29 (December 1951): 22–23, 60–62; Cynthia Flannery Stine, "I Had a Brain Tumor," *Saturday Evening Post* 229 (September 22, 1956), 31, 121–24; Mary Roberts Rinehart, "You Can Have Cancer—and Live!" *Today's Health* 36 (October 1958): 60–63.

19. Fitts and Ravdin, "What Philadelphia Physicians Tell Patient . . . ," 901–4.

20. May, *Homeward Bound*, xxii, 102–3. For other accounts of disease and Cold War ideas of risk and safeguarding the family, see Jane Smith, *Patenting the Sun: Polio and the Salk Vaccine* (New York: Morrow, 1990); David Oshinsky, *Polio: An American Story* (New York: Oxford University Press, 2005). On the expansion of surveillance, see Katherine Simon, "Review: Cancer Illness among Residents of Ten Metropolitan Areas," *Milbank Memorial Fund Quarterly* 31 (October 1953): 484–88, quotes on 487.

21. Southard, *No Sad Songs for Me* (Garden City, NY: Doubleday, Doran and Co., 1944), 166–67.

22. "Carbon 14 into Service," *Science News Letter* 50 (August 10, 1946): 83.

23. Southard, *No Sad Songs*, 50.

24. Thomas Parran, "Our Deadliest Enemy at Home," *American Magazine* 137 (March 1944): 40–41, 118, 121, quote on 40.

25. "Statement of Dr. Alfred G. Levin, Miami, Fla.," *Hearings before a Subcommittee of the Committee on Foreign Relations, United States Senate, Seventy-Ninth Congress, Second Session on S. 1875* (Washington, DC: U.S. Government Printing Office, 1946), 42.

26. Daugherty, "Buddy Adler," X5.

27. Southard, *No Sad Songs*, 52, 119.

28. Parke, "The Sickle's Shadow," BR5.

29. Southard, *No Sad Songs*, 153.

30. Parran, "Our Deadliest Enemy," 40.

31. Southard, *No Sad Songs*, 6.

32. "Columbia Tackles Unusual Subject," *Los Angeles Times* (May 16, 1950), 19.

33. Ora Marshing, "Breast Cancer," *Hygeia* 23 (March 1945): 176–77, 201–2.

34. Francis Ashley Faught, "Foretell Cancer!" *Hygeia* 17 (December 1939): 1067.

35. Southard, *No Sad Songs*, 6.

36. Paul Boyer, *By the Bomb's Early Light: American Thought and Culture at the Dawn of the Atomic Age* (New York: Pantheon Books, 1985).

37. "Cancer Research," *Science News Letter* 44 (November 6, 1943): 303.

38. S. Gordon Castigliano, "Inoperability versus Incurability in Tumor Management," *Penn Medical Journal* 42 (September 1949): 1364–70, quote on 1364.

39. Leslie J. Reagan, "Engendering the Dreaded Disease: Men, Women, and Cancer," *American Journal of Public Health* 87 (November 1997): 1779–87.

40. Southard, *No Sad Songs*, 159.

41. Bosley Crowther, "Mortal Flesh: Contemplating Illness in 'No Sad Songs for Me,'" *New York Times* (May 7, 1950), 111.

42. Tinee, "Cancer Movie Daring," C10.

43. Richard L. Coe, "Film Casts Cancer As Gentle Victim," *Washington Post* (May 18, 1950), 14.

44. It adds "nothing whatever to anyone's real understanding of this ghastly disease," he wrote. Coe, "Film Casts Cancer," 14.

45. Daugherty, "Buddy Adler," X5.

46. Gladys Denny Shultz, "Women Need No Longer Die of the No. 1 Cancer Foe!" *Ladies' Home Journal* 72 (April 1955), 61.

47. Ruth D. Abrams and Jacob E. Finesinger, "Guilt Reactions in Patients with Cancer," *Cancer* 6 (May 1953): 474–82, quote on 478.

48. "Let's Tell the Truth About Dying" (letter to the editor), *Ladies' Home Journal* (January 1960), 77.

49. As one nurse noted, the majority of women with pelvic lesions she encountered were stunned to be in a cancer ward because they had "led such clean lives," "never abused themselves," and "maintained at all times good hygiene." Ibid., 478. For insight on the lingering stigma of cancer, see Isaac F. Marcosson, "The Cured Cancer Club," *Hygeia* 17 (August 1939): 694–96, quote on 694.

50. As one critic noted about the film, "The results may not be too imaginative . . . or documentary on the other hand, but it is always in good taste." Philip K. Scheuer, "Actress Inspiring in 'No Sad Songs,'" *Los Angeles Times* (May 22, 1950), B7.

51. Frank wrote that "lack of contact between middle and upper class Negroes and whites is one of the features of the problem of Negro-white relationship," and he quoted W. E. B. Du Bois: "The very representatives of the two races, who for mutual benefit . . . ought to be in complete understanding and sympathy, are . . . strangers . . . one side thinks that all whites are narrow and prejudiced, and the other thinks educated Negroes dangerous and insolent." Jerome D. Frank, "Adjustment Problems of Selected Negro Soldiers," *Journal of Nervous and Mental Disease* 105 (June 1947): 647; see also George P. Banks, "The Effects of Race on One-on-One Helping Interviews," *Social Service Review* 45 (June 1971): 137–46; and Ellen Dwyer, "Psychiatry and Race During World War II," *Journal of the History of Medicine and Allied Sciences* 61 (April 2006): 117–43.

52. Lorna Doone Burks, *I Die Daily: The Story of a Woman Whose Love Will Live Forever* (New York: Rockport Press, 1946), 15, 17, 19. Edited by Arthur J. Burks, dedication by Arthur J. Burks.

53. Ibid., 19.

54. Henry F. Pringle, "What Do the Women of America Think bout Medicine," *Ladies' Home Journal* 55 (September 1938), 14–15, 42–43, quote on 15.

55. Lala L. Handorf and Thyra E. Pedersen, "Nursing Care in Terminal Cancer," *American Journal of Nursing* 50 (October 1950): 643–46, quote on 645.

56. "Statement of Dr. Charles Cameron," *Hearings Before the Committee on Interstate and Foreign Commerce, House of Representatives* (October 1, 2, and 3, 1953) (Washington, DC: U.S. Government Printing Office, 1953), 198.

57. As Herman and Anne Somers wrote in 1958, "The hospital stands for the oxygen tent, the blood bank, the operating room, and other miraculous instruments . . . The American people have insisted on taking advantage of this life-saving institution in greater and greater numbers . . . At the same time, hospital care, rightly or wrongly, is generally associated with high, even catastrophic costs." Herman M. Somers and Anne R. Somers, "Private Health Insurance: Part One. Changing Patterns of Medical Care Demand and Supply in Relation to Health Insurance," *California Law Review* 46 (August 1958): 376–410, quote on 391.

58. Anne R. Somers and Herman M. Somers, "Health Insurance: Are Cost and Quality Controls Necessary?" *Industrial and Labor Relations Review* 13 (July 1960): 581–95.

59. Ray Hosier to Dr. Ochsner, March 14, 1955, Box 21, Folder 5, Alton Ochsner Papers, Williams Research Center, Historic New Orleans Collection.

60. Edward Nichols, "Confronting the Fear of Cancer," *Hartford Courant* (April 6, 1955), 16.

61. Owen Wangensteen, "Editorial: Should Patients Be Told They Have Cancer?" *Surgery* 27 (June 1950): 944–47, quote on 944.

62. Ibid., 944. In 1953, according to one survey in Philadelphia, only 41 percent of surgeons "tended to tell their patients they had cancer." Psychiatrists, at 60 percent, were much more likely to disclose the diagnosis. But most other medical specialists were deeply reluctant. Only 12 percent of radiologists told their patients; 19 percent of specialists in obstetrics and gynecology; 21 percent of internists; 25 percent of nonspecialists; and 30 percent of university-based physicians. Fitts and Ravdin, "What Philadelphia Physicians Tell Patients . . . ," 901–4.

63. "'Mr. Glencannon' Kills Self and His Ill Wife," *Washington Post* (July 8, 1950), 12; "Gilpatric, Wife Die: Suicide Pact Seen," *New York Times* (July 8, 1950), 28; "Breaking the News," *Time* (July 17, 1950), 45.

64. "No Gilpatric Inquest," *New York Times* (July 9, 1950), 52. See also "Guy Gilpatric Slays Stricken Wife and Self," *Chicago Daily Tribune* (July 8, 1950), 10.

65. Rosemary M. Kent, *An Evaluation of the Health Education Program of the American Cancer Society, North Carolina Division, Inc.* (MPH thesis, University of North Carolina School of Public Health, 1949), 95, 109–10.

66. "The Truth or Not: Should a Patient Be Told He Has Cancer?" *Newsweek* (November 5, 1955), 83.

67. Arthur Sutherland, a pioneering figure in psycho-oncology in the early 1950s, was one among those who called for frank discussions with patients before such surgery. "Some Perils Noted in Surgery," *New York Times* (October 21, 1952), 32. See,

for example, Arthur M. Sutherland, Charles E. Orbach, Ruth B. Dyk, and Morton Bard, "The Psychological Impact of Cancer and Cancer Surgery," *Cancer* 5 (September 1952): 857–72. On radical surgery, see George T. Pack, "Argument for Radicalism in Cancer Surgery," *American Surgeon* 17 (April 1951): 271–78.

68. "Parts of the face like the nose, ears, lips, jaws or other parts of the head may be partially or completely destroyed by the lesions or by therapeutic measures used in an attempt to delay the progress of the disease or to give the patient relief," noted two nurses in 1950. Lala L. Handorf and Thyra E. Pedersen, "Nursing Care in Terminal Cancer," *American Journal of Nursing* 50 (October 1950): 643–46, quote on 645. Other graphic examples are described in Joseph H. Morris, M.D., to Alton Ochsner, August 10, 1960, Box 46, folder 1, Ochsner Papers.

69. Marian Miller Kean with Steven M. Spencer, "I've Had Cancer 32 Years," *Saturday Evening Post* 227 (August 14, 1954), 27, 88–90, quote on 88. See also, King, "I Lost My Voice to Cancer," 71–73.

70. Kean with Spencer, "I've Had Cancer 32 Years," 90. By the late 1950s, one medic could note "in some centers the classic operation has been giving way to local mastectomy and radiation therapy; in others to still more radical surgery." D. W. Smithers, "Cancer of the Breast: A Study of Short Survival in Early Cases and of Long Survival in Advanced Cases," *American Journal of Roentgenology, Radium Therapy, and Nuclear Medicine* 80 (November 1958): 740–58.

71. Kean with Spencer, "I've Had Cancer 32 Years," 90.

72. Edna Kaehele, *Living with Cancer* (Garden City, NY: Doubleday, 1952), 17.

73. Ibid., 13, 17, and 130. As Kaehele noted, "The conscientious doctor makes an examination, performs a biopsy, and gives up before he opens his mouth to further intimidate the cowering wretch on his table."

74. Mary Margaret McBride, "They Survived Death," *Los Angeles Times* (March 7, 1955), B6.

75. One chapter of Barron Lerner's recent book focuses, for example, on Dulles's cancer. Barron Lerner, *When Illness Goes Public: Celebrity Patients and How We Look at Medicine* (Baltimore: Johns Hopkins University Press, 2006).

76. Quentin Reynolds, "The Girl Who Lived Again," *Reader's Digest* 65 (October 1954), 50–55, quote on 52.

77. Susan E. Cayleff, *Babe: The Life and Legend of Babe Didrikson Zaharias* (Chicago: University of Illinois Press, 1995), 1–3.

78. "A Gallant Competitor," *New York Times* (April 13, 1953), 26; "Babe Zaharias' Sports Career Ended! Hit By Malignant Malady," *Chicago Daily Tribune* (April 10, 1953); "Illness May End Career of Didrickson: Malignancy Hinted," *Washington Post* (April 10, 1953), 32.

79. "Ike and Babe Zaharias Open Cancer Drive, Chat about Golf," *Washington Post and Times Herald* (April 3, 1954), 14.

80. Reynolds, "The Girl Who Lived Again," 51. See also "Babe Is Back," *Time* (August 10, 1953), 44; "I'm Not Out of the Rough Yet," *Cosmopolitan* (October 1953), 78–83.

81. "Mrs. Zaharias Resting: Stricken by Cancer Again, She Vows to Return to Golf," *New York Times* (August 7, 1955), 10; Walter Trojan, "Heart Attack Strikes

Ike," *Chicago Daily Tribune* (September 25, 1955), 1; Laurence Burd, "Condition Listed 'Good'; Call in Specialist," *Chicago Daily Tribune* (September 25, 1955), 1.

82. "Fights Second Cancer: Unflinching Babe Zaharias Wages Her 'Greatest Battle,'" *Washington Post and Times Herald* (August 7, 1955), C3.

83. "Babe Again Has Cancer, Doctors Say," *Chicago Daily Tribune* (August 6, 1955), B1; "Fights Second Cancer," C3.

84. "Eisenhower Tries Golf Putting at White House," *Los Angeles Times* (November 13, 1955), 1; "Babe Having Trouble; Back to Hospital," *Chicago Daily Tribune* (November 26, 1955), B1; "Babe Zaharias Suffers Attack of Pneumonia," *Washington Post and Times Herald* (December 29, 1955), 18; "Mrs. Zaharias X-Rayed," *New York Times* (March 31, 1956), 10; "Babe Zaharias Still in Pain, But Keeps Hope," *Chicago Daily Tribune* (May 24, 1956), E3; "Babe Undergoes Five-Hour Pain-Relieving Operation," *Los Angeles Times* (July 14, 1956), A5.

85. Bob Considine, "Babe Fights Cancer in Texas Hospital," *Washington Post and Times Herald* (August 5, 1956), F1.

86. Cayleff, *Babe*, 232.

87. "Babe Zaharias Dies," *New York Times* (September 28, 1956), 1; quote on 30. For both Eisenhower and Zaharias (and for their admiring public), their return to golfing and the "club life" was a benchmark for recovery. "From One Ailing Golfer to Another," *Washington Post and Times Herald* (November 4, 1955), 26. As one article in 1937 had noted, "Golf, which is the backbone of club life, ranks just behind yachting and polo in conspicuous consumption when it is played in the beautiful surroundings of the metropolitan private club." Proctor Hall, "The Country Club Comes 'Out of the Rough,'" *New York Times* (August 1, 1937), 115. Laurence Burd, "Ike Plays Golf for First Time Since Attack," *Chicago Daily Tribune* (February 18, 1956), 4.

88. Enoch Callaway, "Should Doctors Tell the Truth to a Cancer Patient?" *Ladies' Home Journal* (May 1961), 65, 108.

89. The *Ladies' Home Journal* revisited the issue again in 1963, where one doctor declared frankly: "'I lie,' one doctor says bluntly. 'In some cases I go on lying even in the face of a direct question. I never destroy hope.'" Bruno Gebhard, "Tell Me Doctor: Is There Too Much Secrecy in Medicine?" *Ladies' Home Journal* (July 1963).

90. Callaway, "Should Doctors Tell . . . ," 65.

91. Ann Landers, "Lies Breed Fear and Unrest," *Hartford Courant* (April 29, 1962), 14E. Even the noted French feminist Simone de Beauvoir defended the need to withhold knowledge, recalling that "Maman [my mother] had dreaded cancer all her life, and perhaps she was still afraid of it at the nursing-home." She was told that she "had been operated on for peritonitis—a grave condition, but curable . . . We ought to have told her, 'You have cancer. You are going to die,'" thought de Beauvoir at one point, but "Maman did not want these intimate conversations." Simone de Beauvoir, *A Very Easy Death* (New York: G. P. Putnam's Sons, 1966), 89.

92. De Beauvoir, *A Very Easy Death*, 89.

93. Charles Oberling, "Why Should Cancer Interest Us?" *Yale Review* (Winter 1944).

94. Charles Geschickter, "Mammary Cancer," in *Diseases of the Breast, 2nd ed.* (Philadelphia: J. B. Lippincott Company, 1945), 410.

95. "Self Examination for Cancer of the Breast," *Ladies' Home Journal* (August 1952).

96. Geschickter, "Mammary Cancer," 410.

97. "Cancer and a Woman's Sex," *Reader's Digest* (September 1955); in "Tell Me, Doctor," *Ladies' Home Journal* (April 1965), the author writes, "Because, after all, you provide your own first line of defense, and, as a wife and mother, you are also your family's first line of defense."

98. "Self-Examination . . . ," 84; R. D. Johnson, M.D., "Self-Inspection Against Cancer," *Today's Health* 30 (January 1952): 22–23.

99. C. H. Smith, "You Can Escape Breast Cancer," *Hygeia* 28 (1950): 30–31, quote on 31. "Film Teaches Women to Examine Selves for Cancer," *Science News Letter* 53 (1950): 18.

100. "Self-Examination of the Breasts," *American Journal of Nursing* 52 (April 1952): 441.

101. "Film Teaches Women to Examine Selves for Cancer," *Science News Letter* 53 (1950): 18. "Women Can Discover Own Breast Cancer," *Science News Letter* 52 (June 13, 1953): 363.

102. "Movie May Help Save Lives of Cancer Victims," *Science News Letter* 53 (March 4, 1950): 142.

103. Eftychia Vayena, "Cancer Detectors: An International History of the Pap Test and Cervical Cancer Screening, 1928–1970," (PhD diss., University of Minnesota), 10. As Gladys Denny Shutz noted, "Though the Papanicolaou smear technique has been practically a household word since 1947, its benefits have been limited to the hundreds of thousands of women, instead of to the millions who should have them." Shultz, "Women Need No Longer Die . . . ," 164.

104. Leonard B. Greentree, "Cancer of the Cervix: A Realistic Program of Cancer Control for the General Practitioner," *American Journal of Obstetrics and Gynecology* 61 (January 1951): 178–82, quote on 181. See also E. Novak, "Comments on Supplementary Value of Surface Biopsy," in *1949–1950 Yearbook of Obstetrics and Gynecology* (July–August 1949): 477–78. Vayena, "Cancer Detectors," 19.

105. Herbert Klarman, "Economic Aspects of Hospital Care," *Journal of Business of the University of Chicago* 24 (January 1951): 1–24.

106. "Many gynecologists must find it difficult to decide how far they can apply . . . especially in . . . ostensibly normal women, the newer techniques which will help disclose an occasional subclinical lesion of intraepithelial or invasive type," noted one physician in 1949. Novak, "Comments . . . ," 477–78.

107. Shultz, "Women Need No Longer Die . . . ," 164.

108. "Penny Cancer Kit," *Today's Health* 33 (February 1955): 15.

109. Ora Marshing, "Breast Cancer," *Hygeia* 23 (March 1945): 176–77, 201–2.

110. Marshing, "Breast Cancer," 201–2.

111. Burks, *I Die Daily*, 34.

112. Johnson, "Self-Inspection Against Cancer," 22–23. See also Vayena, "Cancer Detectors," 27–34. J. Heller, "Cancer—A Public Health Problem," *Journal of the International College of Surgeons* 23 (1955): 463–69. See also Joseph Meigs, "The History of the Inter-Society Cytology Council," *Annals of the New York Academy of Science* 63 (1956): 1041–45.

113. Paul Fluck, "Gossip Can Be a Killer! Beware of It!" *Chicago Daily Tribune* (July 12, 1953), D1.

114. Marion Flexner, "Cancer—I've Had It," *Ladies' Home Journal* (May 1947), 57, 150.

115. Ibid., 57.

116. "Cancer Test Will Depend on Women," *New York Amsterdam News* (October 21, 1950), 7. See also "Cancer Film to Be Shown Here, March 21," *Atlanta Daily World* (March 20, 1953), 8.

117. "Attention Ladies," *Atlanta Daily World*, May 9, 1952, 2.

118. "Cancer Society Names a Negro Affairs Aide," *New York Times* (January 3, 1956), 19; "New Appointment," *New York Amsterdam News* (January 21, 1956), 8.

119. Robert L. Brown, "Tragedy of Cancer: Breast Cancer Detection Personal Responsibility," *Atlanta Daily World* (March 27, 1962), 8.

120. "Housewife Applauds Two Films on Cancer," *Chicago Daily Defender* (March 14, 1960), A14; "Theatres Show 'For Women Only' Movies," *Chicago Daily Defender* (March 1, 1960), A14.

121. "Housewife Applauds . . . ," A14.

122. James Baldwin, "The Devil Finds Work," in James Baldwin and Toni Morrison, *James Baldwin: Collected Essays* (New York: Library of America, 1998), 493. "The Devil Finds Work" was first published in 1976.

123. Walter Ames, "All-Star Revue Reverting to Delayed, Kinescope Program," *Los Angeles Times* (April 29, 1952), 24.

124. "Hattie McDaniel, Beulah of Radio," *New York Times* (October 27, 1952), 27.

125. "Hattie McDaniel, Negro Star, Dies," *Los Angeles Times* (October 27, 1952), A1. McDaniel's role-playing (and the stereotypes of the African-American mammy it promoted) was the topic of enduring criticism and commentary. Marshall Hyatt and Cheryl Sanders, "Film as a Medium to Study the Twentieth-Century Afro-American Experience," *Journal of Negro Education* 53 (Spring 1984): 161–72; Clayton R. Koppes and Gregory D. Black, "Blacks, Loyalty, and Motion-Picture Propaganda in World War II," *Journal of American History* 73 (September 1986): 383–406.

126. Milton A. Smith, "Korea GIs Swat Beulah," *Chicago Defender* (May 12, 1951), 20.

127. Charles R. Metzger, "Pressure Groups and the Motion Picture Industry," *Annals of the American Academy of Political and Social Science* 254 (November 1947): 110–15, quotes on 112, 113. As historians Clayton R. Koppes and Gregory D. Black have noted, although activists like the NAACP's Walter White struggled for fairer depictions of blacks in the cinema, "the struggle . . . ended in frustration." Koppes and

Black, "Blacks, Loyalty, and Motion-Picture . . . ," 404. See also Stephen Vaughn, "Ronald Reagan and the Struggle for Black Dignity in Cinema, 1937–1953," *Journal of Negro History* 77 (Winter 1992): 1–16.

128. "Some instinct caused me to profoundly distrust the sense of life they projected," he wrote. Baldwin, "The Devil's Work," 493.

129. Adrienne L. McLean, *Being Rita Hayworth: Labor, Identity, and Hollywood Stardom* (New Brunswick, NJ: Rutgers University Press, 2004).

130. Bill Davidson, "Probing the Secrets of Life," *Collier's* (May 14, 1954), 78–83, quote on 79–80. For more on this story, see Michael Gold, *A Conspiracy of Cells: One Woman's Immortal Legacy and the Medical Scandal It Caused* (Albany: State University of New York Press, 1986); and Hannah Landecker, "Immortality, in Vitro: A History of the HeLa Cell Line," in Paul E. Brodwin, ed., *Biotechnology and Culture: Bodies, Anxieties, Ethics* (Bloomington: Indiana University Press, 2001), 53–72.

131. Davidson, "Probing the Secrets of Life," 79–80. Rebecca Skloot, *The Immortal Life of Henrietta Lacks* (New York: Crown Books, 2010).

132. Ibid., 79–80. See also Joan Fujimura, *Crafting Science: A Sociohistory of the Quest for the Genetics of Cancer* (Cambridge, MA: Harvard University Press, 1996), 41.

133. Gold, *A Conspiracy of Cells*, 18.

134. Davidson, "Probing the Secrets of Life," 79–80.

135. Gold, *A Conspiracy of Cells*, 14.

136. Daugherty, "Buddy Adler," X5.

137. Crowther, "Disability Pictures," 131.

138. Howard Thompson, "Case History: 'Young Doctors' in New York," *New York Times* (January 29, 1961), X7.

139. Edmund Fuller, "Hospital Microcosm," *New York Times* (September 20, 1959), BR50; Jerry Crowe, "Life in a Big Hospital," *Chicago Daily Tribune* (December 13, 1959), C3.

140. Arthur Hailey, *Final Diagnosis* (Garden City, NY: Doubleday, 1959), 218.

141. Ibid., 52, 304.

142. *The Young Doctors* (United Artists: Release, August 1961).

Chapter 4

1. Rosemary M. Kent, *An Evaluation of the Health Education Program of the American Cancer Society, North Carolina Division, Inc.* (MPH thesis: University of North Carolina School of Public Health, 1949), xii.

2. For more on racial ideology in the interwar period, see Elazar Barkan, *The Retreat of Scientific Racism: Changing Concepts of Race in Britain and the United States Between the World Wars* (New York: Cambridge University Press, 1992). See also Robert Proctor, *The Nazi War on Cancer* (Princeton, NJ: Princeton University Press, 1999).

3. Kent, *An Evaluation*, 70, 75.

4. Ibid., 72–73.

5. Ibid., 72–73, 95.

6. Sigismund Peller, *Cancer in Man* (New York: International Universities Press, 1952), 226–27. See also Sigismund Peller, *Not in My Time: The Story of a Doctor* (New York: Philosophical Library, 1979).

7. Isaac Berenblum, *Science Versus Cancer* (London: Sigma Books, 1946), 36. Paul E. Steiner, *Cancer: Race and Geography* (Baltimore: Williams and Wilkins, 1954).

8. "More attention has been paid to this problem than almost any other," he noted, but "the results have on the whole been disappointing." Berenblum, *Science Versus Cancer*, 36, 37.

9. Paul Coe, "Nonwhite Population Increases in Metropolitan Areas," *Journal of the American Statistical Association* 50 (June 1955): 283–308, quote on p. 283.

10. As Melissa Nobles has noted in her study of race and U.S. Census, the logic of race changed markedly in the latter half of the twentieth century. Melissa Nobles, *Shades of Citizenship* (Stanford, CA: Stanford University Press, 2000), 168.

11. "Crusade Against Cancer," *Hartford Courant* (September 3, 1947), 12.

12. "No Discrimination Is Shown by Cancer in Attacking People," *New York Amsterdam News* (November 3, 1945), 13.

13. Peller, *Cancer in Man*, 226–27.

14. Ibid.

15. Steiner, *Cancer*, 13.

16. Ibid., 6–7.

17. Ibid., 326.

18. Ibid., 14.

19. Franz Boas, "Race and Progress," *Science* 74 (July 3, 1937): 1–8.

20. Steiner, *Cancer*, 14.

21. Quotes in this paragraph are found in Steiner, *Cancer*, 13, 41, 319.

22. Quotes in this paragraph are found in ibid., 12, 14.

23. No difference was found in stomach, uterus, pancreas, skin, kidneys, gall-bladder (males), larynx (male), and penis, bone tumors (female), soft tissue, and malignant melanomas. Ibid., 316.

24. Ibid., 13.

25. See Michael Keevak, "East Asian Bodies in Nineteenth-Century Medicine: The Mongolian Eye, the Mongolian Spot, and Mongolism," chapter 4 of *How East Asians Became Yellow* (unpublished manuscript).

26. As Steiner noted, the Mongoloid group "are subdivided into 239 (0.7 per cent) Japanese; 70 (0.2 per cent) Chinese; and 83 (0.2 per cent) Filipinos." *Cancer*, 12.

27. Ibid., 14.

28. Nobles, *Shades of Citizenship*, 188.

29. Ariela Gross, "Texas Mexicans and the Politics of Whiteness," *Law and History Review* 21 (Spring 2003): 195–205, quote on 197. See also Neil Foley, *The White Scourge: Mexicans, Blacks, and Poor Whites in the Texas Cotton Culture* (Berkeley: University of California Press, 1997); David Montejano, *Anglos and Mexicans in the Making of Texas, 1836–1986* (Austin: University of Texas Press, 1987).

30. From "Appendix: Race Categories and Instructions to Census Enumerators of U.S. Population Censuses, 1850–1960," in Nobles, *Shades of Citizenship*, 190.

31. William Haenszel, "Cancer Mortality among the Foreign-Born in the United States," *Journal of the National Cancer Institute* 26 (January 1961): 49.

32. Steiner, *Cancer*, 7.

33. Charles S. Cameron, *The Truth about Cancer* (Englewood Cliffs, NJ: Prentice-Hall, 1956).

34. In 1950, the nonwhite population numbered 16 million (or 10.5 percent of the entire population), of which around 94 percent, or 15 million, were black. In 1960, the nonwhite population had grown to 20 million (11.2 percent of the U.S. population), of which again 94 percent (or 18.8 million) were black. Preston Valien, "General Demographic Characteristics of the Negro Population in the United States," *Journal of Negro Education* 32 (Autumn 1963): 329–36. See especially 329. By 1970, black Americans now made up 88 percent of the nationwide nonwhite population. For 1970, see U.S. Department of Commerce, Bureau of the Census, "1970 Census of Population: Supplementary Report—Negro Population in Selected Places and Selected Counties" (Washington, DC, 1971), 17. www2.census.gov/prod2/decennial/documents/31679801n1-40ch01.pdf.

35. Harold Dorn and Sidney Cutler, *Morbidity from Cancer in the United States; Variation in Incidence by Age, Sex, Race, Marital Status, and Geographic Region—U.S. Department of Health Education and Welfare/Public Health Monograph* 29 (Washington, DC: U.S. Government Printing Office, 1955), 12.

36. Paul Coe, "Nonwhite Population Increases in Metropolitan Areas," *Journal of the American Statistical Association* 50 (June 1955): 283–308, quote on 283. As Coe noted, this "tremendous population explosion" sending nonwhites "surging into central cities . . . introduces new problems of interracial adjustment in many northern and western cities where previously these problems have been absent." Paul F. Coe, "The Nonwhite Population Surge to Our Cities," *Land Economics* 35 (August 1959): 195–210, quote on 195–96.

37. Dorn and Cutler, *Morbidity from Cancer*, 12.

38. The term "non-white," Paul Coe wrote in 1959, included "Negroes, Indians, Japanese, Chinese, Philipinos, Koreans, Asiatic Indians, Polynesians, and other Asiatics." Coe, "The Nonwhite Population Surge . . . ," 195. Writing in 1963, another researcher noted, "the non-white population consists of Negroes, American Indians, Japanese, Chinese, Filipinos, Koreans, Asian Indians, and Malayan races." Preston Valien, "General Demographic Characteristics . . . ," 329.

39. William Haenszel, Samuel Marcus, and Edmund Zimmerer, *Cancer Mortality in Urban and Rural Iowa*, Public Health Monograph No. 37 (Washington, DC: U.S. Government Printing Office, 1956), 2.

40. *Census Tract Statistics: Dallas and Adjacent Area*, 1950 Population Census Report, vol. 3, chapter 14 (Washington, DC: U.S. Government Printing Office, 1952), 2.

41. According to the *1940 Census of Dallas and Adjacent Area*, 1950 Population Census Report, vol. 3, chapter 14 (Washington, DC: U.S. Government Printing Office, 1952), 36.

42. See, for example, the discussion of the low rate of cancer among Eskimos ("the healthiest people in the world") and their "exclusive meat diet," in F. E.

Chidester, *Nutrition and Glands in Relation to Cancer* (Milwaukee: Lee Foundation for Nutritional Research, 1944), 55.

43. See, for example, chart in Sidney J. Cutler and Samuel C. Marcus, *Cancer Illness among Residents of Philadelphia, Pennsylvania* (Bethesda, MD: Public Health Service, National Cancer Institute of the National Institutes of Health, 1948), 15.

44. Irving I. Warran, *Cancer Illness among Residents of New Orleans, Louisiana* (Bethesda, MD: Public Health Service, National Cancer Institute of the National Institutes of Health, 1947), 3–4.

45. Samuel C. Marcus, *Cancer Illness among Residents of Birmingham, Alabama* (Bethesda, MD: Public Health Service, National Cancer Institute of the National Institutes of Health, 1947), 17.

46. Sidney J. Cutler, *Cancer Illness among Residents of Pittsburgh, Pennsylvania* (Bethesda, MD: Public Health Service, National Cancer Institute of the National Institutes of Health, 1947), 16.

47. Cutler, *Cancer Illness . . . Pittsburgh*, 16.

48. Sidney J. Cutler, *Cancer Illness Among Residents in Atlanta, Georgia, 1947*, Cancer Morbidity Series—No. 1, 1950 (Bethesda, MD: National Cancer Institute of the National Institute of Health, 1950), 5.

49. Sidney J. Cutler, *Cancer Illness . . . in Atlanta*, 17.

50. Jerry W. Combs and Kingsley Davis, "Differential Fertility in Puerto Rico," *Population Studies* 5 (November 1951): 104–16, quote on 104.

51. Karen Brodkin, *How Jews Became White Folks and What That Says about Race in America* (New Brunswick, NJ: Rutgers University Press, 1999), 141.

52. Maurice Sorsby, *Cancer and Race: A Study of the Incidence of Cancer among Jews* (London: John Bale, Sons and Danielsson, 1931).

53. Albert Rothman, Leonard Rapaport, and Israel Davidson, "Carcinoma of the Cervix in Jewish Women," *American Journal of Obstetrics and Gynecology* 62 (July 1951): 160–62, quote on 162.

54. On the problems of assimilation, intermarriage, and immigration, see Berenblum, *Science Versus Cancer*, 38.

55. Albert Rothman, Leonard Rapaport, and Israel Davidson, "Carcinoma of the Cervix in Jewish Women," *American Journal of Obstetrics and Gynecology* 62 (July 1951): 160–62, quote on 160.

56. Peller, *Cancer in Man*, 232.

57. Writing on how different groups responded to expanding radiation therapy, one author insisted that "the only racial consideration which is of importance is the rarity of cancer of the cervix among Jewish women." S. T. Cantril, ed., *Radiation Therapy in the Management of Cancer of the Uterine Cervix* (Springfield, IL: Charles C. Thomas, 1950).

58. Alfred C. Kinsey, Wardell B. Pomeroy, and Clyde E. Martin, *Sexual Behavior of the Human Male* (Philadelphia: W. B. Saunders, 1948); Alfred C. Kinsey et al., *Sexual Behavior of the Human Female* (Philadelphia: W. B. Saunders, 1953).

59. "Silence of Educated Negroes Slants Sex Report, Kinsey Says," *Chicago Defender* (November 27, 1948), 1.

60. Quoted in L. F. Palmer, "Sex Study Snubs Negroes, Experts Claim," *Chicago Defender* (August 29, 1953), 1. See also "Omission of Negroes from Sex Study Arouses Scholars," *Chicago Defender* (August 29, 1953), 1. See also Nate Haseltine, "Dr. Kinsey Reports on Study of Women's Sexual Behavior," *Washington Post* (August 21, 1953), 1.

61. Doris Blake, "The Blake Report: Dr. Kinsey Talked to the Wrong Women," *Los Angeles Times* (August 24, 1953), B1. As Doris Blake noted at the time, "Despite the title, Kinsey admits his book does not report the sex behavior of all American women, much less women of other countries. It excludes Negro women, because not enough of them were interviewed."

62. Bruce Bliven, "Appraising 'The Kinsey Report,'" *New York Times* (May 16, 1948), BR4.

63. Berenblum, *Science Versus Cancer*, 38. See also Alfred Joseph Cantor, *Cancer Can Be Cured* (New York: Didier, 1946), 79. "Cancer of the penis is practically unknown among the Hebrews," Cantor pronounced.

64. Peller, *Cancer in Man*, 232.

65. E. L. Kennaway, "Racial and Social Incidence of Cancer of Uterus," *British Journal of Cancer* 2 (1948): 177–212.

66. Irwin Weiner, Louis Burke, and Morris Goldberger, "Carcinoma of the Cervix in Jewish Women," *American Journal of Obstetrics and Gynecology* 61 (February 1951): 418–22, quote on 421.

67. William Ober and Leopold Reiner, "Cancer of the Cervix in Jewish Women," *New England Journal of Medicine* 251 (September 30, 1954): 555–59.

68. A. Brzezinsky and Y. M. Bromberg, "Significance of Postmenopausal Bleeding in Jewish Women," *Obstetrics and Gynecology* 1 (March 1953): 359–63, quote on 363. Hospital surveys continued to confirm that carcinoma of the cervix was somewhere between five and nine times more frequent in non-Jewish than in Jewish women. I. Weiner et al., "Carcinoma of Cervix in Jewish Women," 418–22; Ober and Reiner, "Cancer of the Cervix in Jewish Women," 555–59. See also S. B. Gusberg and J. S. Corscaden, "Pathology and Treatment of Adenocarcinoma of the Cervix," *Cancer* 4 (1951): 1006–72; and J. Scapier, E. Day, and G. R. Durfee, "Intraepithelial Carcinoma of Cervix: Cytohistological and Clinical Study," *Cancer* 5 (1952): 315–23.

69. Weiner et al., "Carcinoma of the Cervix in Jewish Women," 418.

70. "Women Need No Longer Die of Their No. 1 Cancer Foe!" *Ladies' Home Journal* (April 1955).

71. Richard Doll, "In Memoriam: Ernst Wynder, 1923–1999," *American Journal of Public Health* 89 (December 1999): 1798–99.

72. "Sex Habits Probed in Their Relation to Cancer," *Science News Letter* (May 1953).

73. Elizabeth Ikin, H. Lehmann, and A. E. Mourant, "An Investigation of Blood-Groups and a Search for Sickle-Cell Trait in Yemenite Jews," *Lancet* (November 22, 1952): 1010–12, quote on 1010. The authors here were particularly interested in "these Yemenite Jews [who] have recently migrated to the new state of Israel and thus become much more readily accessible for anthropological investigation."

74. Alfred Plaut and Alice C. Kohn-Speyer, "The Carcinogenic Action of Smegma," *Science* 105 (April 11, 1947): 391–92.

75. Weiner et al., "Carcinoma of the Cervix in Jewish Women," 421–22.

76. "Circumcision and Cancer," *Time* (April 5, 1954), 96–97. There was also speculation about circumcision's impact on prostate cancer rates among Jews. See Herbert Kenyon, *The Prostate Gland* (New York: Random House, 1950).

77. As *Time* reported, Wynder had found that in women "whose husbands have been routinely, ritually circumcised, cervical cancer is only one-tenth to one-fifth as common as among non-Jewish women of similar age and social status." Ibid., 96–97.

78. Ernest Kennaway, "Some Biological Aspects of Jewish Ritual," *Man* 57 (May 1957): 65–72, quotes on 67 and 71.

79. Bemoaning the absence of black women from the Kinsey 1953 study, sociologist Edward N. Palmer supported the need for a separate study of black women: "I think such a study if adequately conducted, would determine, once and for all, whether there are any differences in the sexual behavior of Negroes and whites—in this instance, the female." See Palmer, "Sex Study Snubs Negroes . . . ," 1.

80. *Proceedings of the First National Cancer Conference* (American Cancer Society and the National Cancer Institute of the U.S. Public Health Service, Federal Security Agency), 131–32.

81. J. Towne, "Carcinoma of the Cervix in Nulliparous and Celibate Women," 1955–1956 *Yearbook of Obstetrics and Gynecology* (1955): 430–31.

82. John Moseley, "Cancer and the Negro," *Crisis* 56 (May 1949): 138–39, 156.

83. *Meeting the Challenge of Cancer: A Supplement to The Challenge of Cancer* (Washington, DC: U.S. Department of Health, Education, and Welfare; Public Health Service; National Cancer Institute, 1955), 19.

84. "Statement of Dr. Charles Cameron," *Hearings before the Committee on Interstate and Foreign Commerce, House of Representatives, October 1, 2, and 3, 1953* (Washington, DC: U.S. Government Printing Office, 1953), 198.

85. Milton Rosenblatt and James Lisa, *Cancer of the Lung* (New York: Oxford University Press, 1956), 25–26.

86. "The clinical impressions on racial susceptibility are gradually being revised as more data are accumulated on the non-white population," insisted the authors. Ibid., 25–26.

87. John S. LaDue, "Bronchogenic Carcionoma," in Roscoe Pullen, ed., *Pulmonary Diseases* (Philadelphia: Lea and Febinger, 1955), 207–8.

88. Alton Ochsner, Michael DeBakey, Charles E. Dunlap, and Irving Richman, "Bronchogenic Carcinoma," *Rocky Mountain Medical Journal* (November 1948): 1009–13, quote on 1009.

89. John S. LaDue, "Bronchogenic Carcionoma," 208.

90. E. Cuyler Hammond and Willard Machle, "Environmental and Occupational Factors in the Development of Lung Cancer," in Edgar Mayer and Herbert Maier, eds., *Pulmonary Carcinoma: Pathogenesis, Diagnosis, and Treatment* (New York: New York University Press, 1956), 141.

91. Doll, "In Memoriam: Ernst Wynder . . . ," 1798–99.

92. William S. Barton, "AMA Groups Discuss Sex, Colds and Heart Disease," *Los Angeles Times* (June 26, 1950), 19.

93. Hammond and Machle, "Environmental and Occupational Factors," 141.

94. Alton Ochsner, M.D., to Dr. A. L. Exline, Austin, TX, December 12, 1957. Box 21, Folder 1, Alton Ochsner Papers, Williams Research Center, Historic New Orleans Collection.

95. Rosenblatt and Lisa, *Cancer of the Lung*," 31. "Although the incidence of smoking among females has steadily increased since World War I," they noted, "the ratio of lung cancer between the sexes is still predominantly in favor of the males."

96. John H. Schaefer, M.D., Assistant Medical Director, State of California, Department of Employment, to Alton Ochsner, M.D., May 5, 1955. Box 21, Folder 5, Ochsner Papers.

97. Alton Ochsner, M.D., to Dr. Cleon W. Symonds, November 5, 1955, Box 21, Folder 5, Ochsner Papers.

98. By the mid to late 1940s, for example, there was growing interest in the role of estrogen and testosterone in the growth of tumors and in the genesis of some cancers. See, for example, "Tumorigenesis," in E. C. Hamblen, *Endocrinology of Woman* (Springfield, IL: Charles C. Thomas, 1945), 526.

99. On the rise in cancer mortality being accounted for primarily by the rise in men's cancers, see "The Battle Against Disease," *American Mercury* 60 (January 1945): 134.

100. Haenszel, "Cancer Mortality . . . ," 49.

101. Cameron, *The Truth about Cancer*. See also, popular coverage of these emerging trends: "Cancer Symposium Studies Incidence," *New York Times* (July 31, 1950), 19; "Some Diseases Rare with Yemenite Jews," *New York Times* (March 10, 1955), 5; "Yemen Jews Free of Lung Cancer; Smoking Habits Eyed for Reason," *New York Times* (February 1, 1955), 31.

102. Charles S. Johnson, "The Socio-Economic Background of Negro Health Status," *Journal of Negro Education* 18 (Summer 1949): 429–35, quote on 429.

103. One observer in 1942 insisted, for example, that the "loss of young men from war casualties will cause a relative increase in age groups susceptible to cancer." "Cancer Expected to Increase," *Science News Letter* 42 (October 3, 1942): 211.

104. Johnson, "The Socio-Economic Background," 429. "The health status of the Negro," he wrote, "cannot be adequately understood without reference to the socio-economic context of the group."

105. One white observer insisted in the Pittsburgh African-American press, "many Negroes who become ill are slowly murdered by jim crowism." Ted Le Berthon, "White Man's Views," *Pittsburgh Courier* (November 4, 1944), 6.

106. J. F. Hynes, *American Journal of Roentgenology and Radium Therapy* (Sept. 1948): 368–81.

107. Peller, *Not in My Time*, 314.

108. Peller, *Cancer in Man*, 226–27.

109. Steiner, *Cancer*, 6.

110. Ann Hallman Pettigrew and Thomas F. Pettigrew, "Race, Disease, and Deseg-regation: A New Look," *Phylon* 24 (4th quarter, 1963): 315–33.

Chapter 5

1. Wednesday May 17, 1972, *ABC Evening News*, headline: "Negroes: Cancer/ Sickle Cell Anemia," *Vanderbilt Television News Archives*. Header Link: 20608.

2. "Cancer in Negroes," *Newsweek* (May 29, 1972); "Cancer Rise in Blacks Reported," *Chicago Tribune* (May 18, 1972), A9.

3. Herbert Seidman, quoted in Victor Cohn, "'Alarming' Increase Is Reported in Cancer Deaths Among Blacks," *Washington Post* (May 18, 1972), A1, A19.

4. "The 'New Negro' of the South: Behind the Birmingham Story," Speech, June 27, 1956, San Francisco, CA, at the Forty-Seventh Annual NAACP Convention, in Clayborne Carson, Stewart Burns, Susan Carson, Pete Holloran, and Dana Powell, eds., *The Papers of Martin Luther King, Jr., vol. 3, Birth of a New Age, December 1955–December 1956* (Berkeley: University of California Press, 1997).

5. See discussion of Dublin in chapter 2.

6. In the year the study gained attention, public debates flared over school busing and the aftermath of urban riots. Noel Greenwood, "School Desegregation—Successes, Failures, Surprises," *Los Angeles Times* (May 21, 1972), B1; John Hebers, "Fear of Busing Exceeds Its Use," *New York Times* (May 28, 1972), 1; Henry Mitchell, "Busing: All Viewpoints," *Washington Post* (May 8, 1972), B13; Louis Mitchell, "The Flames Have Died Down, But . . . Did the Riots Make a Difference?" *Chicago Tribune* (May 10, 1972), 14; "Guardsmen Patrol City in Carolina," *New York Times* (May 30, 1972), 41; Sandra Haggerty, "On Being Black: Color Consciousness Is More than Skin Deep," *Los Angeles Times* (May 24, 1972), B7.

7. Jack Slater, "The Terrible Rise of Cancer Among Blacks," *Ebony* (November 1979), 131–36, quote on 131. Another writer in the *Atlanta Daily World*, an African-American publication, wondered whether the new trend was caused by blacks moving "into more industrialized communities and occupations . . . [with] increased exposure to environmental cancer causes." "Non-whites Three Times More Likely to Get Cancer than Whites," *Atlanta Daily World* (June 16, 1977), 1.

8. LaSalle D. Leffall Jr., *No Boundaries: A Cancer Surgeon's Odyssey* (Washington, DC: Howard University Press, 2005), 89.

9. Victor Cohn, "'Alarming' Increase Is Reported in Cancer Deaths among Blacks," *Washington Post* (May 18, 1972), A1.

10. "Minnie Riperton, 31; Sang, Wrote 'Loving You,'" *Washington Post* (July 13, 1979), D7. Jennings Parrott, "Newsmakers—Rickover Can't See Admirals for Stars," *Los Angeles Times* (April 5, 1977), 2.

11. Quackery, it seemed, had returned in the form of antiestablishment activism, yet Krebiozen was a sort of antiestablishment protest that could also appeal to main-stream Americans. Pamela K. Burkhalter, "Cancer Quackery," *American Journal of Nursing* 77 (March 1977): 451–53, quote on 451. For more on historical controversies surrounding medical quackery, see, for example, James Harvey Young, *Toadstool Millionaires: A Social History of Patent Medicines in American Before Federal Regula-*

tion (Princeton, NJ: Princeton University Press, 1961); Charles O. Jackson, *Food and Drug Legislation in the New Deal* (Princeton, NJ: Princeton University Press, 1970); James Harvey Young, *The Medical Messiahs: A Social History of Quackery in Twentieth-Century America* (Princeton, NJ: Princeton University Press, 1967); Eric S. Juhnke, *Quacks and Crusaders: The Fabulous Careers of John Brinkley, Norman Baker, and Harry Hoxsey* (Lawrence: University of Kansas Press, 2002).

12. Elinor Langer, "Krebiozen: Government Indicts Sponsors of Alleged Cancer Drug," *Science* 146 (December 4, 1964): 1282.

13. Of twenty-two patients treated with the drug Krebiozen (seventeen of whom were deemed to be terminal cases), eight had since died, but twelve had "shown a moderate to marked regression" of the growths, and two showed "no evidence of cancer." Roy Gibbons, "U. of I. Reveals Cancer Control Drug," *Chicago Daily Tribune* (March 27, 1951), 1.

14. "Cancer Control Drug Developed by War Refugee," *Chicago Daily Tribune* (March 29, 1951), 8. As the *Tribune* reported, Durovic "said he carried on the work with krebiozen secretly in Argentina" and "the reason no Argentine doctors ever hear about the preparation . . . is because he never discussed his work or the discovery." Jules Dubos, "Doctors Where Durovic Worked Cool to His Drug," *Chicago Daily Tribune* (March 29, 1951), 7. Clayton Kirkpatrick, "Durovic's Life Story Reveals War Ancestry," *Chicago Daily Tribune* (November 16, 1951), 1. See also Elinor Langer, "Krebiozen: A Dozen Years after Introduction, Controversy over Cancer Treatment Still Flares," *Science* 140 (June 21, 1963): 1294–96.

15. Lee Shassere, "Five Women Give Living Proof of Drug's Power," *Chicago Daily Tribune* (March 27, 1951), 10. "Warns Against 'False Hopes' of Cancer Cure," *Chicago Daily Tribune* (April 29, 1951), 19.

16. "U.S. Outlines Rules on New Cancer Drug," *New York Times* (March 31, 1951), 8.

17. "New Cancer Drug No Aid, A.M.A. Says," *New York Times* (October 26, 1951), 18; "Another Cancer Cure Flops," *Chicago Daily Tribune* (October 27, 1951), 8.

18. "Because real hope is so hard to sustain," noted one reporter, "false hopes come easily." James E. Hague, "A Cancer 'Cure' and Its Backer Found Wanting," *Washington Post* (November 18, 1951), B3.

19. Burkhalter, "Cancer Quackery," 451.

20. Roy Gibbons, "Blast Cancer Society Over Krebiozen Snub," *Chicago Daily Tribune* (May 19, 1959), A1.

21. Roy Gibbons, "Public Warned Cancer Cure Is Yet in Future," *Chicago Daily Tribune* (March 28, 1951), 6.

22. See, for instance, an exchange between Ivy and C. P. Rhoads of the Memorial Center for Cancer and Allied Diseases in New York. C. P. Rhoads and A. C. Ivy, "Comments and Communications: Krebiozen," *Science* 114 (September 14, 1951): 285–86.

23. "Cancer Expert Suspended by Medical Group," *Los Angeles Times* (November 14, 1951), 6; Elinor Langer, "Krebiozen: A Dozen Years after Introduction . . . ," 1295.

24. "Why the Doctors Won't Try the 'Cancer Drug,'" *Los Angeles Times* (December 25, 1952), A4.

25. "Douglas Criticizes A.M.A. on Krebiozen, Urges Test," *Chicago Tribune* (June 13, 1963), A1.

26. Drew Pearson, "The Washington Merry-Go-Round: Bricker Kills Cancer Drug Report," *Washington Post* (August 20, 1953), 39; "Sen. Bricker Drops Probe of Krebiozen Started by Tobey," *Chicago Daily Tribune* (August 21, 1953), A11; "Cancer Inquiry Ends in Senate Dispute," *New York Times* (August 21, 1953), 34.

27. Drew Pearson, "Krebiozen Creates Feud in AMA," *Washington Post* (August 30, 1953), B5; Percy Wood, "Each Side at Krebiozen Hearing Accuses Other of Making Errors in Its Reports," *Chicago Daily Tribune* (October 9, 1953), 1. Percy Wood, "Plot Charges Against Dr. Ivy," *Chicago Daily Tribune* (April 10, 1953), 1; Percy Wood, "Seven Cancer Victims Silent Witnesses at Krebiozen Hearing," *Chicago Daily Tribune* (April 11, 1953), 1; "Illini President Forced Out, Blames Drug Affair," *Los Angeles Times* (July 26, 1953), 18.

28. "Asks Ribicoff O.K. for Test of Krebiozen," *Chicago Daily Tribune* (April 13, 1961), A4; "Kribiozen [*sic*] Evaluation to Be Made," *Washington Post* (April 21, 1961), A12; Elinor Langer, "Krebiozen: Nearly a Decade of Controversy Spent in Pursuit of 'Fair,' Government-Sponsored Test," *Science* 140 (June 28, 1963): 1383–85.

29. Quoted in Ray Lyman Wilbur, "The Health Status and Health Education of Negroes in the United States: A Critical Summary," *Journal of Negro Education* 6 (July 1937): 572–77, quote on 575.

30. John B. West, "The Present Character and Extent of Health Education for Negroes," *Journal of Negro Education* 6 (July 1936): 493–98, quote on 493.

31. Wilbur, "The Health Status and Health Education of Negroes . . . ," 576.

32. James Patterson has argued that the lesson of the Krebiozen story was that "the continuing appeal of unorthodox practitioners . . . depended considerably on the fears and resentments of economically disadvantaged people who were excluded from the modern medical culture." James Patterson, *The Dread Disease: Cancer and Modern American Culture* (Cambridge, MA: Harvard University Press, 1987), 166. "Demonstrator Arrested at White House," *Washington Post* (June 5, 1963), B6.

33. "Cancer Drug Supporters Picket White House," *Los Angeles Times* (August 7, 1963), 3; "Pickets Seek Kennedy's Aid for Krebiozen," *Chicago Tribune* (August 7, 1963), A2. "Pro-Krebiozen Pickets March in Washington," *Chicago Tribune* (November 2, 1964), B7; "10 Fail to See Johnson on Cancer Drug," *Los Angeles Times* (November 2, 1964), 14.

34. "Krebiozen's Backers Open 1st Convention," *Chicago Tribune* (February 2, 1964), 16.

35. Robert C. Toth, "Krebiozen: The Moral Case May Never Be Cleared Up," *Los Angeles Times* (December 15, 1963), L3. One observer noted that President Lyndon Johnson's new vice president, Hubert Humphrey, was "viewed with suspicion [by the Department of Health, Education, and Welfare] . . . because he endorsed a 'fair test' for a Krebiozen resolution in the Senate even after NIH and FDA declared that

allegedly anti-cancer compound to be worthless." Robert C. Toth, "President Holds Key: Powerful Role for Humphrey Indicated," *Los Angeles Times* (November 5, 1964), 2.

36. Andrew Abbott, "Status and Status Strain in the Professions," *American Journal of Sociology* 86 (January 1981): 819–35, quote on 828.

37. John T. Flynn, "Krebiozen and Faith" (letter), *Science* 152 (April 29, 1966): 592.

38. Elinor Langer, "Krebiozen: A Dozen Years after Introduction, Controversy over Cancer Treatment Still Flares," *Science* 140 (June 21, 1963): 1294–96, quote on 1295.

39. Langer, "Krebiozen: Government Indicts Sponsors . . . ," 1282.

40. Langer, "Krebiozen: Nearly a Decade of Controversy . . . ," 1384.

41. Leonard B. Berman Jr., "By No Means Complete Is Truth about Cancer," *Washington Post and Times* (May 6, 1956), E7.

42. Advertisement, *New York Times* (January 30, 1955), BR18; "Feud Over So-Called Cancer Drug on Again," *Los Angeles Times* (January 31, 1955), 13; Percy Wood, "Krebiozen: The Pro-Ivy View of the 'Key' Cancer Drug," *Chicago Daily Tribune* (February 20, 1955), G5; "Cancer Expert Attacks Charges Against AMA," *Los Angeles Times* (February 1, 1955), 14.

43. Robert K. Plumb, "Cancer Drug Test Balked at Parley," *New York Times* (October 25, 1958), 18; Langer, "Krebiozen: Nearly a Decade of Controversy . . . ," 1384.

44. "Cancer Group Rejects Test of Krebiozen," *Chicago Daily Tribune* (March 5, 1959), A9; Percy Wood, "Chances Rise for U.S. Test of Krebiozen," *Chicago Daily Tribune* (February 8, 1961), 3; Langer, "Krebiozen: Nearly a Decade of Controversy . . . ," 1384.

45. Langer, "Krebiozen: Nearly a Decade of Controversy . . . ," 1385.

46. See "Asks Ribicoff O.K. . . . ," A4; "Kribiozen [*sic*] Evaluation . . . ," A12; Langer, "Krebiozen: Nearly a Decade of Controversy . . . ," 1385.

47. Robert C. Toth, "U.S. Investigation of Krebiozen Due," *New York Times* (January 16, 1963), 9.

48. Langer, "Krebiozen: Nearly a Decade of Controversy . . . ," 1383.

49. "FDA Bans Krebiozen, an Anti-Cancer Drug, from Interstate Traffic," *Wall Street Journal* (July 16, 1963), 20.

50. Kenneth M. Endicott, Director of the National Cancer Institute, to Owen Wangensteen, Professor of Surgery, University of Minnesota, October 1, 1963, Department of Surgery Collection #1007, Box 18, Folder: "Krebiozen, 1953," University Archives, University of Minnesota.

51. "U.S. Jury Said to Return Krebiozen Case Indictment," *New York Times* (October 28, 1964), 13; "Krebiozen Doctor Charged with 'Intent to Defraud,'" *Los Angeles Times* (October 30, 1964), 3; Langer, "Krebiozen: Government Indicts Sponsors . . . ," 1282; "A.M.A. Aide Says Krebiozen Was Put on Market," *Chicago Tribune* (October 23, 1963), 22; "Two Doctors to Face Krebiozen Case Hearing," *Los Angeles Times* (November 9, 1963), 16.

52. "Cancer Patients Honor Dr. Ivy," *Chicago Tribune* (February 20, 1965), 6. "Trial Is Under Way in Krebiozen Case," *New York Times* (April 29, 1965), 5.

53. W. Joynes McFarlan, "U.S. Calls Krebiozen Inexpensive Acid, Ineffective in Treatment of Cancer," *Washington Post, Times Herald* (September 8, 1963), A3; Langer, "Krebiozen: Government Indicts Sponsors . . . ," 1282.

54. Langer, "Krebiozen: Government Indicts Sponsors . . . ," 1282. Prosecutors insisted that one patient under Krebiozen treatment, Helen Best, did not die from viral pneumonia in August 1953 (as Ivy and Durovic reported to the FDA) but from cancer in 1954.

55. "A.M.A. Is Accused of Falsifying Data to Block Krebiozen," *New York Times* (May 7, 1965), 11; "Inspector Accused at Krebiozen Trial," *New York Times* (May 21, 1965), 68; "A.M.A. Stopped Krebiozen Test: Ivy," *Chicago Tribune* (December 16, 1965), 18.

56. Langer, "Krebiozen: Nearly a Decade of Controversy . . . ," 1383.

57. Langer, "The Krebiozen Case: What Happened in Chicago," *Science* 151 (March 4, 1966): 1061–64, quote on 1061. Donald Janson, "Krebiozen called 'Pillar of Fraud'; Prosecutor Says Promoters Fit Mold for 'Quackery,'" *New York Times* (January 22, 1966).

58. Langer, "Krebiozen: A Dozen Years after Introduction . . . ," 1294.

59. Sheila Wolfe, "Medic Credits Cancer Cure to Krebiozen," *Chicago Tribune* (October 29, 1965), 7.

60. Sheila Wolfe, "'Cancer' Was Ulcer, Trial Witness Told," *Chicago Tribune* (November 5, 1965), D15; James Strong, "Patient Tells of Krebiozen Aiding Health," *Chicago Tribune* (November 20, 1965), N9.

61. "Krebiozen Backers Win, But Drug Still a Loser," *Chicago Daily Tribune* (February 1, 1966), 4.

62. Langer, "The Krebiozen Case . . . ," 1064, 1061.

63. Arthur Snider, "Competence of Jury in Krebiozen Verdict Hit," *Los Angeles Times* (February 2, 1966), 6.

64. "Cancer 'Cure' Picket Arrested," *Washington Post* (June 23, 1964), C1.

65. See "Asks Ribicoff O.K. . . . ," A4; "Kribiozen [*sic*] Evaluation . . . ," A12; Langer, "Krebiozen: Nearly a Decade of Controversy . . . ," 1385.

66. Robert K. Plumb, "The Question of a Cure," *New York Times* (October 30, 1955), BR36.

67. Bernard Pierre Widman, "The Case of the Incurable Cancer Patient," *Radiology* 61 (1953): 215–21.

68. Sidney J. Cutler, *Cancer Illness among Residents in Atlanta, Georgia, 1947*, Cancer Morbidity Series—No. 1, 1950 (Bethesda, MD: National Cancer Institute of the National Institutes of Health, 1950), 12.

69. Thomas Quinn Curtiss, "Saroyan in Search of a Moral," *New York Times* (November 20, 1949), BR5; William Saroyan, *Don't Go Away Mad, and Two Other Plays* (New York: Harcourt Brace, 1949), 21.

70. Preface to Saroyan, *Don't Go Away Mad*, 7–9.

71. One reviewer called the play a long-winded version of Eugene O'Neill's play *The Iceman Cometh*. See Thomas Quinn Curtiss, "Saroyan in Search of a Moral," *New York Times* (November 20, 1949), BR5.

72. Charles Scruggs, "The Tale of Two Cities in James Baldwin's *Go Tell It On the Mountain*," *American Literature* 52 (March 1980): 1–17, quote on 8.

73. Marjorie Driscoll, "When Black Blood Boils," *Los Angeles Times* (January 21, 1968), O32.

74. Robert Cromie, "Novel Takes an Oblique Look at Racial Situation in U.S.," *Chicago Tribune* (October 30, 1967), 18. See also Mel Watkins, "The Black Revolution in Books," *New York Times* (August 10, 1969), BR8.

75. Cromie, "Novel Takes an Oblique Look . . . ," 18.

76. John A. Williams, *The Man Who Cried I Am* (New York: Signet Press, 1967), 362.

77. Driscoll, "When Black Blood Boils," O32.

78. Williams, *The Man*, 9–10, 151.

79. Ibid., 151–52, 171.

80. Martin Luther King Jr., "Speech at the Great March on Detroit," June 23, 1963, Detroit, Michigan. In Clayborn Carson and Kris Shepard, eds., *A Call to Conscience: The Landmark Speeches of Dr. Martin Luther King, Jr.* (New York: IPM/ Warner Books, 2001).

81. "The 'New Negro' of the South: Behind the Birmingham Story," speech, June 27, 1956, San Francisco, at the Forty-Seventh Annual NAACP Convention. In Clayborne Carson, Stewart Burns, Susan Carson, Pete Holloran, and Dana Powell, eds., *The Papers of Martin Luther King, Jr.*, vol. 3, *Birth of a New Age, December 1955– December 1956* (Berkeley: University of California Press, 1997).

82. *Proceedings from Enhancing Interactions to Reduce Cancer Health Disparities: An NCI-Wide Workshop*, November 2005 (Bethesda, MD: U.S. Department of Health and Human Services, National Institutes of Health, February 2006), 4.

83. Cohn, "'Alarming' Increase . . . ," A1.

84. "Cancer Rise in Blacks Reported," *Chicago Tribune* (May 18, 1972), A9.

85. "Cancer in Negroes," *Newsweek* (May 29, 1972), 47; Cohn, "'Alarming' Increase . . . ," A1.

86. Ulrich Henschke, LaSalle Leffall, Jr., Claudia Mason, Andreas Reinhold, Roy Schneider, and Jack White, "Alarming Increase of the Cancer Mortality in the U.S. Black Population (1950–1967)," *Cancer* 31 (April 1973): 763–68, quote on 768.

87. LaSalle D. Leffall Jr., *No Boundaries: A Cancer Surgeon's Odyssey* (Washington, DC: Howard University Press, 2005), 90.

88. Leffall, *No Boundaries*, 89; Otha Linton, "Ulrich Henschke," *Journal of the American College of Radiology* 3 (August 2006): 639. See also U. K. Henschke, "Radiation Therapy of Cancer of the Colon and Rectum," *Diseases of the Colon and Rectum* 2 (January–February 1959): 84–91; R. D. Brasfield and U. K. Henschke, "Internal Mammary Radiation Implants," *Progress in Clinical Cancer* 10 (1965) 450–452; U. K.

Henschke, "Cesium-131 Seeds for Permanent Implants," *Radiology* 85 (December 1965): 1117–19.

89. Howard University Cancer Center website: www.med.howard.edu/hucc/. Accessed: June 19, 2007.

90. Leffall, *No Boundaries*, 46, 61–62, 65, 89.

91. L. D. Leffall Jr., J. B. Ewing, and J. E. White, "Cancer of the Breast in Young Negro Patients," *American Journal of Surgery* 109 (April 1965): 404–5; L. D. Leffall Jr., J. E. White, and B. Syphax, "Massive Gastrointestinal Hemorrhage: A Clinical Study," *Medical Annals of the District of Columbia* 36 (November 1967): 657–61; M. Crawford, E. B. Chung, L. D. Leffall Jr., and J. E. White, "Soft Part Sarcoma in Negroes," *Cancer* 26 (September 1970): 503–12.

92. U. K. Henschke, L. D. Leffall, C. H. Mason, A. W. Reinhold, R. L. Schneider, and J. E. White, "Comparison of the Cancer Deaths in the Black and White U.S.A. Population from 1949 to 1967," *Medical Annals of the District of Columbia* 41 (5) (1972): 293–98.

93. Henschke et al., "Comparison of the Cancer Deaths . . . ," 293–98.

94. Victor Cohn, "'Alarming' Increase . . . ," A1.

95. Henschke et al., "Comparison of the Cancer Deaths . . . ," 293–98, 297.

96. Henschke et al., "Alarming Increase . . . ," 763–68, 768.

97. Henschke et al., "Comparison of the Cancer Deaths . . . ," 297.

98. Ibid., 297.

99. U.S. Commission on Civil Rights, *Equal Opportunity in Hospitals and Health Facilities: Civil Rights Policies Under the Hill-Burton Program* (Washington, DC: Public Health Service, Department of Health, Education, and Welfare, March 1965) (CCR Special Publication Number 2, March 1965); Elinor Langer, "Hospital Discrimination: HEW Criticized by Civil Rights Groups," *Science* 149 (September 17, 1965): 1355–57.

100. Henschke et al., "Alarming Increase . . . ," 763–68.

101. Ibid., 763–68, 767.

102. Ibid. Here the authors cited D. Waggoner and G. Newell, "Regional Convergence of Cancer Mortality Rates over Time in the United States, 1940–1960," *American Journal of Epidemiology* 93 (1971): 79–93.

103. Cohn, "'Alarming' Increase . . . ," A1. See also, "Rise in Negro Cancer Deaths Held Alarming," *Los Angeles Times* (May 18, 1972), A5.

104. Henschke et al., "Alarming Increase . . . ," 768.

105. Victor Cohn, "Whites Lead in Cancer Survival," *Washington Post* (August 28, 1975), A1.

106. On cancer and these agents, see Robert Vare, "Inhaling Cancer: Asbestos under Fire," *New Republic* (July 8, 1972), 13–15; Ralph Nader, "In the Public Interest: Tainted Meat," *New Republic* (September 2, 1972), 9–10; "Red Food Coloring—How Safe Is It?" *Consumer Reports* (February 1973), 130; Deborah Shapley, "Occupational Cancer: Government Challenged in Beryllium Proceeding," *Science* 198 (December 2, 1977): 898; Thomas H. Maugh III, "Carcinogens in the Workplace: Where to Start Cleaning Up," *Science News* 197 (September 23, 1977): 1268; "Industry's Challenge on

Benzene," *Business Week* (August 22, 1977), 30; "DES Blamed on Mothers' Cancer," *Science News* 112 (December 1977): 422; "Hair Dyes and Cancer: GAO Asks for Action," *Science News* 112 (December 1977): 422; Philip H. Abelson, "The Tris Controversy," *Science* 197 (July 8, 1977): 8; "Tris—A Sleepwear Flame Retardant Banned," *Consumer's Research* (June 1977), 4; Richard F. Spark, "Legislating Against Cancer," *New Republic* (June 3, 1978), 16.

107. Cohn, "'Alarming' Increase . . . ," A1. For Howard University's Paul Cornely, the new lessons of cancer were rooted in social inequality: "The black male has always been at the bottom of the heap. In jobs, he has the lowest paying and dirtiest ones where there is carcinogenic exposure." Cohn, "Whites Lead in Cancer Survival," A10.

108. Henschke et al., "Comparison of the Cancer Deaths . . . ," 296–97.

109. Ibid., 768.

110. Henschke et al., "Alarming Increase . . . ," 768.

111. Ibid., 768.

112. F. Burbank, *Patterns in Cancer Mortality in the United States, 1950–1967*, National Cancer Institute, Monograph 33 (Washington, DC: U.S. Government Printing Office, 1971).

113. Henschke et al., "Comparison of the Cancer Deaths . . . ," 298. One retrospective study tracking similar trends cast the story in white/nonwhite terms, noting that "non-white predominance became in 1950 for females and in 1956 for males." F. Burbank and J. Fraumeni, "U.S. Cancer Mortality: Non-white Predominance," *Journal of the National Cancer Institute* 49 (1972): 649–59.

114. See discussion of this issue in chapter 4. See also *1970 Census of Population, Subject Reports: Persons of Spanish Origin* (Washington, DC: Bureau of the Census, U.S. Department of Commerce, Social and Economic Statistics Administration, June 1973), x. See also Melissa Nobles, *Shades of Citizenship: Race and the Census in Modern Politics* (Stanford, CA: Stanford University Press, 2000), 190.

115. *1970 Census of Population*, ix.

116. Henschke et al., "Alarming Increase . . . ," 768.

117. As one researcher noted about another study of lung cancer in Los Angeles, the authors of the study "of possible effects of air pollution on risk of lung cancer in Los Angeles County, claim to restrict their analysis to Caucasians but they include Mexican-Americans in this group. The problem here is that about one-third of the ancestry of Mexican-Americans in California is Mexican Indian, a fact which may be relevant to this and other epidemiological studies." T. Edwards Reed, "Ethnic Classification of Mexican-Americans," *Science* 185 (July 1974): 283.

118. The NCI created an End Results Program in 1957 in order to provide a "resource for uniformly collected data on survival of patients drawn from more general populations than those attracted to major research centers." Cutler and Latourette, "A National Cooperative Program for the Evaluation of End Results in Cancer," *Journal of the National Cancer Institute* 22 (1959): 633–46. The NCI's lack of a database similarly hampered data collection and comparison. Michael Shimkin, *As Memory Serves: Six Essays on a Personal Involvement with the National Cancer Institute,*

1938–1978 (NIH Publication No. 83–2217, September 1983), 178. See also Cutler et al., eds., *End Results in Cancer, Report No. 4* (Washington, DC: U.S. Government Printing Office, 1972).

119. M. H. Myers and B. F. Hankey, *Cancer Patient Survival Experience: Trends in Survival 1960–1963 to 1970–1973, Comparison of Survival for Black and White Patients, Long Term Effects of Cancer,* NIH Publication 80–2148 (Washington, DC: U.S. Department of Health and Human Services, June 1980), 1.

120. M. A. Haynes and B. D. Smedley, eds., *The Unequal Burden of Cancer: An Assessment of NIH Programs and Research for Minorities and the Medically Underserved* (Washington, DC: Institute of Medicine, National Academy Press, 1999), 47.

121. Ibid., 47.

122. William I. Lourie, ed., *The 1976 SEER Code Manual: Cancer Surveillance, Epidemiology, and End Results Reporting* (Washington, DC: Public Health Service, U.S. Department of Health, Education, and Welfare, 1976), p. 12. Accessed July 25, 2007. http://seer.cancer.gov/manuals/historic/codeman_1976.pdf.

123. Questions of representative sampling continued to reshape the program from year to year. J. L. Young, "Incidence of Cancer in the United States Blacks," *Cancer Research* 35 (November 1975): 3525–36. This study, for example, pointed to the underenumeration of young black men and overenumeration of older black men in the Census and speculated about its impact on cancer statistics. In 1979, the SEER program was expanded again to include ten rural counties in Georgia, again with the goal of adding more African-American representation. In 1983, SEER reorganized yet again: "a four-county area of New Jersey was added to increase coverage of African Americans and Hispanics. New Orleans and New Jersey were subsequently dropped from the program for 'technical reasons.'" In 1992, SEER added Los Angeles County and the San Jose–Monterey area of California to further increase representation of Hispanics and other ethnic groups of interest. "This resulted in a 46 percent increase in the overall population covered by the SEER program, and increases of 41 percent for African Americans and 223 percent for Hispanics." Haynes and Smedley, *Unequal Burden,* 47.

124. Preston Valien, "General Demographic Characteristics of the Negro Population in the United States," *Journal of Negro Education* 32 (Autumn 1963): 329–36.

125. Haynes and Smedley, *Unequal Burden*; Brian D. Smedley, Adrienne Y. Stith, and Alan R. Nelson, eds., *Unequal Treatment: Confronting Racial and Ethnic Disparities in Health Care* (Washington, DC: National Academy Press, 2001).

126. Leffall, *No Boundaries,* 89.

127. Henschke et al., "Alarming Increase . . . ," 767.

128. Cutler, *Cancer Illness . . . Atlanta, Georgia, 1947,* 20–21. The same pattern was found in Marcus's study of Birmingham. See Samuel Marcus, *Cancer Illness among Residents of Birmingham, Alabama 1948,* Cancer Morbidity Series, No. 8. (Bethesda, MD: National Cancer Institute of the National Institutes of Health, 1952), 25.

129. Max Freedman, "The Krebiozen Case: Matters of Public Policy Raised for Study," *Los Angeles Times* (August 26, 1963), A5.

130. Charles S. Johnson, "The Socio-Economic Background of Negro Health Status," *Journal of Negro Education* 18 (Summer 1949): 429–35, 435. As Johnson noted, "for each death there are about 16 illnesses lasting for one week or longer," and illness was a far more complex social problem than mortality.

131. Cohn, "Whites Lead in Cancer Survival," A1.

132. L. A. G. Ries, M. P. Eisner, C. L. Kosary, B. F. Hankey, B. A. Miller, L. Clegg, et al., eds., *SEER Cancer Statistics Review, 1975–2002* (Bethesda, MD: National Cancer Institute, 2005). Robin Marantz Henig, "The Fight Against Cancer: Beating the Odds," *Washington Post* (April 8, 1984), 11. See also Peter Kerr, "Relationships: A Group for Cancer Survivors," *New York Times* (March 29, 1982), B9; Judy Klemesrud, "Life with Cancer: A Survivor's Guide," *New York Times* (October 10, 1982), S.1, 92; "The Struggle of Andrew Silk," *New York Times* (October 18, 1981), S.6, 33.

133. Audre Lorde, *The Cancer Journals* (San Francisco: Aunt Lute Books, 1980).

134. Samuel S. Epstein, *The Politics of Cancer Revisited* (New York: East Ridge Press, 1998), xvii. First published 1978 by Sierra Club Books.

135. Phillip M. Boffey, "Cancer Progress: Are the Statistics Telling the Truth?" *New York Times* (September 18, 1984), C1.

136. Ibid., C1. As Boffey noted, "the last decade has seen a striking shift of opinion among Government officials and scientists in the importance attached to chemical carcinogens."

137. Phillip Boffey, "The Parade of Chemicals that Cause Cancer Seems Endless," *New York Times* (March 20, 1984), C1.

138. Boffey, "Cancer Progress . . . ," C1.

Chapter 6

1. Camille L. Mojica, "Breast Cancer Linked to Lifestyle: Higher Rate Among Bay Area Women Due to Choices, Study Says," *San Jose Mercury* (July 2, 1997), 1B; Chris Shackleford, "Women Taking Responsibility for Their Health; An Expert Panel of Women Physicians Answer Your Questions," *Chattanooga Free Press* (November 4, 1997), C1.

2. "Cancer Strikes Black Men Hardest of Any Population Group," *New Jersey Star Ledger* (April 27, 1996), 3; Raymond Demers et al., "Increasing Incidence of Cancer of the Prostate; The Experience of Black and White Men in the Detroit Metropolitan Area," *Archives of Internal Medicine* 154 (June 13, 1994): 1211.

3. Matt Crenson, "Common Prostate Cancer Test Needs Changes for Black Men," *Chattanooga Times* (August 29, 1996), A18.

4. "Cancer Strikes Black Men Hardest . . . ," 3.

5. Kurt Snipes, "Overview of the Fifth Asian American Network for Cancer Awareness, Research, and Training Cancer Control Academy," *Cancer* 104, S12 (November 7, 2005): 2889–90.

6. Roger E. Hernandez, "Death Statistics Fatal to Assumptions," *Oregonian* (July 15, 1995), D8.

7. Ibid., D8.

8. H.J.RES.119: A joint resolution designating the week of April 19, 1987, through April 25, 1987, as "National Minority Cancer Awareness Week," became Public Law No. 100–27 with the president's signature in April that year.

9. Randolph E. Schmid, "More Charity Stamps Proposed," *Associated Press Online* (October 22, 1997); "Clinton Signs Breast Cancer Stamp Bill," *Patriot Ledger* (August 14, 1997), 5. Steven Woloshin, M.D., and Lisa M. Schwartz, M.D., "The U.S. Postal Service and Cancer Screening—Stamps of Approval?" *New England Journal of Medicine* 340 (March 18, 1999), 884–87.

10. Juanne Nancarrow Clarke, "A Comparison of Breast, Testicular, and Prostate Cancer in Mass Print Media (1996–2001)," *Social Science and Medicine* 59 (2004): 541–51, quote on 548.

11. Barbara Ehrenreich, "Welcome to Cancerland," *Harper's* (November 2001), 43–53, quote on 50.

12. Betti Cuniberti, "On Recliner Row, Breast Cancer Awareness Can Send Wrong Message," *St. Louis Post-Dispatch* (October 13, 2004), F1.

13. Roni Rabin, "Health Disparities Persist for Men, and Doctors Ask Why," *New York Times* (November 14, 2006), F1.

14. Gina Kolata, "Testing for Cancer Risks," *New York Times* (March 28, 1995), A18; Gina Kolata, "Tests to Assess Risks for Cancer Raising New Questions," *New York Times* (March 27, 1995), A1.

15. Raymond Demers et al., "Increasing Incidence of Cancer of the Prostate: The Experience of Black and White Men in the Detroit Metropolitan Area," *Archives of Internal Medicine* 154 (June 13, 1994): 1211.

16. A. L. Potosky, B. A. Miller, P. C. Albertsen, and B. S. Kramer, "The Role of Increasing Detection in the Rising Incidence of Prostate Cancer," *Journal of the American Medical Association* 273 (February 15, 1995): 548–52.

17. Leonard Gomella, "The Will Rogers Phenomenon in Prostate Cancer: A Good Thing," *Cancer Journal from Scientific American* 4 (January/February 1998): 19-21; Schuman and Mandel, "Epidemiology of Prostatic Cancer in Blacks," *Preventive Medicine* 9 (1980): 630–49.

18. Rabin, "Health Disparities Persist for Men, and Doctors Ask Why."

19. M. C. Wang, L. A. Valenzuela, G. P. Murphy, and T. M. Chu, "Purification of a Human Prostate Specific Antigen," *Investigative Urology* 17 (1979): 159–63; T. A. Stamey, N. Yang, A. R. Hay, J. E. McNeal, F. S. Freida, and E. Redwine, "Prostate Specific Antigen as a Serum Marker for Adenocarcinoma of the Prostate," *New England Journal of Medicine* 317 (1987): 909–16; M. K. Brewer, M. P. Chetner, J. Beatie, B. M. Buchner, R. L. Vessella, and P. H. Lange, "Screening for Prostatic Carcinoma with Prostate Specific Antigen," *Journal of Urology* 147 (1992): 841–45; W. J. Catalona, D. S. Smith, T. L. Ratliff, K. M. Dodds, D. E. Coplen, J. J. Yuan, et al., "Measurement of Prostate-Specific Antigen in Serum as a Screening Test for Prostate Cancer," *New England Journal of Medicine* 324 (1991): 1156–61.

20. For more on the complicated clinical history of prostate cancer, see W. F. Whitmore Jr., "The Natural History of Prostate Cancer," *Cancer* 31 (1973): 1104–12.

21. Already in the 1980s there was a pronounced tendency toward radical prosta-tectomy for benign prostate enlargement (known as benign prostatic hyperplasia). See Thomas McDade, "Prostates and Profits: The Social Construction of Benign Prostatic Hyperplasia in American Men," *Medical Anthropology* 17 (1996): 1–22.

22. Robert Aronowitz, "The Rise of Surveillance," chapter 9 in *Unnatural History: Breast Cancer and American Society* (New York: Cambridge University Press, 2007), 211–34.

23. Mary McNaughton Collins, Floyd J. Fowler, J., Richard G. Robers, Joseph E. Oesterling, and George J. Annas, eds., "Medical Malpractice Implications of PSA Testing for Early Detection of Prostate Cancer," *Journal of Law, Medicine, and Ethics* 25 (1997).

24. Gina Kolata, "Tests to Assess Risks for Cancer Raising Questions," *New York Times* (March 27, 1995), A1. John Roberts, "Cancer Tests Don't Always Raise Survival Rates," *New York Times* (March 31, 1995), A30.

25. "FDA Approves New "Free PSA" Blood Text," March 11, 1998, press release by the Urological Sciences Research Foundation, http://www.usrf.org/breakingnews/bn_980311_freepsa.html. The Foundation had strong ties to industry.

26. Kim Painter, "Younger Women Weigh Worth, Worries about Mammograms; Doctors Divided on Risks for Patients Under 50," *USA Today* (January 21, 1997), 1D; Sabin Russell, "Mammogram Study Yields Cautionary Note," *San Francisco Chronicle* (July 3, 1996), A4.

27. Potosky et al., "The Role of Increasing Detection in the Rising Incidence of Prostate Cancer," 552.

28. Sreekanth Reddy, Marc Shapiro, Ronald Morton Jr., and Otis Brawley, "Prostate Cancer in Black and White Americans," *Cancer and Metastasis Reviews* 22 (2003): 83–86. See also O. W. Brawley, "Prostate Cancer and Black Men," *Seminars in Urology and Oncology* 16 (1998): 184–86.

29. "Change Sought in Prostate Test to Benefit Blacks with Cancer," *New York Times* (August 2, 1996), A14.

30. Ted O. Morgan, Steven J. Jacobsen, William F. McCarthy, Debra J. Jacobsen, David G. McLeod, and Judd W. Moul, "Age-Specific Reference Ranges for Serum Prostate-Specific Antigen in Black Men," *New England Journal of Medicine* 335 (August 1, 1996): 304–10; "Change Sought in Prostate Test . . . ," A14.

31. "Change Sought in Prostate Test . . . ," A14. See J. E. Oseterling, Y. Kumamoto, T. Tsukamoto, et al., "Serum Prostate-Specific Antigen in a Community-Based Population of Healthy Japanese Men: Lower Values than for Similarly Aged White Men," *British Journal of Urology* 75 (1995): 347–53.

32. Smith, Bullock, and Catalona, "Racial Differences in Operating Characteristics of PC Screening tests," *Journal of Urology* 158 (November 1997): 1861–66.

33. R. F. Kropman, W. de Kieviet, R. C. M. Pelger, and P. L. Venema, "The Effect of Orgasm on Prostate-Specific Antigen," *World Journal of Urology* 12 (December 1994): 313–15; M.-B. Tchetgen, J. T. Song, M. Strawderman, S. J. Jacobsen, and J. E. Oesterling, "Ejaculation Increases the Serum Prostate-Specific Antigen Concentration," *Urology* 47 (1996): 511–16; Joe Manning, "Ejaculation Can Skew Prostate Cancer

Test," *Milwaukee Journal Sentinel* (May 6, 1999), 3; Don Colburn, "Prostate Cancer Aims at Poorer Black Men," *Washington Post* (August 27, 1996), Z05.

34. Potosky et al., "The Role of Increasing Detection in the Rising Incidence of Prostate Cancer," 548–52. See also R. M. Merrill, E. J. Feuer, and J. L. Warren, et al., "Role of Transurethral Resection of the Prostate in Population-Based Prostate Cancer Incidence Rates," *American Journal of Epidemiology* 150 (1999): 848–60.

35. William S. Kubricht III, B. Jill Williams, Terence Whatley, Patricia Pinkard, and James A. Eastham, "Serum Testosterone Levels in African-American and White Men Undergoing Prostate Biopsy," *Urology* 54 (1999): 1035–38, quote on 1037.

36. Ibrahim Abdalla, Paul Ray, Vera Ray, Florin Vaida, and Srinivasan Vijayakumar, "Comparison of Serum Prostate-Specific Antigen Levels and PSA Density in African-American, White, and Hispanic Men without Prostate Cancer," *Urology*, 51 (1998): 300–305, quote on 304. By this point, the literature on prostate cancer and socioeconomic inequality had grown. See, for example, S. Vijayakumar, R. Weichselbaum, F. Vaida, W. Dale, and S. Hellman, "Prostate-Specific Antigen Levels in African-Americans Correlate with Insurance Status as an Indicator of Socio-economic Status," *Cancer Journal from Scientific American* 2 (1996): 225–33.

37. S. Vijayakumar, F. Vaida, R. Weichselbaum, and S. Hellman, "Race and the Will Rogers Phenomenon in Prostate Cancer," *Cancer Journal from Scientific American* 4 (January–February 1998): 27–35.

38. I. J. Powell and F. L. Meyskens, "African American Men and Hereditary/ Familial Prostate Cancer: Intermediate-Risk Populations for Chemoprevention Trials," *Urology* 57 (April 2001): 178–81.

39. Vijayakumar et al., "Race and the Will Rogers Phenomenon," 35.

40. Ibrahim Abdalla et al., *"Comparison,"* , 304.

41. Peter Albertsen, "Editorial: Unraveling the Epidemiology of Prostate Cancer," *Journal of Urology* 157 (June 1997): 2223.

42. Elizabeth Ward, Michael Thun, Lindsay Hannan, and Ahmedin Jemal, "Interpreting Cancer Trends," *Annals of the New York Academy of Science* 1076 (2006): 29–53, quote on 34–35, 36–37.

43. A. R. Feinstein, D. A. Sosin, and C. K. Wells, "Will Rogers Phenomenon. Stage Migration and New Diagnostic Techniques as a Source of Misleading Statistics for Survival in Cancer," *New England Journal of Medicine* 312 (1985): 1604–8.

44. For a short discussion of the Will Rogers phenomenon, see for example, Harvey Motulsky, *Intuitive Biostatistics* (New York: Oxford University Press, 1995), 274.

45. Gomella, "The Will Rogers Phenomenon . . . ," 20.

46. Vijayakumar et al., "Race and the Will Rogers Phenomenon," 35.

47. Ian Thompson, Robin J. Leach, Brad H. Pollock, and Susan L. Naylor, "Prostate Cancer and Prostate-Specific Antigen: The More We Know, the Less We Understand," *Journal of the National Cancer Institute* 95 (July 16, 2003): 1027–28.

48. "Prostate-cancer Test Misses Most Tumors, Findings Show," *Seattle Times* (January 24, 2003), A1.

49. "No Lifesaving Boost from Prostate Tests," *Chicago Sun Times* (January 15, 2006), A6.

50. Gina Kolata, "Tests to Assess Risks for Cancer Raising Questions," *New York Times* (March 27, 1995), A1.

51. G. L. Lu-Yao, M. Friedman, and M. S. L. Yao, "Use of Radical Prostatectomy among Medicare Beneficiaries before and after the Introduction of Prostate Specific Antigen Testing," *Journal of Urology* 157 (June 1997): 2219–22.

52. I. J. Powell, M. Banerjee, M. Novallo, W. Sakr, D. Grignon, D. P. Wood, J. E. Pontes, "Should the Age Specific Prostate Specific Antigen Cutoff for Prostate Biopsy Be Higher for Black than for White Men Older than 50 Years?" *Journal of Urology* 163 (January 2000): 146–49.

53. I. M. Thompson, D. K. Pauler, P. J. Goodman, et al., "Prevalence of Prostate Cancer Among Men with a Prostate-Specific Antigen Level < or = 4.0 ng per Milliliter," *New England Journal of Medicine* 350 (May 27, 2004): 2239–46.

54. Sreekanth Reddy, Marc Shapiro, Ronald Morton Jr., and Otis Brawley, "Prostate Cancer in Black and White Americans," *Cancer and Metastasis Reviews* 22 (2003): 83–86, quote on 83. See also O. W. Brawley, "Prostate Cancer and Black Men," *Seminars in Urology and Oncology* 16 (1998): 184–86.

55. Thomas Stamey, Mitchell Caldwell, John E. McNeal, Rosalie Nolley, Marcie Hemenez, and Joshua Downs, "The Prostate Specific Antigen Era in the United States Is Over for Prostate Cancer: What Happened in the Last 20 Years?" *Journal of Urology* 172 (October 2004): 1297–1301.

56. Laurie Barclay, M.D., "End of an Era for PSA Screening: A Newsmaker Interview with Thomas Stamey, M.D.," *Medscape Medical News* (September 17, 2004), www.medscape.com/viewarticle/489474; accessed on June 1, 2007.

57. "Patient with Prostate Cancer Voices Doubts about PSA Test," *Globe and Mail* (Toronto) (August 22, 206), A11.

58. Stamey et al., *"The Prostate Specific Antigen Era,"* 1298.

59. Dorsey Griffith, "Cancer News Mostly Good for State's Asians," *Sacramento Bee* (October 22, 2004), A1.

60. Grace Ma and Linda Fleisher, "Awareness of Cancer Information Among Asian Americans," *Journal of Community Health* 28 (April 2003): 115–30, quote on 127.

61. Taunya English, "Cervical Cancer Tests Urged," *Oregonian* (August 17, 2001), B1.

62. Mark D. Somerson, "OSU-led Team Will Study Asian-Americans' Health: $7.6 Million Research Project to Target Cancer," *Columbus Dispatch* (April 7, 2000), 2B.

63. Warren E. Leary, "Study Urged on Cancer and Races," *New York Times* (January 21, 1999), A11.

64. See, for example, G. A. Alexander, K. C. Chu, and R. C. S. Ho, "Representation of Asian Americans in Clinical Cancer Trials," *Annals of Epidemiology* 10 (2000): 561–67; R. Ho, "Disparities in Cancer Treatment Outcomes among Asian Americans: Implications for the Asian American Network for Cancer Awareness, Research, and Training," *Asian American Pacific Islander Journal of Health* 8 (2000): 39–42; and Debra A. Paterniti, Moon S. Chen et al., "Asian Americans and Cancer Clinical

Trials: A Mixed Methods Approach to Understanding Awareness and Experience," *Cancer* 104 (December 15, 2005): 3015–24.

65. Leary, "Study Urged on Cancer and Races," A11.

66. The "poorly understood" claim is from Miok C. Lee, "Knowledge, Barriers, and Motivators Related to Cervical Cancer Screening Among Korean-American Women: A FOCUS Group Approach," *Cancer Nursing* 23 (3) (June 2000): 168–75. On being lumped together, see English, "Cervical Cancer Tests Urged," B1.

67. Leary, "Study Urged on Cancer and Races," A11.

68. English, "Cervical Cancer Tests Urged," B1.

69. Nancy J. Burke, J. Carey Jackson, Hue Chan Thai, Frank Stackhouse, Tung Nguyen, Anthony Chen, and Victoria M. Taylor, "'Honoring Tradition, Accepting New Ways': Development of a Hepatitis B Control Intervention for Vietnamese Immigrants," *Ethnicity and Health* 9 (May 2004): 153–69, quote on 155.

70. Data on increasing population drawn from Marc J. Perry and Paul Maclun, "Population Change and Distribution, Census 2000 Brief" (Washington, DC: U.S. Census Bureau, Department of Commerce, April 2001), www.census.gov/prod/2001pubs/c2kbr01–2.pdf; Mark E. Pfeifer, "U.S. Census 2000: An Overview of National and Regional Trends in Vietnamese Residential Distribution," *Review of Vietnamese Studies* 1 (2001): 1–8.

71. Betty L. Martin, "Survey Shows Asian Health Attitudes," *Houston Chronicle* (January 27, 2005), 20.

72. Justin Gest, "Health and Medicine: A Closer Look at Care for Asians," *Houston Chronicle* (July 29, 2004), B2.

73. "Cancer and Race," *Atlanta Constitution* (January 21, 1999), 12C.

74. Cathy Pascual, "Culture Puts Vietnamese Women at Increased Cancer, Risk," *Los Angeles Times* (October 12, 2000), B2. As one 1996 Bay Area California study argued, "74 percent of those the registry classified as Vietnamese agreed with this classification on interview, while 90 percent of those identifying themselves as Vietnamese were so classified . . . Misclassification was associated with age, sex, year of immigration, education, and language use." See also K. C. Swallen, S. L. Glaser, S. L. Stewart, D. W. West, G. N. Jenkins, and S. J. McPhee, "Accuracy of Racial Classification of Vietnamese Patients in a Population-Based Cancer Registry," *Ethnicity and Disease* 8 (1998): 218–27. See also S. Gomez and S. Glaser, "Misclassification of Race/Ethnicity in a Population-Based Cancer Registry," *Cancer Causes and Control* 17 (August 2006): 771–81. In this study, the authors found that "case counts were underestimated in Chinese by 16 percent, Vietnamese by 37 percent, and American Indian by 63 percent," 775.

75. T. D. Sterling and A. Arundel, "A Review of Recent Vietnamese Studies on the Carcinogenic and Teratogenic Effects of Phenoxy Herbicide Exposure," *International Journal of Health Services* 16 (1986): 265–78.

76. Phillip Boffey, "The Parade of Chemicals that Cause Cancer Seems Endless," *New York Times* (March 20, 1984), C1.

77. Sallie Han, "For Asian Women, It's a Risky Move," *New York Daily News* (September 11, 1997), 44.

78. Regina Ziegler et al., "Migration Patterns and Breast Cancer Risk in Asian-American Women," *Journal of the National Cancer Institute* 85 (November 17, 1993): 1819–27, 1825. The study concluded (p. 1825) that "it is . . . reasonable to expect that exposure to the West does not generate an instantaneous effect, but instead it causes a gradual increase in risk over time, similar to that noted for most 'carcinogens.'"

79. Han, "For Asian Women . . . ," 44.

80. "Asians in U.S. Adopt Unhealthy Habits," *Chicago Sun Times* (October 19, 1992), 10.

81. As the reporter noted, "the immigrants left a land where cancer attacked many people at the back of the throat or in the liver and they resettled in a country where those cancers are rare." Paul Watson, "Asian, Canadian Scientists Try to Solve Cancer Riddle," *Toronto Star* (November 2, 1996), A2.

82. "Asians in U.S. Adopt Unhealthy Habits," 10.

83. "U.S. Cultural Gap Increases Asian Women's Cancer Risk," *Chicago Sun Times* (June 25, 1996), 21.

84. Neal L. Benowitz, Eliseo J. Perez-Stable, Brenda Herrera, and Peyton Jacob III, "Slower Metabolism and Reduced Intake of Nicotine from Cigarette Smoking in Chinese-Americans," *Journal of the National Cancer Institute* 94 (January 16, 2002): 108–115, quote on 111. Kawanza Griffin, "Asian Smokers' Risk of Lung Cancer Studied," *Milwaukee Journal Sentinel* (January 21, 2002), 4G.

85. Benowitz et al., "Slower Metabolism . . . ," 113.

86. Cicero Estrella, "English Fluency Linked to Asian Women's Cancer Risk," *San Francisco Chronicle* (October 22, 2004), B3.

87. See also Jane Brody, "Finding Tea's Place at a Healthful Table," *New York Times* (March 20, 2001), F8; Sabin Russell, "Herbs Tested on Breast Cancer," *San Francisco Chronicle* (July 16, 2001), A4; Karen Herzog, "Soy in Diet May Provide a Number of Health Benefits," *Milwaukee Journal Sentinel* (October 17, 1999), 4.

88. C. N. Jenkins, S. J. McPhee, J. A. Bird, and N. T. Bonilla, "Cancer Risks and Prevention Practices Among Vietnamese Refugees," *Western Journal of Medicine* 153 (September 1990): 331; V. M. Taylor, J. C. Jackson, S. M. Schwarts, S. P. Tu, and B. Thompson, "Cervical Cancer among Asian American Women: A Neglected Public Health Problem?" *Asian American Pacific Island Journal for Health* 4 (Autumn 1996): 327–42.

89. My Linh D. Huynh, Stephen S. Raab, and Eric J. Suba, "Association Between War and Cervical Cancer Among Vietnamese Women," *International Journal of Cancer* 110 (2004): 775–77. See also D. C. Skegg, P. A. Corwin, C. Paul, and R. Doll, "Importance of the Male Factor in Cancer of the Cervix," *Lancet* (1982): 581–83.

90. Huynh et al., "Association Between War and Cervical Cancer . . . ," 777.

91. Grace X. Ma et al., "Risk Perceptions and Barriers to Hepatitis B Screening and Vaccination Among Vietnamese Immigrants," *Journal of Immigrant and Minority Health* 9 (July 2007): 213–20; Grace X. Ma et al., "Knowledge, Attitudes, and Behaviors of Hepatitis B Screening and Vaccination and Liver Cancer Risks Among Vietnamese Americans," *Journal of Health Care for the Poor and Underserved* 18 (February 2007): 62–73.

92. See Maren Klawiter, *The Biopolitics of Breast Cancer: Changing Cultures of Disease and Activism* (Minneapolis: University of Minnesota Press, 2008).

93. Katherine Ellison, "Breast Cancer Puzzle in Marin," *Washington Post* (October 23, 2002), A3.

94. Joan Ryan, "Unseen Killer Stalks Marin," *San Francisco Chronicle* (March 24, 2002), D3; Dana Wilkie, "Feinstein Looks into 'Cancer Clusters,'" *San Diego Union-Tribune* (June 6, 2001), A3; Diana Marszalek, "Marin's Cancer Mystery," *San Francisco Chronicle* (August 13, 1999), 1; Katherine Ellison, "Breast Cancer Puzzle in Marin," A3; Ulysses Torassa, "Breast Cancer Amid Affluence," *San Francisco Chronicle* (January 26, 2003), A1.

95. Ryan, "Unseen Killer Stalks Marin," D3.

96. Ellison, "Breast Cancer Puzzle in Marin," A3.

97. Marszalek, "Marin's Cancer Mystery," 1

98. Wilkie, "Feinstein Looks into 'Cancer Clusters.'"

99. Susan Sachs, "Public Clamor Puts Focus on 'Clusters' in Cancer Research," *New York Times* (September 21, 1998), A1.

100. Kevin Johnson, "Cancer Clusters Are Difficult to Nail Down," *USA Today* (April 13, 1999), 8D; Jan Hollingsworth, "Cancer Cluster Still Puzzles Investigators," *Tampa Tribune* (February 12, 1999), 1; Andrea Kannapell, "Drinking Water, and What Else? From Wells in South Jersey Flow Radium, and Anxiety," *New York Times* (August 30, 1998), 14NJ1; "There Is Something in the Water in Toms River," *Newark Star-Ledger* (April 19, 1996), 20.

101. Christine Russell, "Risk versus Reality: How The Public Perceives Health Hazards," *Washington Post* (June 14, 1988), Z14.

102. Kevin Johnson, "Cancer Clusters . . . ," 8D; Susan Sachs, "Public Clamor Puts Focus on 'Clusters' in Cancer Research," *New York Times* (September 21, 1998), A1.

103. Ellison, "Breast Cancer Puzzle in Marin," A3.

104. Ibid., A3.

105. Adair Lara, "The Risks of Relief: Hormone Replacement Is Hotly Debated—Are the Benefits Worth the Danger?" *San Francisco Chronicle* (January 18, 2004), E1; Thomas H. Maugh II, "Death Rate for Breast Cancer Bolsters Theory," *Los Angeles Times* (April 19, 2007), A9.

106. Ulysses Torassa, "Cancer Linked to Hormone Therapy on the Rise," *San Francisco Chronicle* (March 19, 2003), A4.

107. Marszalek, "Marin's Cancer Mystery," 1.

108. Ruth Rosen, "What Causes Breast Cancer?" *San Francisco Chronicle* (May 15, 2003), A23.

109. Maugh, "Death Rate for Breast Cancer Bolsters Theory," A9.

110. Ellison, "Breast Cancer Puzzle in Marin," A3.

111. Nancy Krieger, "Is Breast Cancer a Disease of Affluence, Poverty, or Both? The Case of African-American Women," *American Journal of Public Health* 92 (April 2002): 611–12.

112. Elliot Diringer and Elaine Herscher, "One County, One Disease, Two Realities," *San Francisco Chronicle* (November 2, 1997), 1/Z1.

113. Daniel G. Kopans, "The Mammography Screening Controversy," *Cancer Journal of the Scientific American* 4 (January/February 1998): 22–24. As Kopans noted, "the most recent controversy became acute when, in 1993, the National Cancer Institute (NCI) withdrew support for breast cancer screening for women ages 40 to 49." But in April 1997, "the NCI reversed its position of the past three years, and once again came out in support of screening women ages 40 to 49." See also Barron Lerner, *Breast Cancer Wars* (New York: Oxford University Press, 2001); and Candis Morrison, *Breast Cancer Detection Behaviors in Low-Income Women over Forty: Characteristics Associated with Frequency and Proficiency of Breast Self-Examination* (PhD diss, University of Maryland, College Park, 1994). And for more on this controversy, which reemerged in late 2009, see Robert Aronowitz, "Addicted to Mammograms," *New York Times* (November 20, 2009), www.nytimes.com/2009/11/20/opinion/20aronowitz.html.

114. Kimlin Tam Ashing-Giwa et al., "Understanding the Breast Cancer Experience of Women: A Qualitative Study of African-American, Asian-American, Latina, and Caucasian Cancer Survivors," *Psychooncology* 13 (June 2004): 408–28, quote on 409.

115. See for example, President's Cancer Panel, 2002 Annual Report, *Facing Cancer in Indian Country: The Yakama Nation and Pacific Northwest Tribes* (Washington, DC: U.S. Department of Health and Human Services, National Institutes of Health, National Cancer Institute, December 2003).

116. Elizabeth Ward, Michael Thun, Lindsay Hannan, and Ahmedin Jemal, "Interpreting Cancer Trends," *Annals of the New York Academy of Science* 1076 (2006): 29–53, 34–35, 36–37.

117. Jennifer Bill, "Breast Self-Exam Backers Rip Study," *Toronto Sun* (June 27, 2001), 7.

118. Warren King, "Hutch Study Questions Usefulness of Breast Self-Exams," *Seattle Times* (October 2, 2002), B1.

119. One study of low-income women in 1994, for example, argued that "proficiency scores of white women were significantly higher than those of African-American women; 4.6 and 3.4 respectively." Married women performed the practice better than divorced or widowed women. Morrison, *Breast Cancer Detection.*

120. Carol Vaughn, "Trying to Beat Cancer in the Long Run," *Houston Chronicle* (October 23, 2003), 2.

121. "The Failure of Breast Self-Exams," *New York Times* (October 6, 2002), 12.

122. Bill, "Breast Self-Exam Backers Rip Study," 7.

123. Russell Harris and Linda Kinsinger, "Routinely Teaching Breast Self-Examination Is Dead. What Does This Mean?" *Journal of the National Cancer Institute* 49 (October 2, 2002): 1420–21.

124. Harris and Kinsinger, "Routinely Teaching Breast Self-Examination . . . ," 1421.

Conclusion

1. Ann Woofter, Certified Reporter, Transcript of *President's Cancer Panel: Real People, Real Problems*, Langford Auditorium, Vanderbilt-Ingram Cancer Center, Vanderbilt University, Nashville, TN, November 16, 2000, 201.

2. Ibid., 201–3, 239.

3. Ibid.

4. "Oscar Winner Louis Gossett Jr. Addresses Prostate Cancer Stigma," March 4, 2010, Grio website, www.thegrio.com/news/oscar-winner-gossett-jr-addresses-prostate-cancer-stigma.php.

5. Steven Woloshin and Lisa M. Schwartz, "The U.S. Postal Service and Cancer Screening—Stamps of Approval?" *New England Journal of Medicine* 340 (March 18, 1999): 884–87.

6. Sylvia Noble Tesh, *Hidden Arguments: Political Ideology and Disease Prevention Policy* (New Brunswick, NJ: Rutgers University Press, 1988).

7. Leslie Reagan, "Engendering the Dread Disease: Women, Men, and Cancer," *American Journal of Public Health* 87 (November 1997): 1779.

8. "Science News: Breast Cancer in Relation to Childbearing and Nursing," *Science* 80 (September 1934): 8–9.

9. Susan Sontag, *Illness as Metaphor* (New York: Farrar, Straus and Giroux, 1978), 1.

10. Woofter, Transcript of *President's Cancer Panel*, 423, 447–48.

11. Ibid., 411, 454, 447.

12. Matthew Pratt Guterl, *The Color of Race in America, 1900–1940* (Cambridge, MA: Harvard University Press, 2001), 70.

13. "By committing this common error [or reading difference as necessarily "racial"]—forgetting the environmental influence in the etiology of disease—the Jews have repeatedly been described as the best example of a race which shows striking immunities or susceptibilities to certain diseases." Maurice Fishberg, *The Jews: A Study of Race and Environment* (New York: Charles Scribner's Sons, 1911), 272.

14. Woofter, *Transcript of President's Cancer Panel*, 368.

15. "Questions and Answers for Census 2000 Data on Race," *U.S. Census Bureau Public Information Office*, March 14, 2001, www.census.gov/Press-Release/www/2001/raceqandas.html.

16. Katie McFadden and Larry McShane, "Use of Word Negro on 2010 Census Forms Raises Memories of Jim Crow," *New York Daily News* (January 6, 2010). www.nydailynews.com/news/2010/01/06/2010–01–06_census_negro_issue_use_of_word_on_forms_raises_hackles_memories_of_jim_crow.html.

17. Jonathan Kahn, "Patenting Race in a Genomic Age," in Barbara Koenig, Sandra Soo-Jin Lee, and Sarah Richardson, eds., *Revisiting Race in a Genomic Age* (New Brunswick, NJ: Rutgers University Press, 2008), 129–48.

18. Barbara Koenig, Sandra Soo-Jin Lee, and Sarah Richardson, "Race and Genetics in a Genomic Age," in Koenig et al., *Revisiting Race in a Genomic Age*, 4.

19. "He represents what is great about America not because we have finally elected a black man as president, but because we've recognized the greatness of our mixed-breed heritage." Elizabeth Wurtzel, "Obama's Triumph Is America's Too," *Wall Street Journal* (November 6, 2008), A17.

20. "White Americans Majority to End by Midcentury," *USA Today*, December 17, 2009, www.usatoday.com/news/nation/census/2009–12–16-White-minority_N.htm.

ACKNOWLEDGMENTS

This study of disease and racial perceptions took years to develop and has benefited from many insightful colleagues, readers, reviewers, research assistants, and friends. Over the years, the book also profited from suggestions I received after lectures on the work in academic and nonacademic venues. Looking back over this long road, I owe many debts to a wide array of individuals whose comments on drafts, or insightful suggestions following presentations or in research groups, helped sharpen and refine the project: Garland Allen, Robert Aronowitz, Robin Bachin, David Barnes, Ronald Bayer, Ruha Benjamin, Lundy Braun, Theodore Brown, David Cantor, Joel Cantor, Curt Cardwell, James Colgrove, Angela Creager, Christopher Crenner, Stephen Crystal, Ronit Elk, Steven Epstein, Amy Fairchild, Susan Fitzpatrick, Joseph Gabriel, Carolina Giraldo, Gillian Hadfield, Dolores Hayden, Dorothy Hodgson, Allan Horwitz, Judith Houck, Jeffrey House, Joel Howell, Nancy Scheper-Hughes, Linda Jack, Jonathan Kahn, John Kasson, Joy Kasson, Peter Keating, Richard Keller, David Jones, Susan Lawrence, Howard Leventhal, Susan Lindee, Bruce Link, Justin Lorts, Hal Luft, Elizabeth Lunbeck, Robert Martensen, Danielle McGuire, Rachel McLaughlin, Jonathan Metzl, Clyde Milner, Richard Mizelle, Khalil Muhammad, Jane Park, Stefani Pfeiffer, Dorothy Porter, Paul Rabinow, Karen Rader, Leslie Reagan, Susan Reverby, Naomi Rogers,

Charles Rosenberg, David Rosner, Alex Rothman, Carolyn Rouse, Rebecca Scales, Walton Schalick, Victor Schoenbach, Daniel Segal, Donald Spivey, Claude Steele, Greg Swedberg, Karen Sue Taussig, William Vega, John Harley Warner, Elizabeth Watkins, and Christine Zemla.

Another group of colleagues and friends provided sustained advice and close readings for which I'm particularly grateful: Isra Ali, Mia Bay, Jeffrey Dowd, Gerald Grob, Bridget Gurtler, Alison Isenberg, Shakti Jaising, Ann Jurecic, Mia Kissil, Nancy Krieger, Catherine Lee, Barron Lerner, Julie Livingston, David Mechanic, Stephen Pemberton, Melissa Stein, Anantha Sudhakar, Dora Vargha, Fatimah Williams-Castro, and Troy Duster. In particular, I must single out Susan Ferber at Oxford University Press for special thanks for her smart shepherding of the project, Audra Wolfe for her incredibly sharp editorial eye, Shakti Jaising for her remarkable observations on everything from narrative flow to word choice, imagery, and argument, and, finally, Alison Isenberg for her always incisive commentaries on just about every aspect of the book.

A number of grants, fellowships, and visiting appointments provided crucial support relating to the research and writing phases of this project. These include the Center for Advanced Study in the Behavioral Sciences at Stanford University, the Center for African-American Studies at Princeton University, the Institute for Health, Health Care Policy, and Aging Research at Rutgers University, the Robert Wood Johnson Foundation Investigator Award in Health Policy Research, and the James S. McDonnell Foundation Centennial Fellowship in the History of Science. No acknowledgement would be complete without thanking members of my family—my parents, Bert and Lynette Wailoo, my brother, Christopher Wailoo, my better half, Alison Isenberg, and our wonderful children, Elliot and Myla—for their exemplary good humor, patience, persistence, and loving support. At the end of the day, any errors or oversights in these pages are purely my own.

Page numbers in italics denote illustrations.

African Americans: (*continued*)
dichotomy; Howard University report on
black mortality; mass migrations; race;
racial classifications; Riperton, Minnie;
specific individuals
African American women: breast cancer
in, 2, 8, 170, 171, 200n95; and breast
self-examination, 83, 85–86, 170; and
cancer awareness, 1, 3, 5, 34, 36, 62, 65,
85–86; cervical cancer in, 60–61, 103, 111;
and doctor-patient relationships, 93–94;
in films and literature, 67–68, 86–87, 131;
inner lives of, 3, 34; mortality trends, 144;
ovarian cancer in, 99; personalized cancer
portraits, 1–2, 3, 5, 92, 93–94, 143, 144, 182;
survival rates, 144; uterine cancer in, 57,
86, 199n84. *See also* African Americans;
Riperton, Minnie; *specific individuals*
Africans, 97, 102
Albertsen, Peter, 157
American Cancer Society (ACS): on
black mortality, 120; on breast self-
examination, 83, 172; cancer awareness
campaigns, 67; as cancer "establishment,"
143, 144; first black outreach by, 2, 11,
85; first black president, 2, 122, 142–43;
and Krebiozen debate, 125, 126; Minnie
Riperton as spokesperson, 1, 122, 143;
parent organization of, 9. *See also*
American Society for the Control of
Cancer (ASCC)
American Eugenics Society, 9, 16
American Indians: gall bladder cancer in,
141; and Mexican Americans, 99, 223n117;
as nonwhites, 103
American Journal of Cancer, 56, 64
American Journal of Nursing, 26
American Medical Association: attention
to smoking, 113–14; on breast self-
examination, 84; health magazine of, 38;
and Krebiozen debate, 123, 124, 125, 126,
127, 128, 129
American Public Health Association, 14
American Society for the Control of
Cancer (ASCC): cancer awareness
campaigns, 16–17, 22, 34, 36, 66, 67;
founding of, 9; as predecessor to
American Cancer Society, 9, 67; and
Women's Field Army, 36, 66. *See also*
American Cancer Society (ACS)
American South: cancer rates in, 44, 53;
fictional accounts of, 46–47; health care
for blacks in, 49, 50; health of blacks in,

41, 43, 44–45; infectious diseases in, 36;
mortality in, 44, 56; skin cancer in, 97, 102
Anglo-Americans, 24, 34, 183. *See also* whites
Appalachia, 42–43, 180
Aronowitz, Robert, 21, 186n16
ASCC. *See* American Society for the
Control of Cancer (ASCC)
Asian Americans: breast cancer in, 164, 165,
181; breast self-examination by, 165, 166,
170, 172; cancer awareness in, 161–62;
cancer causation theories for, 164–66,
181; ethnic and cultural differences
among, 162, 163; heart disease in, 162; and
immigration to U.S., 43–44, 148–49, 163,
164–65, 178, 181; in Los Angeles study,
10, 100; lung cancer in, 149, 165–66;
men, 166; as nonwhite, 6, 105–6; racial
classifications for, 6, 100, 105–6, 151,
161–64, 174–75; in U.S. census, 6; women,
11, 148–49, 162, 164–65, 166, 170, 172, 181.
See also Chinese Americans; Filipinos;
Japanese Americans; Korean Americans;
Vietnamese Americans
Atlanta, Ga., 142, 143
Auden, W.H., 29

Baldwin, James, 86, 87, 131
Baltimore, Md., 42–43
Barker, J. Ellis, 9, 40
Barnett, J.C., 20
Beckman Coulter (company), 153
Benn, Gottfried, 27–28
Berenblum, Isaac, 95, 107, 108, 110
Bernardi, Daniel, 67–68
Black: as census category, 6, 184. *See also*
African Americans
Black Valley (Weaver), 30
bladder cancer, 102
Blake, Doris, 108
Bloodgood, Joseph Colt, 36
Boas, Franz, 98
Bogart, Humphrey, 80
Bogen, Emil, 14, 19
bone cancer, 99
Bousfield, M.O., 59
Bradley, Mary Hastings, 29–31
Bradley, Tom, 2
BRCA-1 and BRCA-2 genes, 151, 154
breast cancer: 1955 statistics, 73; in African
Americans, 2, 8, 170, 171, 200n95; in
Asian Americans, 164, 165, 181; in cancer
scholarship, 186n16; comparisons with
prostate cancer, 150, 152–53; genetic

testing for, 151, 154; and hormone replacement therapy, 151, 168–69; in Jane Addams, 13–14; mammograms, 151, 153, 154, 157, 171, 233n113; mortality, 8, 17, 170, 171; national awareness efforts, 150; and reproductive choices, 9, 14, 15, 19, 23, 25, 34, 73, 148, 178, 189n11, 189n16; research funding for, 150, 152; treatments, 20, 151, 154, 205n70; in whites, 8, 11, 103, 113, 170, 171. *See also* breast self-examination (BSE); Marin County breast cancer epidemic; Riperton, Minnie

breast self-examination (BSE): by African Americans, 83, 85–86, 170; by Asian women, 165, 166, 170, 172; cultural origins of, 10, 69–70, 82–84, 85; film messages about, 10, 67, 68, 82–83, 85–86, 90; by Hispanics, 170, 172; lack of lifesaving benefit, 159, 173; by married women, 170, 172; as self protection and empowerment, 10, 69, 83, 84, 85, 170, 172, 173; study questioning efficacy of, 171–73; whiteness as framework for, 2, 68, 85, 90, 170–71; and white women, 10, 82, 83, 85, 170, 172

Brodkin, Karen, 106

Broun, LeRoy, 26, 28

BSE. *See* breast self-examination (BSE)

Budapest, 52, 53, 54

Burks, Lorna Doone, 75–76, 84–85

Burt, A.M., 21

Bush, Hayden, 144

Cabot, Richard, 20, 21, 28, 31

Callaway, Enoch, 49

Callen, Maude, 65

Cameron, Charles: on affluent society, 76; on cancer as multifaceted disease, 112; as director of American Cancer Society, 10, 84; on early detection, 83, 84; *The Truth About Cancer,* 102–3

Cancer: Its Origins, Its Development, and Its Self-Perpetuation (Meyer), 41

Cancer: Race and Geography (Steiner), 95–101

cancer: crossing color line, 3–4, 6, 12, 40–41, 65, 179, 182; as egalitarian, 5, 9, 47, 61, 92, 94–96, 115, 118, 143; "epidemics" of, 7, 11–12, 157, 171, 174; fear of, 1, 6, 13, 15, 22, 28, 74, 80, 81, 82, 177; personalized portraits of, 1–2, 3, 4, 5, 46–47, 66, 68, 80–81, 89, 143, 144, 170, 175, 176–78, 179, 182; stigma associated with, 2, 26–29, 31, 32, 38, 68, 73–74, 84, 165, 172, 178, 179, 193n61, 193n64,

203n49. *See also* cancer awareness; cancer causation theories; cancer establishment; diagnosis; mortality; survival; treatments; *specific cancers*

Cancer (journal), 136

Cancer and Race (Sorsby), 52–55

cancer awareness: "awareness contexts" in, 8; class divisions in, 25–26; cultural origins of, 4–5; deception and paternalism in, 31–32, 74–80, 81–82, 83, 178, 204n62; divergent trajectories for white women and blacks, 8–9, 68, 179; doctor-patient relationships, 31–32, 70, 74–80, 81–82, 85; fictional dramatizations, 22–23, 29–31, 32–33; identity politics in, 11, 145, 150, 171, 174, 178, 179–80; in immigrants, 34, 161–62; military imagery in, 9–10, 67, 68, 69–70, 71, 83, 89, 90, 91; national campaigns, 150; public cynicism, 122–23, 125; racial undercurrents in, 3, 35, 36, 68; "right living" as key to, 21–23; and self-surveillance campaigns, 70, 72, 82–86, 179; as social ideology, 3, 4–5, 178; as struggle for resources and equal access, 94, 121, 142, 143–44, 150, 178–79; wealth-poverty divide in, 180. *See also* diagnostic tools; media; men; public health; women; *specific racial and ethnic groups*

cancer causation theories: affluence, 2–3, 76, 167, 169; aging, 7, 115, 195n9; behavior, 112, 115, 163; civilization, 2–3, 10, 14, 18, 21–24, 63, 86, 97, 112, 149, 164–65, 181; culture, 150, 163; diet, 18, 32, 95, 139, 163, 165; diversity in, 107, 112, 114; environmental and occupational exposures, 112, 113–14, 115, 139, 144, 145, 148, 149, 163, 164, 216n7, 223n107; ethnicity, 112, 149, 150, 151, 165–66; genetic difference, 5, 95, 110, 137, 138, 139, 151, 154, 163, 168, 171, 182, 183, 184; hormones, 114, 156, 168–69; racial biology, 5, 14–15, 53, 93, 95, 97, 110, 114, 115–16, 137, 149, 150, 151, 152, 154–57, 178, 181; reproductive choices, 9, 14, 15, 19, 23, 25, 34, 38, 73, 148, 149, 169, 189n11, 189n16, 191n46; sexual behavior, 10, 54, 95, 107–11, 112, 114, 166; social inequalities, 113, 114, 115, 116, 118, 137–38, 142, 156; viruses, 114; white female vulnerability, 3, 4–5, 9, 14–18, 19, 25–26, 29, 32, 34, 35–36, 37, 38, 39, 94, 95, 178, 179, 181, 190n26. *See also* Howard University report on black mortality; Jewish cervical cancer anomaly; mass migrations cancer diagnosis. *See* diagnosis; diagnostic tools; early detection

cancer establishment: blind to black cancer experience, 11, 146; Howard University critique of, 11, 135–36; main entities in, 143, 144, 146; medical paternalism of, 129, 178; public skepticism toward, 11, 121–22, 129, 144–45, 177, 178. *See also* American Cancer Society (ACS); National Cancer Institute (NCI); U.S. Public Health Service (PHS)

The Cancer Journals (Lorde), 144

cancer survival. *See* survival

cancer treatments. *See* treatments

Cansino, Margarita Carmen (Rita Hayworth), 87

Carson, Rachel, 125

Carter Administration, 145

Carter, Jimmy, 1

Cathcart, Gary, 128

Caucasoids, 100–101. *See also* whites

Cayleff, Susan, 80, 81

Census. *See* U.S. Census

Central Americans, 6

cervical cancer: 1920s statistics, 17; 1940s statistics, 73; 1950s statistics, 73; in African Americans, 60–61, 103, 111; delaying diagnosis, 36; and Henrietta Lacks, 87; and human papillomavirus, 166; in Japanese Americans, 11, 149, 163, 174–75; in Jews, 10, 53–54, 95, 102–3; in lower class women, 26, 111; in middle class women, 73; and Pap smears, 84, 90, 115, 137; reproductive choices linked to, 25, 60–61; sexual behavior linked to, 54, 95, 107–11, 166; in Vietnamese Americans, 11–12, 149, 161, 163, 166, 171, 174; in whites, 25, 102–3, 108, 163. *See also* Jewish cervical cancer anomaly

chemotherapy: as improved cancer therapy, 76, 90, 124; life extension from, 96, 121, 137, 143; for prostate cancer, 152. *See also* treatments

Chicago Defender, 86

Chicago Medical Society, 124

Chicago Tribune: on cancer awareness, 2; on Howard University report, 134; on Krebiozen trial, 128; movie review, 67, 73

Chinese Americans: breast cancer in, 165; cancer awareness in, 161; cancer of nasopharynx, 97, 141; immigration to U.S., 164, 165; in Los Angeles study, 96–97, 98, 100; lung cancer in, 149,

165–66; as nonwhite, 103; smoking by, 149, 165–66

chorioepithelioma, 99

Civilization Against Cancer (Little), 61

civilization-primitivism dichotomy: African Americans as "immune" to cancer, 5, 9, 11, 34, 40, 41–42, 43, 45, 60, 63, 64, 94, 98, 105, 148, 152, 178, 181; civilization as cause of cancer, 2–3, 10, 14, 18, 21–24, 40–44, 63, 86, 97, 112, 149, 164–65, 179, 181, 195n9; civilization as unhealthy for African Americans, 36–37, 40–44, 58–59, 62–63, 64; mortality in, 9, 36–37. *See also* primitive groups

Clarke, Elizabeth, 168, 169

Clark, Juanne, 150

Classic Hollywood, Classic Whiteness (Bernardi), 67–68

Clinton, Bill, 150

Coe, Paul, 103

Coe, Richard, 73

Cohn, Isidore, 51, 61, 63

Colbert, Claudette, 68, 86

Cold War imagery, in cancer awareness campaigns, 9–10, 67, 69–70, 91

Collier's (magazine), 87

colon cancer, 17, 165

"colored": as racial classification, 6, 104. *See also* African Americans

"color line": cancer crossing, 3–4, 6, 12, 40–41, 65, 179, 182; and W.E.B. Du Bois, 2, 12

Considine, Bob, 81

Crowther, Bosley, 67, 73, 88

Cuban Americans, 6, 142

cure rates. *See* survival

Cutler, Sidney, 103, 143

Davenport, Charles, 23–24

death. *See* mortality

Department of Health, Education and Welfare, in Krebiozen debate, 127

Depression era, public health in, 47–50

detection. *See* diagnosis

Detroit, 43

DeVita, Vincent T., Jr., 144–45

"Diagnosis" (Wharton), 32–33

diagnosis: of female cancers, 10, 187n24; of internal cancers, 7, 17, 18, 21, 56, 115, 178, 188n35, 190n34; of male cancers, 10, 18, 178; uncertainties in, 88–89; in urban areas, 45, 97, 176; in whites vs. blacks, 56, 105. *See also* diagnostic tools; early detection

gastrointestinal cancer, 18
gender: as central motif in cancer
    awareness, 6; identity politics of, 11, 150,
    170. *See also* men; women
genetic testing: for breast cancer, 151, 154; as
    early detection, 151; ethical and practical
    considerations, 154; and ideas of racial
    biology, 184
Georgia, 49, 50
Georgia Federation of Colored Women's
    Clubs, 50
Germans, 24
Gey, George, 87
Gey, Margaret, 87
Gilded Caravan (Woods), 30
Gilpatric, John Guy, 78
Gilpatric, Louise, 78
Gines, Venus, 182
Glaser, Barney, 8
Gomella, Leonard, 158
Gossett, Louis, Jr., 175, *175*, 177, 179
Go Tell It on the Mountain (Baldwin), 131
Gover, Mary, 53, 188n35
Grant, Cary (Archibald Leach), 87
Green, Paul, 46–47, 196n28
Gross, Ariela, 101

Haenszel, William, 102, 115
Hailey, Arthur, 88–89
Hamer, Fannie Lou, 143
Harlem, 42, 43, 124
Hayworth, Rita, 87
Health and Human Services, 145
HeLa strain, 87
Henschke, Ulrich, 135
Hernandez, Lourdes, 172
Hernandez, Roger, 149
Hispanics: breast self-examination by, 170,
    172; as distinct from Latinos, 182; groups
    classified as, 6; health paradox of, 149;
    and U.S. Census, 6, 103, 140. *See also*
    Latinos
Hoffman, Frederick: on mortality from
    civilization, 18, 36–37; predictions of
    black extinction, 45–46, 57; as statistician
    for Prudential Life, 18, 24, 36, 45–46, 48;
    on white vulnerability, 24
Holleb, Arthur, 84
Holmes, Samuel Jackson: on health
    education for blacks, 49; *The Negro's
    Struggle for Survival: A Study in Human
    Ecology,* 49, 56, 64; photo, 64; on primitive
    immunity, 60, 64; on racial survival,

57–60, 62, 64, 199n84; statistical analyses
    of, 55–58, 199n79
Hosier, Ray, 77
Houston Chronicle, 172
Houston, Tx., 163
Howard University report on black
    mortality: authors, 135, 142–43;
    cancer causation theories in, 134–35,
    136–40, 142; critique of cancer
    establishment, 11, 121–22, 135–36, 140–41;
    critique of racial classification system,
    140–41, 142; findings, 11, 120, 134, 146; as
    turning point in cancer awareness, 134,
    142–43
HRT (hormone replacement therapy), 151,
    168–69
human papillomavirus (HPV), 166
Hunt, Florence, 50
Hygeia (magazine): on cancer awareness
    in women, 16, 25; fictionalized cancer
    story, 26–27, 38–39; as magazine of
    AMA, 38

"I Am Not Afraid of Cancer," 26–27,
    38–39
identity politics: in cancer awareness, 11,
    145, 149, 150, 171, 174, 178, 179–80; and
    diagnostic tools, 7, 11, 151, 171–72, 175; and
    gender, 11, 150, 170
I Die Daily (Burks), 75–76, 84–85
Illness as Metaphor (Sontag), 144, 178
immigrants: cancer awareness in, 34,
    148–49; and civilization theories, 181;
    in competition with blacks, 43, 59;
    and racial classifications, 119; and
    representative sampling, 142;
    U.S. legislation restricting, 59. *See also*
    mass migrations; *specific immigrant
    groups*
Institute of Medicine (IOM), report on
    race, 162–63
internal cancer: diagnosing, 17, 18, 56, 115,
    178, 188n35, 190n34; mortality from, 18,
    56, 190n34
Irish Americans: cancer mortality in, 24;
    cancer rates in, 24, 100–101; in New York
    City study, 24, 100; racial classifications,
    12, 24, 100–101, 183; women, 24
Italians: in Los Angeles study, 97; migration
    to urban life, 43–44; in New York City
    study, 24, 100; racial classifications,
    24–25, 97
Ivy, Andrew, Krebiozen saga, 123–29

Japanese Americans: cervical cancer in, 11, 149, 163, 174–75; immigration and cancer incidence, 164; in Los Angeles study, 96, 98, 100; as nonwhite, 103; and PSA test, 155; racial classifications, 96, 98, 100, 103, 174–75; women, 11, 149, 163, 164, 174

Jewish cervical cancer anomaly: behavior and customs in, 53–54, 108; and circumcision, 110–11; described, 10, 106–7; as epidemiological mystery, 10, 53, 95, 106; new disease theories spawned by, 107, 108, 109, 119; race biology discredited in, 109, 110; sexual behavior and, 54, 107, 108–9, 110–11

Jewish women: breast cancer in, 151; cervical cancer in, 10, 53, 95, 106–7, 111; hysterectomies in, 109–10; uterine cancer in, 53–54, 109–10. *See also* Jewish cervical cancer anomaly; Jews

Jews: Ashkenazi, 151; cancer rates in, 24, 51–55; and circumcision, 110–11; European, 51–55, 109, 151; intermarriage by, 108; in Los Angeles study, 97; migration to urban areas, 43–44, 52–53; in New York City study, 24, 100; penile cancer in, 108; in postwar U.S., 106; prostate cancer in, 214n76; as race vs. ethnic group, 100, 109, 110; racial classifications of, 12, 52–53, 55, 97, 106, 183; Russian, 109; as white, 12, 96–97, 106, 183. *See also* Jewish cervical cancer anomaly; Jewish women

The Jews: A Study of Race and Environment (Fishberg), 181

Johnson, Charles Spurgeon, 107–8, 115

Journal of the National Cancer Institute, on breast self-exam, 172, 173

Jung, Karl, 22, 23

Kaehele, Edna, 79–80, 81
Kean, Marian Miller, 79
Kellogg, John Harvey, 40, 44
Kennaway, Ernest, 107, 108
Kennedy, John F., 125
Kent, Rosemary, 92–94, 95, 116
King, Martin Luther, Jr., 121, 133, 134
Kinsey, Alfred, 107
Kinsey Reports, 107–8, 214n79
Kline, Wendy, 24
Koenig, Barbara, 184
Kolata, Gina, 150–51
Korean Americans, 161–62, 175

Krebiozen: announcement of, 122–23; FDA involvement, 124, 126, 127, 128; indictments and criminal trial, 122, 127–29; public support for, 123–24, 125, 126, 143, 218n32; as rallying cry against cancer establishment, 122–23, 125–26, 129, 216n11; scientific assessments of, 123–24, 126–27, 217n13; sponsors of, 123

Krieger, Nancy, 170

Lacks, Henrietta, 87
Ladies' Home Journal: on breast self-examination, 82, 90; on female cancer, 73; on female stoicism, 74, 85; on medical deception, 76, 81; on Pap smears, 84

Laetrile, 125
Lancet, 110
Landers, Ann, 82
Langer, Elinor, 127, 128, 129
larynx cancer, 99
Latin Americans: as nonwhite, 140; Spanish ancestry of, 6, 99, 141, 142; as white, 101, 182

Latin Cancer Awareness, 182
Latinos: as distinct from Hispanics, 182; health paradox of, 149; racial classifications, 12, 182, 183. *See also* Hispanics

Lee, Sandra Soo-Jin, 184
Leffall, LaSalle D., Jr.: and American Cancer Society, 2, 122, 142–43; on Howard University report, 121, 134, 146; training and career, 135

leukemia, 70, 95
Life (magazine), 65, 90, *91*
Lisa, James, 112–13, 114
Little, Clarence C.: affiliation with ACSS, 16, 54; on curing cancer, 72; on egalitarian nature of cancer, 9, 61; on heredity as cancer cause, 114; on Jewish cervical cancer anomaly, 54–55

liver cancer: in African Americans, 97, 99, 139; in Africans, 97, 102; and alcohol consumption, 139; difficulty diagnosing, 17

Living with Cancer (Kaehele), 79–80
Lombard, Herbert, 14
Lorde, Audre, 143, 144
Los Angeles cancer study, 10, 96–102
Los Angeles Times: on Krebiozen debate, 125; review of *No Sad Songs for Me,* 67, 71–72, 73

National Cancer Institute (NCI): Asian American initiative, 162; breast self-exam campaigns, 83; cancer awareness films, 69; cancer surveillance program (SEER), 141–42, 144, 223n118, 224n123; Howard University critique of, 140, 141; in Krebiozen debate, 125, 126, 127, 128; origins of, 49, 50; as part of cancer "establishment," 144; prostate cancer study, 148; response to antiestablishment criticism, 141, 144–45; skin cancer survey, 98; use of nonwhite as racial classification, 140

National Institutes of Health (NIH), 50

Native Americans. *See* American Indians

NCI. *See* National Cancer Institute (NCI)

Negro: as census category, 184; civilization as destructive to, 41. *See also* African Americans

The Negro's Struggle for Survival: A Study in Human Ecology (Holmes), 49, 56, 64

New England Journal of Medicine, 109, 158

New Orleans, La., 142

Newsweek (magazine): on breast cancer, 34; on Howard University report, 120, 134; survey on medical deception, 78–79

New York Amsterdam News, 85, 96

New York City insurance survey, 24–25

New York Times: on cancer in whites, 24; on diagnostics industry, 150–51; on environmental cancers, 145; on medical deception, 79; review of *No Sad Songs for Me*, 67

NIH. *See* National Institutes of Health (NIH)

Nixon, Richard, 120, 142

"No Deadly Medicine" (TV show), 88

nonwhites: as Census classification, 6, 12, 103–4; as racial and epidemiological construct, 6, 103–6, 119, 140–41, 181, 182–83, *See also specific nonwhite groups*

No Sad Songs for Me (film): as cancer awareness vehicle, 66–70; end-of-life portrayals in, 72–73, 74; movie reviews, 67, 71–72, 73, 203n50; resilience and personal triumph in, 69, 70, 131. *See also* Scott, Mary (film character)

No Sad Songs for Me (novel), 70, 72

Obama, Barack, 184, 235n19

Ochsner, Alton, 7, 77, 114

Oesterling, Joseph, 155

ovarian cancer, 17, 99

Papanicolaou, George N., 84

Pap smear, 84, 90, 115, 137

Parran, Thomas, Jr., 48, 70, 71

Pattern of Three (Bradley), 29–31

Peller, Sigismund, 10, 94–95, 108, 110, 116

penile cancer: and circumcision, 111; in Indo-Chinese, 102; in Jews, 102, 108, 111

Peto, Richard, 144

Pettigrew, Ann, 117

Pettigrew, Thomas, 117

PHS. *See* U.S. Public Health Service (PHS)

physicians: and African American patients, 74–75, 93–94; and diagnostic uncertainty, 88–89; as moral managers, 17; paternalism and deception by, 31–32, 74–80, 81–82, 93–94, 178, 204n62, 205n73, 206n78, 206n91; and white female patients, 70, 85, 86

Pittsburgh study, 104–5

The Politics of Cancer (Epstein), 144

Potosky, Arnold, 154, 155

Powell, Isaac, 159

Preble, William, 28

Prescott, Henry, 31

President's Cancer Panel (2000), 176, 179, 182

primitive groups: African Americans as, 2, 9, 40–42, 62, 181; cancer occurrence in, 2, 5, 22, 33, 40–42, 94, 178, 194n82; civilization as dangerous for, 9, 36–37, 40–44, 62–63, 64; inner lives of, 5, 33, 41. *See also* civilization-primitivism dichotomy

prostate cancer: in African Americans, 11–12, 136, 148, 152, 154, 159, 161, 171, 174, 175, 181–82; awareness groups, 150; causation theories, 148, 182; chemotherapy for, 152; comparisons to breast cancer, 150, 152–53; difficulty diagnosing, 17; and digital rectal exams, 153, 175, 177; epidemic of, 151–52, 154, 157, 158–59, 161; in Jews, 214n76; Louis Gossett's testimony, 175, 177, 179; mortality, 11–12, 148, 151–53, 154, 157; postage stamp, 150; and race biology, 156, 161, 171, 182; research funding for, 150, 152; Sam Frost's testimony, 176–78; as slow growing, 152–53, 157, 160; treatments for, 152, 159, 227n21. *See also* PSA test (prostate-specific antigen test)

prostate specific antigen, 154

prostate-specific antigen test. *See* PSA test (prostate-specific antigen test)

Prudential Life Insurance Company, 18, 24, 36, 45–46

PSA test (prostate-specific antigen test): in blacks vs. whites, 154–55; as diagnostic tool, 152–53; introduction of, 11; in Japanese, 155; limitations of, 152–61; and racial biology theories, 11, 148, 154–57, 159, 161; Sam Frost's testimony, 176–78; and "Will Rogers Phenomenon," 157–58. *See also* prostate cancer

A Psychological Study of Cancer (Evans), 21–23, 32, 41–42

public health: and cancer surveillance, 42, 48–49, 65; in Depression era, 47–50; and mass migrations, 42, 48–49, 65, 148–49; segregation in, 35, 49, 50, 137; and uneducated patients, 33, 36, 124–25; value of statistics in, 7. *See also* U.S. Public Health Service (PHS)

Public Health Service. *See* U.S. Public Health Service (PHS)

Public Works Administration, 49

Puerto Ricans, 6, 101, 141

race: and intersectionality, 186n17; multiple meanings of, 6, 180–84; and Nazi ideology, 61, 93, 137, 186n16; scientific inaccuracy of, 162–63. *See also* racial biology; racial classifications

race suicide, 15, 24, 25

racial biology: as cancer causation theory, 5, 14–15, 53, 93, 95, 97, 110, 114, 115–16, 137, 149, 150, 151, 152, 154–57, 178, 181; and genetic testing, 184; in historical cancer studies, 5–6; in Howard University report, 137; and prostate cancer, 156, 161, 171, 182; and PSA test, 11, 148, 154–57, 159, 161; and racial immunity, 5, 9, 11, 34, 40, 43, 45, 60, 61, 63, 64, 94, 98, 105, 148, 152, 178, 181

racial classifications: "colored," 6, 104; dynamic nature of, 6, 7, 10, 12, 65, 94–96, 101–6, 151, 181, 182–84, 183–84; and genetics, 184; high social stakes in, 101, 117, 140; limitations of, 101–2, 103, 116, 140–41, 144; in Los Angeles study, 96–97, 98–101; and multiracial families, 12, 61, 184, 235n19; of National Cancer Institute, 140; necessity of, 183; in New York City study, 24–25; "one-drop rule," 12; and politics of recognition, 121, 122, 140–41, 149; and representative sampling systems, 141–42. *See also* nonwhites; U.S. Census; *specific ethnic and racial groups*

racial segregation: cancer imagery describing, 121, 133; health differences as

excuse for, 117; and public health, 35, 49, 50, 137

radiation, 70, 72, 76, 116

Reader's Digest (magazine): on Babe Zaharias, 80; on cancer therapies, 76–77; on female cancer fighters, 9–10

Reagan Administration, 145

Reagan, Leslie, 178

Reddick, Max (fictional character), 130, 131–33, 145, 182

Reed, Greedy (fictional character), 130, 182

Reid, Ira, 42

Reinhardt, James, 44

research: breast cancer vs. prostate cancer, 150; conflation of race in, 182; funding for, 180

Reynolds, Quentin, 80

Richardson, Sarah, 184

Riesman, David, 25

Riperton, Minnie: as landmark in racial and cancer awareness, 3, 4, 5, 8, 143, 145, 176, 179, 182; personalized cancer story of, 1–2, 3, 4, 5, 146; photo, *147*; as spokesperson for American Cancer Society, 1, 122, 143, 146

Rogers, Will, 157

Roosevelt, Franklin D., 50

Rosenau, Milton, 62–63

Rosenblatt, Milton, 112–13, 114

Rose, Nikolas, 3

Rosen, Ruth, 169

Rothman, Albert, 107

Russians, in New York City studies, 24, 100

Ruth, Babe, 77

San Francisco Chronicle, 167, 170

Saroyan, William, 130

Saturday Evening Post (magazine): on female cancer fighters, 9–10; on new cancer therapies, 76–77; personalized cancer story, 79

Schereschewsky, J.W., 49

Science: on cholesterol, 19; on Krebiozen debate, 126, 128, 129; on penile hygiene in cervical cancer, 110

Science Newsletter, 14–15

Science Versus Cancer (Berenblum), 95

Scott, Mary (film character): actresses asked to play, 66, 68–69, 86; character traits personified by, 66–69, 70, 71, 72, 75; cultural significance of, 69, 182

Scruggs, Charles, 131

Seattle-Puget Sound, Wa., 142

U.S. Census: 1920 Census, 34–35; 1930 Census, 194n79; 1970 Census, 141; 2000 Census, 184; 2010 Census, 184; and African Americans, 6, 56–57, 138, 184, 199n79; and Asian Americans, 6; Hispanic classification in, 6, 103, 140; and Mexican-Americans, 6, 99, 101; Negro classification in, 184; nonwhite classification in, 6, 103–4; predictions of white minority, 184; self-identification in, 140, 184; shifting racial classifications in, 6, 12, 101–2, 181, 184

U.S. Congress: breast cancer stamp, 150; immigration laws, 59; and Krebiozen, 124, 218n35; Lou Gossett's testimony, 175, 177, 179; Medicaid passage, 137; Medicare passage, 121, 137; National Breast Cancer Awareness Month, 150; National Cancer Act, 9; National Minority Cancer Awareness Week, 150; prostate cancer stamp, 150; Sam Frost's testimony, 176–77

U.S. Public Health Service (PHS): Atlanta study, 105; and cancer surveillance, 42, 48–49, 65; and Depression era, 50; Louisiana study, 104; 1955 report on cancer morbidity, 103; as part of cancer "establishment," 146

Us TOO, 150

uterine cancer: in blacks, 57, 86, 199n84; early causal theories, 14, 15, 25; ease of diagnosis, 18; in Jews, 53–54, 109–10; in poor women, 25, 26; survival, 86; in whites, 57, 86, 113

Vietnamese Americans: cervical cancer in, 11–12, 149, 161, 163, 166, 171, 174; immigration to U.S., 43–44, 149, 163, 164–65

Vietnam War, 163, 164, 166

Wangensteen, Owen H., 77, 78, 127
"War on Cancer," 9, 120, 142, 146
Warren, Shields, 27
Washington Post: on black immunity, 43; on Howard University report, 120, 139; on Marin County breast cancer epidemic, 167, 169
Waters, Ethel, 86
Weaver, Ollie (fictional character), 46–47, 130, 182, 196n28
Weaver, Raymond, 30
West, John, 124
Wharton, Edith, 32–33

Whatever We Do (Updegraff), 30
White, Jack, 135
white: as complex racial category, 6, 96–97, 182–83; Jews as, 12, 96–97, 106, 183; Latin Americans as, 101, 182; Mexican Americans as, 6, 99, 101–2, 141, 183, *See also* white men; whites; white women

white men: cancer rates in, 104; lung cancer in, 112–14; mortality trends, 39, 46, 57; PSA testing in, 154–55, 156; survival rates, 144. *See also* whites

whites: as benchmark in cancer studies, 5–6, 101, 182–83; and civilization-primitivism dichotomy, 2–3, 40; as future American minority, 184; inner lives of, 3, 8–9, 33–34; in Los Angeles study, 98, 99; mortality trends, 34, 44, 144; in New York study, 24–25; as vulnerable to cancer, 4, 34, 35, 40. *See also* white men; white women

white women: of Appalachia, 180; blamed for failure to detect cancer, 19, 70, 194n84; bravery and stoicism of, 68, 70, 71, 74, 81, 85, 90, 91; breast cancer in, 8, 11, 103, 113, 170, 171; and breast self-examination, 10, 82, 83, 85, 170, 172; as cancer fighters, 9–10, 66, 68, 70, 89, 91, 207n97; cervical cancer in, 25, 102–3, 108, 163; doctor-patient relationships, 70, 75, 85, 86, 194n86; as emotionally able to confront cancer, 34, 35–36, 76, 82, 83; as key to nation's future, 3, 15, 25, 29; lung cancer in, 113; messages of self-control and self-monitoring for, 10, 68, 84–85, 86, 89, 90, 179; mortality trends, 144; perceived inner lives of, 3, 5, 8–9, 33–34, 35–36, 38, 151, 179; and reproductive choices, 9, 14, 15, 19, 23, 25, 29, 34, 38, 73, 189n11, 189n16, 191n46; responsibility for safeguarding family, 16, 19, 68, 85, 91, 207n97; survival rates, 144; as target of cancer awareness campaigns, 2, 3, 4–5, 8, 9–10, 11, 14, 15–17, 19–21, 32, 34, 36, 38, 66–67, 70, 120, 130, 176, 178, 179; uterine cancer in, 57, 86, 113; as vulnerable to cancer, 3, 4–5, 9, 14–18, 19, 25–26, 29, 32, 34, 35–36, 37, 38, 39, 40, 94, 95, 178, 179, 181, 190n26. *See also* whites

Wide Fields (Green), 46–47
Wilbur, Ray Lyman, 125
Willard, Mabel, 20–21
Willcox, Walter F., 18, 45
Williams, John A., 130, 131–33
"Will Rogers Phenomenon," 157–58
Wilson, Harriet, 92–95, 116

Woglom, William, 28

The Woman Citizen (Wood), 39

women: bravery of, 68, 69–74, 78, 81, 131; and cancer risk awareness, 2–5, 9–11, 14–16, 18, 20, 25–39, 44, 46, 50, 53–55, 57, 58, 60, 61, 66–91, 92, 93, 106–11, 130, 146, 148–49, 152, 153, 154, 157, 161–75, 176, 178, 179, 181; educated, 4, 17, 34, 79, 80, 168, 169; elderly, 57; and fear, 21, 26, 38, 130, 179; married, 16, 19, 25, 32; middle class and affluent, 4, 9, 13, 15, 19, 20, 25, 28–29, 32, 34, 38, 66, 70, 73, 79, 80, 82, 85, 86, 167–73; modesty of, 15, 16, 17, 36, 41, 71, 86, 165, 166, 172, 179; nonwhite, 5, 36, 66, 83, 105, 172; and reproduction, 9, 14–16, 17, 23, 25, 29, 34, 38, 53–54, 73, 189n11, 191n46; self-control of, 33, 34, 67, 69, 71, 83, 84, 85, 86, 89, 170, 177; sexuality, 54, 95, 107–11, 119, 166; trust in physicians, 70, 74–75, 77, 79, 82, 85, 86; unmarried, 16, 19, 22, 32, 53; working class, 25, 26, 34. *See also* African American women; Asian Americans, women; breast cancer; breast self-examination (BSE); cervical cancer; Irish Americans, women; Japanese Americans, women; Jewish women; Mexican Americans, women; uterine cancer; white women

Women's Field Army, 36, 66

Wood, Francis C., 14, 39

Woods, Alice, 30

World War II, 9, 65, 70, 90, 119

Wright, Louis T., 44

Wynder, Ernest, 107, 110

X-rays, 90, 114–15

The Young Doctors (film), 88

Zaharias, Babe Didrikson, 77, 80–81, 182, 206n87

Zaharias, George, 80, 81

DATE DUE

Demco